LEGAL
RIGHTS
OF THE
POOR

For my dear son Veerendra.
With very best wishes!
Happy Reading.

Dad.
November, 2021

FOUNDATIONS OF INCLUSIVE AND SUSTAINABLE PROSPERITY

LEGAL RIGHTS OF THE POOR

Naresh Singh

authorHOUSE®

AuthorHouse™
1663 Liberty Drive
Bloomington, IN 47403
www.authorhouse.com
Phone: 1-800-839-8640

Published by AuthorHouse 11/07/2014

ISBN: 978-1-4969-4707-9 (sc)
ISBN: 978-1-4969-4708-6 (e)

Library of Congress Control Number: 2014918718

ACKNOWLEDGMENTS

The idea of this book was first suggested by Bill Ascher of Soka University as part of a development policy series. As the book evolved it no longer fit those requirements and so is being published independently. I am grateful to Bill for his suggestions and encouragement in the early stages of this work and for making available two of his students to assist in the research. I wish to acknowledge the excellent support received from these students Wade Sias and Min Xiang Lee.

The book has its origins and inspiration in the work of the Commission on Legal Empowerment of the Poor, co-chaired by Madeleine Albright and Hernando de Soto. I had the privilege of serving as Executive Director of the Commission. Chapters 4 and 5 are based on the report of the Commission entitled: Making the Law Work for Everyone. Like in any work of this kind an enormous debt of gratitude is owed to many published works from I have drawn extensively. They are acknowledged throughout the text. My daughter Shanaya assisted with the final checking of references for which I am grateful. Any errors or omissions are of course my sole my responsibility for which I apologise in advance.

Naresh Singh.
October, 2014.
Ottawa, Canada.

DEDICATION

For Shanaya, Shea and Veerendra who are an inspiration. I hope they will live in a world that is more just, equitable and prosperous.

CONTENTS

PRAISE FOR LEGAL RIGHTS OF THE POOR

"Dr.Naresh Singh has been at the forefront of global efforts to develop methods and policies that will liberate the poor and the marginalized of the world. In this important new book he first analyzes recent efforts by the global community in this regard, and then building on these lessons of the past and his own vast knowledge Dr. Singh outlines concrete and practical steps for the immediate future—all aimed to lay a foundation for the inclusive and sustainable prosperity of all. He builds on the premise that "the foundations of success lie in anchoring the agenda in the human-rights and development communities of practice, showing how value can be added to the work of each, how synergies can be built, and how common challenges to dominant power relations can be addressed." Dr. Singh's goal is to help us create conditions and strategies to make power a positive-sum game. Such an approach might be the key to the success of peaceful self-empowerment. The analysis and ideas discussed in this book are profound and practical. In this book Dr. Singh lays out a realistic and promising way forward into the post-2015 era, and it is a must-read for those who are concerned about that future era."

Gerald T. G. Seniuk, Retired Chief Judge
of the Provincial Court of Saskatchewan, Canada.

"This book is a must-read for anyone and everyone concerned with one of the most pressing problems that faces the world today: How best to fight and win the global war on poverty, the conditions of which still afflict a large part of humanity. The author is one of the major architects and a practitioner of what has become known as the sustainable livelihoods approach to development. In this book he makes a powerful and persuasive argument about the need to get at the roots of poverty in the structure of social inequality and change the relation of power relations between the haves and the have-nots. A key part of the solution, Singh argues, can be found in the legal empowerment of the poor.

—Henry Veltmeyer, Professor Emeritus, International Development Studies, Saint Mary's University.

"The book is an outstanding contribution to the human rights discourse relating to the empowerment of the poor. Dr. Naresh Singh has systematically addressed the normative, legal, ethical, human rights and development implications of addressing poverty from the standpoint of inclusivity and sustainability. The book goes beyond the mere recognition of the human right to freedom from poverty, but responds to the larger challenges of creating domestic and international legal entitlements for the poor, while formulating policy prescriptions for achieving sustainable prosperity. This book is a welcome addition to the growing literature on linkages between human rights and development as it is valuable for all those who are interested in the study of international law, human rights and development studies."

Professor C. Raj Kumar
Founding Vice Chancellor; O.P. Jindal Global University &
Dean, Jindal Global Law School

The difference between what we do and what we are capable of doing would suffice to solve most of the world's problems.

—Mahatma Gandhi

The significant problems we have cannot be solved at the same level of thinking with which we created them.

—Albert Einstein

The power of the people is greater than the people in power.
—Bono

INTRODUCTION

Two important milestones in the evolution of international development cooperation are converging. On the one hand, it is five years since the landmark report *Making the Law Work for Everyone*, a publication of the Commission on Legal Empowerment of the Poor, was launched in 2008. On the other, it is the eve of 2015, the target year of the millennium development goals (MDGs) and the beginning of the post-2015 era in development cooperation. It is therefore a most opportune time to examine how the struggle for the legal empowerment of the poor can help shape the post-2015 agenda and vice versa with the purpose of helping the poor and marginalized people of the world realize their legal rights and improve their material circumstances. This potentially could make a major contribution to shaping a world that is more prosperous and sustainable and societies that are more just, inclusive, and equitable. That is the goal of this book.

When the commission published its report, there were high hopes that it would make a significant contribution to the legal empowerment of the poor. Looking back five years later, the results are mixed at best. The greatest success of its work has probably been raising awareness of this important agenda, which was not getting widespread global attention from governments, multilateral organizations, civil society, or academia, whether in the north or the south. It has been less successful at integrating itself into the policies and program priorities of governments, the multilateral system, or civil society. In other words, it did not become institutionalized. Yes, the subject has received greater academic attention, and more projects have targeted the legal empowerment of the poor; but the hoped-for systemic sea change has not materialized. One of the reasons for this was that while the United Nations Development Program (UNDP) committed to advancing the agenda after the report's publication, its approach was to stimulate projects on the ground. The project, as a development vehicle, is not suited to systemic change; no wonder, then, that the results have been piecemeal. This book adopts the premise that the foundations of success lie in anchoring the agenda in the human-rights and development communities of practice, showing how value can be added to the work of each, how synergies can be built, and how common challenges to dominant power relations can be addressed.

On the eve of the post-2015 era, there have been periodic reports on the extent to which the MDGs have been achieved. These show that we have had mixed but very encouraging results in many countries. According to the *MDG 2013 Report,* the proportion of people living in extreme poverty has been halved at the global level.[1] The world reached the poverty-reduction target five years ahead of schedule. In developing regions, the proportion of people living on less than $1.25 a day fell from 47 percent in 1990 to 22 percent in 2010. About 700 million fewer people lived in conditions of extreme poverty in 2010 than in 1990. But these are global figures; not all countries reached the targets, especially those in crisis and postcrisis situations. Similarly, as of 2010, 89 percent of the world's population had access to drinking water—another MDG target achieved. On the other hand, we need to do much more to get the poorest kids to school, to respond to HIV/AIDS, to improve environmental sustainability,

---

[1]   United Nations, *MDG Report,* 2013, www.un.org/milleniumgoals.

and to achieve gender equality. Work on the MDGs will have to continue.

Looking forward to the post-2015 era, the UN organized world consultations in which more than a million people participated. The report *The World We Want* captured their views.[2] Equality and nondiscrimination also stood out as key messages: people are demanding justice, participation, and dignity. Inequalities and social exclusion exist particularly for poorer people; for women and girls; for those in rural areas and urban slums; for people living with disabilities; for indigenous people; for migrants and displaced people; and for others marginalized for reasons related to religion, ethnicity, or sexual orientation. The insecurities they face compound each other: for instance, the lack of decent jobs can leave people without access to health services and living in unsafe conditions. In addition, people have said emphatically that the challenges—and, indeed, opportunities—they face are complex and interlinked. The relationships between these various insecurities point to the need to go beyond a silo approach and arrive at a future sustainable-development agenda that is more integrated and holistic. People demand that this new agenda be built on human rights and universal values of equality, justice, and security. Better governance of markets and of the environment underpins many of their calls. There is also a strong call to retain the focus on concrete, measurable goals and yet improve dramatically the way we measure progress against them. Finally, they hope that a data revolution will support an accountability revolution.

The cry for this kind of world has been around forever. Either we have failed to address this agenda in an effective manner,

---

[2]   www.Worldwewant2015.org.

or the world was not yet ready, or both. This book seeks to be relevant to this call to address inequalities, injustice, human rights, and social exclusion in a more integrated, holistic, and transformative manner. It seeks to do so by looking at what we have learned both in the development community and in the legal-rights community and goes on to address fundamental obstacles that neither community has dealt with in this context, such as changing power relations.

Chapter 1 provides the backdrop against which policy and programmatic actions to ensure the legal rights of the poor must take place. It provides a stocktaking of the progress, or lack thereof, that the world has made in reducing poverty, inequality, and exclusion. It also highlights various approaches—including the policy instruments that have been successful in certain contexts—and mentions their limitations. Interestingly, the legal rights of the poor, human rights generally, and access to justice and the rule of law have not featured prominently in the dominant approaches to date.

The chapter starts by taking a look at the global experience of the fight against poverty over the last several decades, drawing from the most influential global reports on poverty and development including the *Human Development Reports (HDR)* of the UNDP and the *World Development Reports (WDR)* of the World Bank. However, it is necessary to go beyond these global reports and look at some in-country assessments to get a more complete picture. After this review, we look at some of the poverty-related challenges to development including inequality, equity, and social exclusion. The chapter concludes with some reflections on the international-development enterprise itself, which then sets the stage for the action required to ensure the legal rights of the poor. Though this agenda can benefit a little from international development support, it is in reality a challenge to be addressed within countries, whether developed or developing.

The central question that this book seeks to answer—how to provide legal rights to the poor—sits squarely in the informal sector, where more than 80 percent of the poor and legally excluded live. Hence, a sound understanding of the characteristics of this sector with its various names is of primary importance. Both the development and the human-rights communities err when they apply formal-sector assumptions to the informal sector without testing their validity in this radically different arena where survival instincts rather than formal rules and laws drive the actions of the people.

Chapter 2 therefore describes the main features of informal systems. It starts with an exploration of the economic sphere dealing mainly with employment, jobs, and small and micro businesses. It next describes social dimensions, such as labor exploitation, lack of health care, the various forms of conflict that arise, sociopolitical alienation, and environmental issues. The case study of the Indian informal sector that follows then brings into vivid focus these economic realities. Extralegality occurs when people in an informal system seek legal goals, such as building a home or running a business to take care of their families, in a socially acceptable manner but do not obey all the provisions of the law, such as registration, taxes, building codes, and so forth. A case study from Tanzania illustrates this phenomenon, in which people living in the informal sector develop their own social rules over time. The most extreme conditions of informality occur in slums, where nearly a billion people live. A brief survey of the living conditions of slums precedes descriptions of two slums, one in Africa and one in India. Those who flee their own countries and are considered refugees constitute a special group of people who are usually without legal rights; the same is true of people displaced within their own countries. The chapter also briefly surveys the challenges facing these groups before concluding.

Economic, social, and cultural rights (ESCR), which are the focus of this book, are socioeconomic human rights, such as the right to housing and an adequate standard of living and the rights to health and education. These are claim rights, implying that they entail responsibilities, obligations, or duties on other parties. Poor people everywhere are generally unable to claim these rights, because of lack of awareness, capability, or organization; state incapacity or unwillingness to meet obligations; or deliberate and systematic exclusion of the poor in order to serve the interests of the elite. This has led to the widespread perception that ESCR are paper rights and to cynicism among the poor when they hear that they are entitled to these rights. The test of whether these rights are legal rights or just moral rights is the degree of *justiciability*. In other words, can poor people go to the courts or similar institutions and win enforceable legal remedies when their ESCR are denied?

Chapter 3 first reviews the justiciability of ESCR in general and, in so doing, makes the case that a growing body of evidence confirms the justiciability of ESCR but with various limitations, caveats, and lessons learned about how to proceed. The discussion is based on a comprehensive Centre of Housing Rights and Evictions 2003 report,[3] which contains case studies from

---

[3]   M. Langford, 2003. *Litigating Economic, Social, and Cultural Rights* (Centre for Housing Rights and Evictions:).

the Asia Pacific, the Americas, Africa, Europe, and international mechanisms. The second half of this chapter illustrates the applications of the principles of ESCR to a major social system, the health system, in order to show how ECSR can be given expression in a systemic manner.

Chapter 4 presents the agenda for the legal empowerment of the poor based mainly on the framework developed by the Commission on Legal Empowerment of the Poor. The approach relies on an integrated-systems strategy in which the poor are central actors in a bottom-up self-empowerment mode supported by an actively engaged developmental state. For the poor to become successful at self-empowerment requires a range of enabling factors, which are discussed at length here and in subsequent chapters. For states to become developmental and pro poor also requires a range of fundamental shifts. These shifts form a large part of the remainder of the book.

The legal-empowerment agenda starts with the self-empowerment process. For this process to succeed, the poor require legal identity, voice, organization in the form of mobilization into action groups, and education and awareness of their rights. We can define the legal reforms required to support this process in terms of four pillars: access to justice and the rule of law, property rights, labor rights, and business rights.

The legal-empowerment agenda as defined in chapter 4 is ambitious and difficult; some may consider it unrealistic. Chapter 5 provides the roadmaps and tools to make it both practical and realistic. The chapter first takes a hard look at the political issues and obstacles that policy reforms generally face. It describes tools for contextual analysis that will help identify obstacles and opportunities as well as likely supporters and opponents of implementing such an agenda. It provides detailed stakeholder analyses and explores different ways of engagement, including the building of coalitions to overcome resistance and support reforms. An analysis of institutional arrangements at the levels of political and administrative state machinery precedes a detailed analysis of policy reform architecture. Throughout these analyses, a point of emphasis is how these institutional and policy arrangements can be made to work with and for the informal sector. The chapter concludes by providing strategies and tactics that could be helpful in different local contexts where the agenda might need to be implemented.

The biggest oversight in the research and practice of human rights and socioeconomic development with regard to the empowerment agenda has been the absence of adequate consideration of the role of power relations. While this issue is mentioned frequently, it never gets the attention it requires and might have become the elephant in the room. Virtually all power analyses, whether in development or human-rights circles, tend to analyze the drivers of change through existing political, contextual, institutional, and stakeholder analyses as described in chapter 6. The underlying assumption usually is that power is a zero-sum game. Not much is available in the literature to help us create conditions and strategies to make power a positive-sum game. Yet this might be the key to the success of peaceful self-empowerment. Chapter 6 seeks to address this oversight. After reviewing the common definitions of power, it describes the typologies of power in an attempt to reveal any chinks in the armor of the concept of power as a zero-sum situation. Following this description, we attempt to marshal some of the theoretical thinking on power as a positive-sum game. The chapter concludes with three case studies that demonstrate practices that could begin to provide guidance for badly needed paradigm-shifting research and practices for making power a positive-sum game.

Chapter 7 gives special attention to half of the 4 billion people who live outside the framework of the rule of law. That more disadvantaged half, women and girls, has been historically disenfranchised relative to their male counterparts and continue to face greater obstacles, but more importantly, they still face skewed power differentials. They lack power in decision making both in the home and in the parliament; they lack control over the assets on which their livelihoods depend and very often over the use of their own bodies. This chapter is not, however, so much about the fight for gender equality as it is an exploration of how the law might be instrumental in helping women to achieve their full potential as they choose to define it. This, of course, requires an examination of how the law continues to fail them as well as a broader discussion of their human-rights deprivations. The chapter begins with a historical overview of the struggle for women's rights and surveys the many areas in which women are better off today as well as the areas in which much more needs to be done. More needs to be done, for example, to give women a louder voice, greater political power, more say in decision making, and more control over resources; more also needs to be done to reduce domestic violence. The chapter describes the Committee on the Elimination of Discrimination against Women (CEDAW) as the most important international legal instrument to support legal empowerment of women and identifies areas requiring further action. The chapter ends with an action agenda in support of the legal empowerment of poor girls and women.

Chapter 8 seeks to bring it all together by seeking to anchor the agenda for action on the legal rights of the poor in the human-rights and development communities as they seek to transform themselves and their work on the eve of the post-2015 era. However, a lot will depend on civil society and state actors within countries, as legal empowerment of the poor requires a reinvention and renewal of the social contract between legally excluded people and the state. The actors will need to work on a different agenda and in a different way if they are to help work toward the world we want. This chapter uses governance and the sustainable-livelihoods framework to design an integrated and holistic approach that is practical yet transformational. After showing how the sustainable-livelihoods (SL) approach puts people at the center of their own development and seeks to unleash their agency through building on their assets, it uses the relatively benign concept of governance to discuss political issues, unpack power issues, and propose a practical self-empowerment agenda. The self-empowerment agenda follows the steps of articulation, mobilization, distribution, and confirmation of issues and rights. The SL approach follows the steps of asset assessment, envisioning a more sustainable livelihood, self-action, and support from others. Together, these steps can produce a truly integrated and transformative agenda to move toward a world that is more just, inclusive, and prosperous.

1

Taking Stock of Poverty and Development Actions

The technocratic illusion is that poverty results from a shortage of expertise whereas poverty is really about a shortage of rights. The emphasis on the problem of expertise makes the problem of rights worse.

—William Easterly

The purpose of this chapter is to provide the backdrop against which policy changes and programmatic actions to ensure the legal rights of the poor must take place. It provides a stocktaking of the progress, or lack thereof, that the world has made in reducing poverty, inequality, and exclusion. It also highlights various approaches—including the policy instruments that have been successful in certain contexts—and mentions their limitations. Interestingly, the legal rights of the poor, human rights generally, and access to justice and the rule of law have not featured prominently in the dominant approaches to date.

We start by taking a look at the global experience of the fight against poverty over the last several decades. This chapter will draw heavily from the most influential global reports on poverty and development including the *HDR* of the UNDP and the *WDR* of the World Bank. However, it is necessary to go beyond these global reports and look at some in-country assessments to get a more complete picture. After this review, we look at some of the poverty-related challenges to development including inequality, equity, and social exclusion. The chapter will conclude with some reflections on the international development enterprise itself, which then sets the stage for the action required to ensure the legal rights of the poor. Though this agenda can benefit a little from international development support, it is in reality a challenge to be addressed within countries, whether developed or developing.

The accelerated progress in reducing poverty in the twentieth century began in Europe and North America in the nineteenth century in what we now can see as the first major wave away from poverty and human deprivation. The ascent started in the foothills of the industrial revolution with rising incomes, improvements in public health and education, and eventually programs of social security. By the 1950s, most of Europe and North America enjoyed full employment and welfare states.

The second major wave of poverty reduction, beginning in the 1950s, took root primarily in previously colonized and newly formed nations around the world. The end of colonialism preceded improvement in education and health and accelerated economic development that led to a dramatic decline in poverty. By the end of the twentieth century, some 3 to 4 billion of the world's people had experienced substantial improvements in their standard of living.[4]

The consensus is that we have made great progress, but much remains to be done. The UN 2013 *HDR* celebrates the rise of the south. According to this report, "China has already overtaken Japan as the world's second biggest economy while lifting hundreds of millions of its people out of poverty. India is reshaping

---

[4]   UNDP, *HDR*, 1997, 2.

its future with new entrepreneurial creativity and social policy innovation. Brazil is lifting its living standards through expanding international relationships and antipoverty programs that are emulated worldwide."[5]

But the rise of the south analyzed in the report is a much larger phenomenon: Turkey, Mexico, Thailand, South Africa, Indonesia, and many other developing nations are also becoming leading actors on the world stage. The report suggests that "the world is witnessing an epochal 'global rebalancing' with higher growth in at least 40 poor countries helping lift hundreds of millions out of poverty and into a new 'global middle class.' Never in history have the living conditions and prospects of so many people changed so dramatically and so fast." [6]

By 2020, according to projections developed for the *HDR*, the combined economic output of three leading developing countries alone—Brazil, China, and India—will surpass the aggregate production of Canada, France, Germany, Italy, the United Kingdom, and the United States. The report also shows that new trade and technology partnerships within the south itself are driving much of this expansion. A key message contained in this and previous *HDRs*, however, is that economic growth alone does not automatically translate into human development progress. Pro poor policies and significant investments in people's capabilities—through a focus on education, nutrition and health, and employment skills—can expand access to decent work and provide for sustained progress.[7]

---

[5]   UNDP, *HDR*, Press Kit Materials, 2013, UNDP /HDR website.

[6]   UNDP. HDR. 2013.

[7]   UNDP, *HDR*, 2013, ii.

The 2013 report identifies three drivers of change: a developmental state, tapping into global markets, and innovative social policies. There are also four specific areas of focus for sustaining development momentum: enhancing equity including gender equity, enabling the voices and participation of citizens including youth, confronting environmental pressures, and managing demographic change.[8] This book will argue that increasing equity and voice will depend heavily on a legal-empowerment agenda within developing countries and that such an agenda will benefit directly from all three of the drivers listed here.

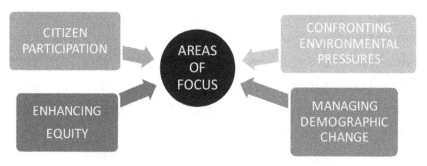

In the same vein, Oxford University's Poverty and Human Development Initiative (OPHI) predicts that countries among the most impoverished in the world could see acute poverty eradicated within twenty years if they continue at present rates.[9]

---

[8]   Ibid., 5–12.

[9]   *The Global Multidimensional Poverty Index* (2013), 5.

It identifies nations like Rwanda, Nepal, and Bangladesh as places where deprivation could disappear within the lifetime of the present generation. Close on their heels in reducing poverty levels were Ghana, Tanzania, Cambodia, and Bolivia.

Their study[10] of the world's poorest billion people used a new measure, the *Multidimensional Poverty Index*, which was recently updated in the 2013 *HDR*. It includes ten

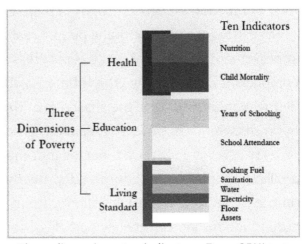

Three dimensions, ten indicators. From OPHI 2013.

indicators to calculate poverty—nutrition, child mortality, years of schooling and attendance, cooking fuel, water, sanitation, electricity assets, and a covered floor. The study found that in 2013, 1.6 billion people were living in "multidimensional" poverty.

The poorest billion people live in one hundred countries. Out of the bottom 1 billion, most live in live in South Asia, with India home to 40 percent, followed by Sub-Saharan Africa with 33 percent. The report also found that 9.5 percent of the billion poorest people lived in developed, upper middle-income countries.

This is not the first time the UNDP *HDR* has celebrated great progress while reminding us of the severity of global poverty that still exists. According to the 1990 *HDR*, "Life expectancy in the South rose from 46 years in 1960 to 62 years in 1987. The adult

---

[10]   www.ophi.org.uk/mpi-2013.

literacy rate increased from 43% to 60%. The under-five mortality rate was halved. Primary health care was extended to 61% of the population, and safe drinking water to 55%. And despite the addition of 2 billion people in developing countries, the rise in food production exceeded the rise in population by about 20%."[11]

Never before have so many people realized such significant improvement in their lives, but this progress should not generate complacency. Removing the immense backlog of human deprivation proved to be the challenge of the 1990s. Despite the optimistic trends in poverty reduction, billions still remained in poverty. The 1990 *HDR* also reported that there were "more than a billion people in absolute poverty, nearly 900 million adults unable to read and write, 1.75 billion without safe drinking water, around 100 million completely homeless, some 800 million who go hungry every day, 150 million children under five (one in three) who are malnourished and 14 million children who die each year before their fifth birthday."[12] Furthermore, during the 1980s, many countries in Africa and Latin America witnessed stagnation or even reversal in human achievements.

While the 1997 *HDR* came to similar conclusions, it went on to comment on the overall progress made in the twentieth century.[13] Even more importantly for this book, it suggested a strategy for the future. The report suggested that the great success in reducing poverty in the twentieth century demonstrated that eradicating severe poverty in the first decades of the twenty-first century was feasible. It went on to say that this might seem

---

[11]   UNDP, *HDR*, 1990, 2.

[12]   Ibid., 2.

[13]   UNDP, *HDR*, 1997.

an extraordinary ambition but was well within our grasp, since almost all countries had committed themselves to this goal at the World Summit for Social Development in 1995. Many countries, even some of the largest, had embarked on this project with all the seriousness necessary to achieve it. And indeed, these countries have delivered as shown in the 2013 report.

But then came the usual refrain: although poverty had been dramatically reduced in many parts of the world, a quarter of the world's people remained in severe poverty. In a global economy of $25 trillion, the 2013 report suggested that poverty levels of this scale are a scandal—reflecting shameful inequalities and an inexcusable failure of national and international policy.

The 1997, the *HDR* considered the progress in reducing poverty over the twentieth century remarkable and unprecedented. China and another fourteen countries whose populations added up to more than 1.6 billion people had halved the proportion of their people living below national income poverty lines in less than twenty years. Ten more countries with almost another billion people had reduced the proportion of their people in poverty by a quarter or more. Beyond mere advances in income, there had been great progress in all these countries in life expectancy and access to basic social services.[14]

Similarly, the *WDR* of the World Bank states that while significant progress has been made, much more remains to be done:

The past three decades have seen some impressive changes in the lives of people in the developing world. Average incomes have doubled. Average life expectancy has increased from 42

---

[14]   *Ibid.*, 2.

to 54 years. The proportion of adults who are literate has risen from about 30 percent to more than 50 percent. There has been a significant closing of the gap between industrialized and developing countries in life expectancy, literacy and primary school enrollment ... More than three-quarters of a billion people have barely enough income to keep themselves alive from week to week. In the low-income countries people on average live 24 years less than they do in the industrialized countries. Some 600 million adults in developing countries are illiterate; a third of the primary school-age children (and nearly half of the girls) are not going to school.[15]

The report then focuses on the role of human development in reducing poverty. It argues that the case for human development is not only, or even primarily, an economic one. Less hunger, fewer child deaths, and a better chance of primary education are almost universally accepted as important ends in themselves. But in a world of tight budgetary and human-resource constraints, the governments of developing countries must ask what these gains would cost—and what the best balance would be between direct and indirect ways of achieving them.

The report then suggests elements of a strategy for the future: the starting point is to empower women and men and to ensure their participation in decisions that affect their lives and enable them to build their strengths and assets. Poor people and poor communities rely primarily on their own energy, creativity, and assets. Such assets are not just economic. They are also social, political, and environmental—for both women and men.

---

[15] World Bank, WDR, 1980.

A people-centered strategy for eradicating poverty should start by building the assets of the poor and empowering them in their fight against poverty. What does such a strategy entail?

Political commitments to securing and protecting the political, economic, social and civil rights of poor people.

Policy reforms and actions to enable poor people to gain access to assets that make them less vulnerable. (Security of tenure for housing and land is as important as access to credit and other financial services.)

Education and health care for all, along with reproductive health services, family planning and safe water and sanitation. (This needs to be achieved soon-not postponed for another generation.)

Social safety nets to prevent people from falling into destitution and to rescue them from disaster.

The World Bank's flagship report on poverty provides a comprehensive analysis of where we were and what we needed to do: it states that poverty is the result of economic, political, and social processes that interact with each other and frequently reinforce each other in ways that exacerbate the deprivation in which poor people live. Meager assets, inaccessible markets, and scarce job opportunities lock people in material poverty. That is why, it argues, promoting opportunity—by stimulating economic growth, making markets work better for poor people, and building up their assets—is key to reducing poverty.[16]

In a world where political power is unequally distributed and often mimics the distribution of economic power, the way state institutions operate may be particularly unfavorable to poor people. For example, poor people frequently do not receive the benefits of public investment in education and health. And they

---

[16]   World Bank, WDR, 2001.

are often the victims of corruption and arbitrariness on the part of the state. Poverty outcomes also are greatly affected by social norms, values, and customary practices that—within the family, the community, or the market—lead to exclusion of women, ethnic and racial groups, or the socially disadvantaged. That was why, the report went on to say, facilitating the empowerment of poor people—by making state and social institutions more responsive to them—is also key to reducing poverty.

Like the 1997 *HDR*, the 2001 *WDR* outlines a broad strategy for reducing poverty. It acknowledges that the approach to reducing poverty has evolved over the last fifty years in response to deepening understanding of the complexity of development. In the 1950s and 1960s, many viewed large investments in physical capital and infrastructure as the primary means of development.[17] In the 1970s, awareness grew that physical capital was not enough and that health and education were at least as important.

In addition to the focus on health and education, the 1980s saw another shift of emphasis following the debt crisis and global recession and the contrasting experiences of East Asia and Latin America, South Asia, and Sub-Saharan Africa. Development efforts emphasized improving economic management and allowing greater play for market forces. The 1990 *WDR* on poverty proposed a two-part strategy: promoting labor-intensive growth (through economic openness and investment in infrastructure) and providing basic services to poor people in health and education.

In the 1990s, governance and institutions moved toward center stage—as did issues of vulnerability at the local and

---

[17]   Albert O. Hirschman, *Development Projects Observed* (Brookings, 1968).

national levels. Building on the earlier strategies in the light of the cumulative evidence and experience of the previous decade, the 2001 WDR proposed a strategy for attacking poverty in three ways: promoting opportunity, facilitating empowerment, and enhancing security. The first two of these are of direct relevance to legal empowerment and inclusion.

Promoting opportunity means creating jobs, credit, roads, electricity, markets for produce, and the schools, water, sanitation, and health services that underpin the health and skills essential for a life worth living. Overall economic growth is crucial for generating opportunity; so is the pattern or quality of growth. Market reforms can be central in expanding opportunities for poor people, but effective reforms need to reflect local institutional and structural conditions. In addition, mechanisms need to be in place to create new opportunities and compensate the potential losers in transitions. In societies with high inequality, greater equity is particularly important for rapid progress in reducing poverty. This requires action by the state to support the buildup of human, land, and infrastructure assets that poor people own or to which they have access.

In order to facilitate empowerment, we must recognize that the choice and implementation of public actions that are responsive to the needs of poor people depend on the interaction of political, social, and other institutional processes. State and social institutions often strongly influence access to market opportunities and to public-sector services, and these institutions must be responsive and accountable to poor people. Achieving access, responsibility, and accountability is intrinsically political and requires active collaboration among poor people, the middle class, and other groups in society. Changes in governance that make public administration, legal institutions, and public service delivery more efficient and accountable to all citizens can greatly facilitate collaboration. Strengthening the participation of poor people in political processes and local decision making also is a necessary step toward collaboration. Also essential to empowering the poor is removing the social and institutional barriers that result from distinctions of gender, ethnicity, and social status. Sound and responsive institutions not only are an important benefit to the poor but also are fundamental to the overall growth process.

It is also relevant for us to look at some of the nuances as they relate to rural poverty as compared to urban poverty. Access to or ownership of land is critical to avoiding poverty, and hunger is never far away for the rural poor.

According to the International Fund for Agricultural Development (IFAD), the population of the developing world is still more rural than urban:

Some 3.1 billion people, or 55 percent of the total population, live in rural areas. However between 2020 and 2025, the total rural population will peak and then start to decline, and the developing world's urban population will overtake its rural population. In Latin America and the Caribbean, and in East and South East Asia, the number of rural people is already in decline. Elsewhere, the growth of rural populations is slowing. Numbers will start to decline around 2025 in the Middle East, North Africa and in South and Central Asia, and around 2045 in sub-Saharan Africa. Despite massive progress in reducing poverty in some parts of the world over the past couple of decades—notably in East Asia—there are still about 1.4 billion people living on less than US$1.25 a day, and close to 1 billion people suffering from hunger.[18]

At least 70 percent of the world's very poor people are rural, and a large proportion of the poor and hungry are children and young people. Neither of these facts is likely to change in the immediate future despite widespread urbanization and demographic changes in all regions. South Asia, with the greatest number of poor rural people, and Sub-Saharan Africa, with the highest incidence of rural poverty, are the regions worst affected by poverty and hunger. Levels of poverty vary considerably, however, not just across regions and countries but also within countries.

The livelihoods of poor rural households are diverse across regions and countries and within countries. The rural poor derive their livelihoods, to varying degrees, from smallholder farming (including livestock production and artisanal fisheries), agricultural wage labor, wage or self-employment in the rural nonfarm economy, and migration. While some households rely primarily on one type of activity, most seek to diversify their livelihood bases as a way to reduce risk. Agriculture plays a vital role in most countries—more than 80 percent of rural households farm to some extent, and typically the poorest households rely most on farming and agricultural labor. However, nonfarm income sources are increasingly important across regions, and income gains at the household level are generally associated with a shift toward more nonagricultural wages and self-employment income.

Rural poverty results from a lack of assets, limited economic opportunities, and poor education and capabilities as well as

---

[18]   IFAD, *Rural Poverty Report*, 2011, 3–4.

disadvantages rooted in social and political inequalities. Yet large numbers of households move in and out of poverty repeatedly, sometimes within a matter of years. While there are rural households that find themselves in chronic, or persistent, poverty, relatively large proportions of people are poor only at specific points in time. Households fall into poverty primarily because of shocks like ill health, poor harvests, social expenses, or conflict and natural disaster.

Mobility out of poverty is associated with personal initiative and enterprise. It is highly correlated with household characteristics like education and ownership of physical assets, and it is also dependent on good health. Beyond household-level factors, economic growth and the local availability of opportunities, markets, infrastructure, and enabling institutions—including good governance—are all important. All these factors tend to be unequally distributed within each country.

Until recently, rural people's capabilities often have been treated separately from investment in creating opportunities for rural development. However, these issues need to be tackled together in order to facilitate broad-based mobility out of poverty and to achieve inclusive, pro poor rural growth.

So far in this chapter, we have examined the situation of global poverty over the last several decades. We will now briefly examine the national situations of some of the counties that have been most successful in reducing poverty, starting in Brazil. Then we will look at a comparison between Pakistan and China. Lastly, a comparison of China, India, and Brazil will provide some insights at the country level, where the complexities and obstacles of poverty eradication are most evident.

Brazil

During the decade from the early 1990s to the early 2000s, Brazil introduced extensive macroeconomic monetary and institutional reforms including trade liberalization, contractionary monetary policies, high interest rates, and deficit-cutting policies. These fundamentals set the stage for rapid growth when global economic conditions became favorable in the mid-2000s. These conditions included rising commodity prices due to increased demand from China and other developing countries, abundant international credit, and increased foreign direct investment (FDI). This growth, combined with social policies and well-targeted programs including public education, social security, conditional cash transfers, and a minimum-wage law, resulted in significant reduction in poverty and inequality. The Gini coefficient dropped 9 percent between 2001 and 2009, and in 2007, Brazil achieved its own MDG to reduce poverty to a quarter of its 1990 levels by 2015.[19]

Encouraged by such success, Brazil launched in mid-2011 a comprehensive national poverty alleviation plan to lift 16.2 million Brazilians out of extreme poverty through cash-transfer initiatives; increased access to education, health, welfare, sanitation, and electricity; and productive inclusion. This flagship program of the federal government promised to create new programs and expand existing initiatives in partnership with states, municipalities, public and private companies, and civil society organizations to extend the opportunities generated by Brazil's strong economic growth to its neediest citizens. What

---

[19] Pedro De Souza, "Poverty, Inequality and Social Policies in Brazil," IPEA Working Paper, 2012.

was once considered a matter of ethics and human rights became an important economic principle based on the conviction that inclusion would make growth sustainable.[20]

China and Pakistan[21]

Although comparing two countries' poverty situations can be problematic, China and Pakistan provide a clear opportunity of comparison due to the similar geographical locations of the two nations, the similar timing of poverty alleviating measures, and the types of reforms the two countries enacted.

Looking at the two countries from the period of 1978–2010, interesting differences arise. China has been successful in poverty reduction, while poverty in Pakistan has fluctuated during the last three decades. In 2012, poverty in Pakistan was as high as it was in the early 1990s, although in the middle of the first decade of the twenty-first century there was significant poverty reduction. So why has Pakistan lagged behind?

The recent debate on poverty reduction seeks inclusive growth in both low-income and middle-income countries. The concept of inclusive growth demands widespread expansion of opportunities so that all segments of society can benefit from economic expansion. The focus is usually on productive employment as a means of increasing incomes for excluded

---

[20]   "Brazil Launches Poverty Alleviation Plan," June 2, 2011, www.brazil.gov.br.

[21]   This section is adapted from G.M. Arif and S. Farooq, Poverty Reduction in Pakistan: Learning from the Experience in China, Pakistan Institute of Development Economics, 2012.

groups based on maximization of economic opportunities and provision of equal access to these opportunities.

How has China been successful in creating such opportunities? In 1978, China adopted a major ideological shift and introduced reforms in rural areas that resulted in the economic empowerment of its people through the provision of land. The success of the Chinese government in reducing poverty is rooted in its solid political determination and powerful organizational ability. Over the last seventy-plus years, the Chinese government has ruled with centralized and dominant political authority. However, its role has changed to that of a motivator as it has delegated all economic powers to the local governments.

The counties are the basic units for all decisions and implementations of rural poverty-reduction policies. Since the late 1970s, the government of China has comprehensively implemented sustainable poverty-reduction programs.

Around the 1980s, rural dwellers were allowed to move to small towns only. Township and village enterprises (TVEs) were encouraged, and they became initial drivers of China's economic growth. This form of labor mobility has been referred to as a plan to "leave the land but not the village." It absorbed a large quantity of surplus agricultural labor in the manufacturing sector by adopting labor-intensive techniques. At present, TVEs have the leading role in various industries. For example, the share of TVEs in the construction material industry measured in production value and employees is 74 percent and 69 percent, respectively. It lifted millions of people out of poverty. Over the last three decades, the rural nonfarm sector has not only played a leading role in rural poverty reduction by contributing in the national economy but also has played an important role in diversifying rural income.[22]

Originating in 1978, the nine-year compulsory schooling system has improved the quality of the labor force. The late 1980s saw further developments in government investments in roads, education, and irrigation, which later stimulated agricultural production and created employment opportunities in farm and nonfarm sectors.

Since 1993, China has boasted the largest FDI flow of all developing countries, which not only has fueled industrialization by diffusing new technologies and management skills and establishing global networks but also has contributed to institutional reforms.[23] In Pakistan, the situation has differed. The rising militancy during the past decade has created an overall uncertainty that has led to lower investment and a decline in FDI.

The government of Pakistan in the past has also distributed state-owned land among the landless peasants. However, this has had little impact on the rural poor, because the amount of distributed land was too small compared to the size of the needy, landless rural population.[24] The last land reforms were carried out in 1977.

Unlike China, where the land reforms initiated in the 1980s benefited the entire rural population, the beneficiaries of land distribution in Pakistan were limited in number, and the landless were not included in the list of beneficiaries. In addition, Pakistan has been politically unstable for decades. For example, in 1977, martial law was imposed in Pakistan, and under the military regime,

---

[22]   from G.M. Arif and S. Farooq, Poverty Reduction in Pakistan: Learning from the Experience in China, Pakistan Institute of Development Economics, 2012

[23]   Dollar, 2007, quoted by Arif and Farooq.

[24]   Qureshi, 2001, quoted by Arif and Farooq.

the process of nationalization implemented by the Pakistan People Party's government (1972–77) not only stopped but was reversed.

The numbers provide evidence of Pakistan's lack of fiscal support for the poor. Pakistan is hardly spending 2 percent of its GDP on education, and allocation for the health sector is stagnant at only 0.6 percent of GDP. During recent periods, education expenditure as a percentage of GDP has declined. Pakistan is unlikely to achieve health- and education-related MDG targets. The skill level of the labor force has not improved over time. This neglect of the social sector has negative implications for achieving sustained high economic growth and reducing poverty.

This study shows, then, that many of the strategies that China used to reduce poverty, such as nonfarm rural enterprises, public investment in infrastructure and education, land reform, and so on, were also carried out in Pakistan but largely failed there due to a weak central government, unstable politics, and poor management.

China, India, and Brazil

A World Bank report by Ravallion[25] looked at the strategies and policies used by China, India, and Brazil during their reform periods to support growth and reduce poverty and their respective outcomes. It concludes that all three countries learned the importance of macroeconomic stability. However, initial conditions in China favored more equitable access to the opportunities provided by reform, while the relatively better off in Brazil and India had better access to these opportunities. The

---

[25] M. Ravallion, A Comparative Perspective on Poverty Reduction in Brazil, China and India, 2009, elibrary.worldbank.org.

report also discovered that high growth rates do not necessarily result in higher inequalities and that growth rates can even increase while inequality falls.

All three countries reduced their poverty rates but through different mixes of approaches. The report used a common poverty line of $1.25 per person per day at purchasing parity power for consumption in 2005. Using that metric, the report evaluated the period between 1981 and 2005 and found that the poverty rate in China dropped from 84 percent to 16 percent, in India from 60 percent to 42 percent, and in Brazil from 17 percent to 8 percent.

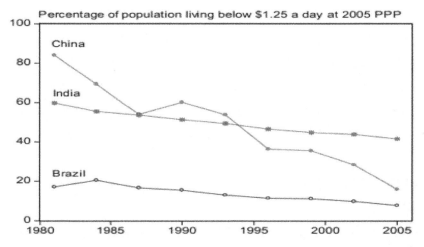

Headcount indices of poverty for a common international poverty line. From M. Ravallion.

The report sketches an overall scorecard of the countries on the two basic dimensions of pro poor growth and pro poor policy intervention:

China clearly scores well on the pro-poor growth side of the card, but neither Brazil nor India do; in Brazil's case for lack of growth and in India's case for lack of poverty-reducing growth.

Brazil scores well on the social policies side, but China and India do not; in China's case progress has been slow in implementing new social policies more relevant to the new market economy (despite historical advantages in this area, inherited from the past regime) and in India's case the bigger problems are the extent of capture of the many existing policies by non-poor groups and the weak capabilities of the state for delivering better basic public services.[26]

The survey of global poverty and the actions taken globally and nationally in some countries that have successfully reduced poverty show that poverty is decreasing in significant ways, but a lot remains to be done. We have learned several lessons about what works. Most importantly, it seems that the enabling environment, which includes factors like initial conditions, governance arrangements, politics, culture, perseverance in implementing bold reforms, and so on, is of central importance in determining the success or failure of possible strategic interventions. It is of note that the various development programs mentioned above have done little to address the legal rights and empowerment of the poor. The potential of a legal-empowerment agenda to help reduce poverty still awaits full exploration. Furthermore, such an agenda has significant potential to address challenges complementary to fighting poverty, such as inequality, marginalization, and exclusion. In the following section of this chapter, we will briefly examine these issues; they will be examined in more detail in chapter 4, in which we review the legal-empowerment agenda itself.

---

[26]   *Ibid*

Social Exclusion

According to a Department for International Development (DFID) review, social exclusion is a concept that can describe, on the one hand, a condition or outcome and, on the other, a dynamic process.[27] As a condition or outcome, social exclusion is a state in which excluded individuals or groups are unable to participate fully in their society. This may result from their social identity (e.g., race, gender, ethnicity, caste, or religion) or social location (e.g., in areas that are remote, stigmatized, or suffering from war or conflict).

> As a multidimensional and dynamic process, social exclusion refers to the social relations and organizational barriers that block the attainment of livelihoods, human development and equal citizenship. It can create or sustain poverty and inequality, and can restrict social participation. As a dynamic process, social exclusion is governed by social and political relations, and access to organizations and institutional sites of power. It was recognized as a way of looking at political and power relations and how they mediated policy dialogue, programmed design and delivery. At a pragmatic level, social exclusion was seen as: less 'threatening' than demanding gender equality; less 'intimidating' than a rights-based approach; and providing the space to address difficult issues of social discrimination such as caste or race. Social exclusion is therefore a broad term which includes political and economic exclusion.[28]

---

[27] J. Beall and L.H. Piron, DFID Social Exclusion Review, www.odi.org.uk/publications.

[28] *Ibid.*

The working definition proposed by the DFID review is this: "Social exclusion is a process and a state that prevents individuals or groups from full participation in social, economic and political life and from asserting their rights. It derives from exclusionary relationships based on power."[29]

Exclusion from social participation includes restricted access to infrastructure, services and amenities, social services, social security and protection, public safety, and social cohesion. Political exclusion refers to restricted access to organizations, consultation, decision making, and the rights and privileges of citizenship. Exclusion from the economy includes restricted access to labor markets, factors of production (such as land or tools), and a wide range of livelihood opportunities. Of course, people sometimes exit formal social systems when potential benefits are greater in the informal system. This process is described in detail in chapter 2.

According to a study for the Inter-American Development Bank, residents in socially excluded communities in Latin America and the Caribbean cannot depend on those institutions designed to protect them, and violence becomes an instrument to achieve certain outcomes, such as justice, security, and economic gain.[30] When conventional methods of obtaining and working for increased social status, higher income, and wider influence are limited, as they often are in marginalized areas, some feel compelled to resort to violent acts.

In India, there is a broad category of poor people, but certain socially excluded groups, such as scheduled castes and scheduled

_____

[29]   *Ibid.*

[30]   H. Berkman, "Social Exclusion and Violence in Latin America and the Caribbean," IADB Working Paper, 613, www.iadb.org/res/publications.

tribes (who make up 16.2 and 8.25 percent of the population respectively, according to the 2001 census), face much greater difficulty in accessing rights, entitlements, and opportunities. Women and girls and the disabled within these groups face even greater exclusion.[31] According to a World Bank study on poverty and exclusion in India, despite impressive rates of growth and poverty reduction, rising inequality is in part the result of historically excluded groups, such as tribes, scheduled castes, and women.[32]

Economic Inclusion

Over the last decade or so, inclusive growth has become the mantra of development agencies as well as of many developing countries' governments, especially in the BRICS nations (Brazil, Russia, India, China, and South Africa).

In most cases, an inclusive growth strategy is based on "the need to generate widespread productive employment, which enables economic growth to reduce both poverty and inequality. In this context, macroeconomic and structural policies play a key role in the creation of sustainable growth and productive employment, while social policies, social protection and labor market policies play a vital supporting role by enabling equal access to these new economic opportunities."[33] In addition, a pro poor investment policy environment that focuses on stimulation of domestically owned, labor-intensive medium, small, and

---

[31]   www.pacsindia.org.

[32]   World Bank, *Poverty and Social Exclusion in India,* 2011.

[33]   P. Martins and T. McKinley, Social Inclusiveness in Asia's Middle Income Countries, ODI, 2011.

microenterprises is required.[34] Other important dimensions in making growth inclusive are inclusive markets,[35] making markets work for the poor,[36] and inclusive business models.[37]

Almost all of these approaches focus on redistribution of employment and income and not much on the redistribution of assets like land and water or inclusion in political processes. Yet political and economic transformation are inseparable. Therefore, any discussion of the redistribution of assets must include the redistribution of power and provision of political voice that are required for such changes to take place.[38], [39]

Later in the book, we will show how legal empowerment of the poor is an effective instrument for combating social exclusion and creating economic inclusion for the betterment of underdeveloped countries and their peoples.

Inequality and Equity

Social exclusion very often leads to social and economic inequality, which is the variation in standards of living across a whole society. The most common measure of inequality is the Gini coefficient, which tracks variations in income and wealth in a population.

---

[34] E. Suart, Making Growth Inclusive: Lessons from Countries and the Literature, www.oxfam.org.

[35] UNDP, www.growinginclusivemarkets.org.

[36] www.m4phub.org.

[37] www1.ifc.org, 2012.

[38] D. Green, *From Poverty to Power* (Oxfam Publishing, 2008).

[39] CLEP, *Making the Law Work for Everyone*, UNDP, 2008.

While the debate on the relationship between inequality, growth, and poverty reduction continues, Stuart concludes there is apparent agreement among academics on the following: "Extreme income inequality is bad for growth as are other forms of inequality including education, insecure land rights and limited access to justice; inequality is bad for poverty reduction even in the presence of growth; it reduces people's capacity to cope with and recover from shocks and stresses; inequality is morally repugnant from a human rights perspective and extreme inequalities reduce political legitimacy, corrode institutions and increase political instability which can lead to violent conflicts."[40]

Another important concept in development, closely related to equality but different, is that of equity. The World Bank explains the concept as "the pursuit of equal opportunities and the avoidance of severe deprivation."[41] The report goes on:

> Equity is *not* the same as equality in income, or in health status, or in any other specific outcome. It is the quest for a situation in which personal effort, preferences, and initiative—rather than family background, caste, race, or gender—account for the differences among people's economic achievements. A situation in which all institutions are color-blind and nonmarket institutions are equally responsive to the rich and the poor. In which personal and property rights are enforced equally for all. And in which all have access to the public services and the

---

[40] E. Stuart, Making Growth Inclusive: Lessons from Countries and the Literature, 2011, www.oxfam.org.

[41] World Bank, *World Development Report: Equity and Development*, 2006.

infrastructure to leverage their productivity and their chances of success in the markets.[42]

The 2010 *HDR* introduced the Inequality Adjusted Human Development Index (IHDI).[43] The IHDI accounts for inequalities in life expectancy, schooling, and income by discounting each dimension's average value according to its level of inequality.

Generally, countries with less human development have more multidimensional inequality and thus larger losses in human development, though there is significant variation. For instance, among the low-HDI countries, Mozambique loses more than 45 percent of its HDI value, whereas Ghana loses 25 percent. Among the high-HDI countries, Peru loses 31 percent compared with 8 percent for Ukraine. The highest loss among developed countries is for South Korea, which loses almost 17 percent. People in Sub-Saharan Africa suffer the largest HDI losses because of substantial inequality across all three dimensions followed by South Asia and the Arab States. South Asia shows high inequality in health and education: India's loss in HDI is 41 percent in education and 31 percent in health. Considerable losses in the Arab States can generally be traced to the unequal distribution of education. Egypt and Morocco, for example, each lose 28 percent of their HDI largely because of inequality in education. In other regions, the losses are more directly attributable to inequality in a single dimension.

---

[42]   *Ibid.*

[43]   UNDP, *HDR*, 2010, www.hdr.undp.org/en/reports.

Naresh Singh

Loss in HDI due to multidimensional inequality

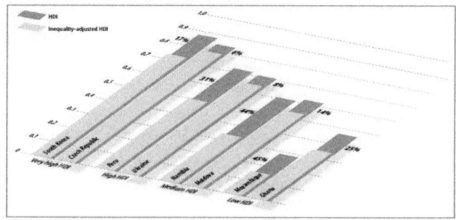

Note: Numbers beside bars are percentage loss due to multidimensional inequality (see statistical table 5).
Source: HDRO calculations using data from the HDRO database.

Loss in the HDI and its components due to inequality, by region

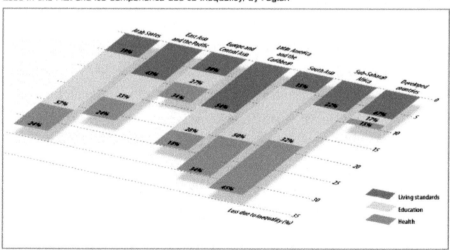

Note: Numbers inside bars are the percentage share of total losses due to inequality attributable to each HDI component.
Source: HDRO calculations using data from the HDRO database.

Conclusion

While many of the foregoing policy and pragmatic interventions have demonstrated some successes, they suffer from two fundamental shortcomings in terms of what policies and what groups they address. In terms of policy, they have focused on social protection policies and attempts at making growth more inclusive but have failed to address the structural injustices that create and maintain poverty and inequity. They will thus continue to address only the symptoms of poverty unless a radical new agenda designed to address the causes is added to the mix.

Sobhan has identified many structural injustices for deprived individuals. They include inequitable access to assets beyond traditional land, water, and forest resources including corporate assets. Also recognized are unequal participation in markets, unjust access to health and education, and undemocratic processes of governance.[44] Thus, access to justice, public services, and political participation remain highly inequitable. Exclusion from these facets of society traps the poor in inescapable poverty, because they participate on unequal terms.

The rights agenda has only been used to a limited extent to help prioritize resources for the poor. Even then, the agenda has primarily the judicial and not the political process. The core challenge to the structural injustices facing the poor is changing the power relations between those who have and those who have not. This book will argue that using a legal-rights approach through the political process is central to addressing this challenge.

---

[44] R. Sobhan, "Designing the MDGs for a More Just World," *Southern Voices* 1 (2013), www.cpd.org.bd.

These policies and programs have been designed and articulated primarily based on assumptions applicable to the formal or durable sector. Underlying assumptions, such as the idea that target populations have legal identities, registered small and micro businesses, titles to their properties, or collective bargaining rights, are largely untrue. A majority of the world's poor people live in the extralegal and informal sectors of society, where social norms and culture can differ vastly from those in the formal sector. The next chapter addresses some of these realities and what they mean for designing poverty-reduction programs.

2

One of the main findings of the Commission on the Legal Empowerment of the Poor (CLEP) was that a staggering 4 billion people on the planet are not able to use the law to improve their livelihoods. The systems in which they make their living are variously described as informal, underground, black market, cash economy, slum, and extralegal. These descriptors are not exactly synonymous, although they share many common characteristics. Informality is a "way of doing things characterized by (a) ease of entry; (b) reliance on indigenous resources; (c) family ownership; (d) small scale operations; (e) labor intensive and adaptive technology; (e) skills acquired outside of the formal sector; (g) unregulated and competitive markets."[45]

The central question that this book seeks to answer—how to provide legal rights to the poor—sits squarely in the informal sector where more than 80 percent of the poor and legally excluded live. Hence, a sound understanding of the characteristics of this sector with its various names is of primary importance. Both the development and the human-rights communities err when they apply formal-sector assumptions to the informal sector without testing their validity in this radically different arena where survival instincts rather than formal rules and laws drive the actions of the people.

---

[45] K. Hart, Employment, Income and Inequality: A Strategy for Increasing Productive Employment in Kenya, ILO, 1972.

This chapter therefore describes the main features of informal systems. It starts with an exploration of the economic sphere dealing mainly with employment, jobs, and small businesses and micro businesses. It next describes social dimensions, such as labor exploitation, lack of health care, the various forms of conflict that arise, sociopolitical alienation, and environmental issues. The case study of the Indian informal sector that follows then brings into vivid focus these economic realities. Extralegality occurs when people in the informal system seek legal goals, such as building a home or running a business to take care of their families, in a socially acceptable manner but do not obey all the provisions of the law, such as registration, taxes, building codes, and so forth. A case study from Tanzania illustrates this phenomenon, in which people living in the informal sector develop their own social rules over time. The most extreme conditions of informality occur in slums, where nearly a billion people live. A brief survey of the living conditions of slums precedes descriptions of two slums, one in Africa and one in India. Those who flee their own countries and are considered refugees constitute a special group of people who are usually without legal rights; the same is true of people displaced within their own countries. Before concluding, the chapter also briefly surveys the challenges these groups face.

The Informal Sector from an Economic Perspective

Economically, the informal sector broadly consists of units engaged in the production of goods or services with the primary objective of generating employment and income for the persons concerned. These small-scale units typically operate at a low level of organization, with little or no division between labor and capital as factors of production. Labor relations—where they exist—are based mostly on casual employment, kinship, or personal and social relations rather than contractual arrangements with formal guarantees.[46]

We can categorize the informal-sector workforce into three broad groups: (a) owner-employers of microenterprises that employ a few paid workers, with or without apprentices; (b) own-account workers who own and operate one-person businesses, who work alone or with the help of unpaid workers, generally family members and apprentices; and (c) dependent workers, paid or unpaid, including wageworkers in microenterprises, unpaid family workers, apprentices, contract labor, home workers, and paid domestic workers.

Employment in the informal sector includes all jobs in informal-sector enterprises or all persons who, during a given reference period, were employed in at least one informal sector enterprise, irrespective of their employment status or whether it was their main or secondary job. The International Labour Organisation (ILO) considers all forms of unprotected labor informal: "Employees are considered to have informal jobs if their employment relationship is, in law or in practice, not subject to labor legislation, income taxation, social protection or entitlement to certain employment benefits (advance notice of dismissal, severances of pay, paid annual or sick leave, etc.)."[47] Thus all unprotected workers, whether from the formal or informal sector, are informal workers.

For national accounting purposes, an institutional sector is different from a branch of economic activity (i.e., an industry). A

---

[46] OECD, 2003, stats.oecd.org/glossary

[47] ILO, Fifteenth International Conference of Labour Statisticians, 1993.

sector simply groups together similar kinds of production units that, in terms of economic objectives, have certain functions and behaviors with common characteristics. The result is not necessarily a homogeneous set of production units.[48]

The term *enterprise* is used here in a broad sense, referring to any unit engaged in the production of goods or services for sale or barter. It covers not only production units that employ hired labor but also production units owned and operated by single individuals working as self-employed persons either alone or with the help of unpaid family members. Enterprises may function inside or outside the enterprise owner's home, in identifiable premises, unidentifiable premises, or without a fixed location.[49]

The World Bank on its website on transition economies describes the informal sector as covering a wide range of labor market activities with two characteristics: "On the one hand, the informal sector is formed by the coping behavior of individuals and families in economic environments where earning opportunities are scarce. On the other hand, the informal sector is a product of rational behavior of entrepreneurs that desire to escape state regulations."[50]

Coping strategies (survival activities) include casual jobs, temporary jobs, unpaid jobs, subsistence agriculture, and holding multiple jobs. Unofficial business activities include tax evasion, avoidance of labor regulations and other government

[48] R. Hussmanns, Defining and Measuring Informal Employment, 2001, www.ilo.org/public/.

[49] *Ibid.*

[50] Inweb90.worldbank.org/eca.

or institutional regulations, and failure to register companies; underground activities include crime and corruption.

Coping Strategeis	Unofficial Bussiness Activities	Underground Activites
• Survival • Temporary/Multi Jobs • Sutinance Agriculture • Unpaid/Family jobs	• Tax Evasion • Avoidance of instituational regulations • Non-Registered	• Crime • Corruption

The World Bank goes on to describe the informal sector as "playing an important and controversial role. It provides jobs and reduces unemployment and underemployment, but in many cases the jobs are low-paid and the job security is poor. It bolsters entrepreneurial activity, but at the detriment of state regulations compliance, particularly regarding tax and labor regulations. The size of the informal labor market varies from the estimated 4–6% in the high-income countries to over 50% in the low-income countries. Its size and role in the economy increases during economic downturns and periods of economic adjustment and transition."[51]

Most descriptions and definitions of the informal sector aim to determine its size for the purposes of national accounting systems and to assess potential contributions to the national tax system, the formal economy, or GNP. They focus almost exclusively on jobs, employment, and income measures. Some, however, go beyond these narrow economic measures to try to understand the informal sector as a valid social system in which

---

[51] *Ibid.*

the large majority of the world's poor live and work. It is also important to consider the large numbers of nonpoor who are not able to cope in the formal system as well as some who deliberately avoid the formal system to escape taxation and other rules and regulations. In many developing countries, the formal and the informal systems work hand in hand, and we find the informal in the formal and vice-versa.

Broader Social Dimensions of the Informal Sector[52]

Taking a broader view to include other social dimensions, we see that the informal sector is also characterized by the following traits.

Fear and insecurity. Squatter populations in big cities are highly vulnerable to dispossession. The consequences of these evictions are severe: besides destroyed property and lost assets, dispossession destroys social networks. Such populations have limited or no access to essential services.

Environmental and sociopolitical repercussions. Urban migration is expanding the number and size of informal settlements, creating serious environmental and sociopolitical implications that affect not only the residents of informal areas but also the growing urban population as a whole. Informal settlements increasingly encroach on environmentally sensitive areas near protected water reservoirs, on public land, and on terrain that cannot be made habitable at reasonable cost.

Labor exploitation. Many of the world's poor are forced into the informal labor sector including illegal spheres like child

---

[52] Regional Dialogue on Legal Empowerment of the Poor in Asia-Pacific Region, www.snap-undp.org.

labor, where they receive fewer benefits and lower wages than formal workers and endure longer hours and more hazardous working conditions. They also have less bargaining power and representation than the formal workforce achieves through unions and other labor organizations.

Lack of health care. More and more of the world's poor—especially those in the informal sector—lack adequate access to health care. The poor, who already bear the brunt of the world's worst maladies from malnutrition to HIV/AIDS, are made more vulnerable by their inability to access and pay for medical care.

Social and political alienation. Informality affects more than individual needs and rights. Security of individual property rights, for example, must be combined with a broader, collective approach to promote socio-spatial integration. Informality also breeds gender inequality, corruption, and political disenfranchisement—all of which compound the position of the underclass.

Conflict. The poor are highly vulnerable to conflicts over scarce assets, such as land.

The poor living in the informal sector have developed informal justice systems, which they seem to trust more than formal systems. Some of the strengths of informal justice systems include the following:

- They are understandable and culturally comfortable.
- They focus on consensus, reconciliation, and social harmony.
- They can be good partners with the formal justice systems by reducing court congestion for nonserious offences.
- They offer swift solutions to disputes.
- They tend to enjoy social legitimacy, to be trusted, and to understand local problems.

- Informal justice systems often survive violent conflict.
- They provide geographical and financial accessibility.

Despite many communities viewing informal justice systems as the most likely way of achieving an outcome that satisfies their sense of justice, there are situations in which they fall well short of realizing that ideal. The main weaknesses of informal justice systems are as follows:

- They often involve unequal power relations and are susceptible to elite capture; where power imbalances exist between disputing parties, the weaker party is vulnerable to exploitation.
- They tend to promote unfair and unequal treatment of women and disadvantaged groups.
- They lack accountability.
- Their decisions may be arbitrary.
- They do not necessarily adhere to international human rights standards.
- They are unsuitable for certain disputes that are important for security and sustainable development; informal justice systems do not work when dealing with government service delivery; large companies; serious crimes; and intervillage, intercommunity, and third-party disputes, as the authority of the informal justice actors rarely extends beyond their own spheres of influence.

With all of these challenges, why would people still turn to the informal sectors, where they are less likely to enjoy legal rights? Do people opt for informality, or are they forced into it? The answers to these questions seem to involve a mixture of contextual and pragmatic motivations, and there is no consensus. However, some patterns seem to exist. For example, in Latin America and the Caribbean, Perry et al. found that self-employed workers, typically owners of micro businesses, opt for the informal sector.[53] They are especially attracted to the informal in situations of low access to human capital and other assets. The lack of access lowers their chances in the formal sector; at the same time, they gain perceived benefits, such as mobility, autonomy, and flexibility, in the informal sector.

On the other hand, salaried workers in the informal sector often would prefer an equivalent or better job in the formal sector, from which they have been excluded because the firms in which they could find work have opted to operate in the informal sector. People also move to the informal sector when the laws and regulations of the formal sector do not provide net benefits to them. We will discuss this further in the section on extralegality below.

India's Informal Economy: A Case Study

A National Commission on the Unorganised Sector report focuses on the informal or unorganized economy that accounts for an overwhelming proportion of the poor and vulnerable population in an otherwise shining India. It concentrates on a detailed analysis of the conditions of work and the lives of the unorganized workers that make up about 92 percent of the total workforce of

---

[53] G.E. Perry et al., Informality: Exit and Exclusion, World Bank Latin America and Caribbean Studies, 2007, www.worldbank.org.

about 457 million (as of 2004–2005). For most of them, conditions of work are utterly deplorable and livelihood options extremely few.[54] Such a sordid picture coexists uneasily with a shining India that has successfully answered the challenge of globalization powered by increasing economic competition both within the country and across the world.

However, a majority of the people, who did not have even INR 20 per day for consumption, were not touched by this euphoria. At the end of 2005, about 836 million people, or 77 percent of the population, were living on less than INR 20 per day and constituted most of India's informal economy. About 79 percent of the informal or unorganized workers belonged to this group without any legal regulation of their jobs, working conditions, or social security, living in abject poverty and excluded from all the glory of a shining India.

When 92 percent of the country's workforce is employed in the informal or unorganized economy (i.e., those who work in the unorganized sector plus the informal workers in the organized sector), it is but natural that there is a high congruence between the poor and the vulnerable segments of the society. However, it is an empirical challenge to demarcate the segments of the population that make up the poor and the vulnerable and then to link them with the informal economy. The commission therefore attempts, as a first approximation, to measure this category by dividing the total population of the country into six groups based on their consumption and expenditure.

---

[54]   National Commission for Enterprises in the Unorganised Sector, *Report on the Conditions of Work and Promotion of Livelihoods in the Unorganized sector,* 2007, www.prsindia.org/uploads/media.

The high congruence between informal work status and poverty and vulnerability is almost complete in the case of casual workers, 90 percent of whom belong to the group of the poor and vulnerable. The report's analysis of the conditions of informal workers is also a commentary on the conditions of life for those whom we have chosen to characterize as poor and vulnerable, who constitute the common people of the country.

Employees with informal jobs generally do not enjoy employment security (they have no protection against arbitrary dismissal), work security (they have no protection against accidents and illnesses at the workplace), or social security (they receive no maternity or health-care benefits, pensions, etc.). Therefore, any one or more of these characteristics can be used to identify informal employment.

An Agenda for Livelihood Promotion

The commission recognizes that livelihood promotion is the only way to deal with poor working conditions and other aspects of poverty and vulnerability that afflict the self-employed. Livelihood issues relate to one's capabilities, access to assets and entitlements, and opportunities for income generation. The empirical reality around the world is that the self-employed largely consist of individual workers with or without assistance from family labor. The commission claims that the notion of livelihood promotion takes on a broader meaning than simple enterprise promotion. Self-employed workers are workers as well as micro entrepreneurs. Their conditions of work are similar to those of wageworkers (e.g., a street vendor or a rickshaw puller pulling his or her own vehicle), and they often strive to make a meager income through self-exploitation by lengthening the working day.

However, they also need to employ the skills of an entrepreneur in sourcing inputs and selling their products. Moreover, for the wageworkers too, especially those working in the unorganized sector, it is impossible to divorce the conditions of work from the conditions of the small enterprises (usually run by the self-employed) in which they are employed. Hence, the promotion of livelihoods and the growth of enterprises have relevance for them as well.

Sixty-four percent of agricultural workers are self-employed farmers. Within the category of farmers, 86 percent are marginal or small farmers (i.e., those that operate on up to two hectares of land), and they account for 45 percent of the area cultivated. Outside agriculture, the self-employed constitute around 63 percent of the unorganized sector. This includes self-employed workers assisted by family workers (also referred to as unpaid workers) and those who employ one to nine workers. The fact that the self-employed form the majority of workers in the Indian economy has not, it seems, sufficiently dawned on the popular consciousness. Thus, the political support for policy and program changes is likely to be weak. The challenge is to ensure a sustained and improving minimum livelihood for workers.

Further, out of this range of security needs of unorganized-sector workers, what can legislation provide, and what can promotional policies or programs achieve? The commission takes the position that acceptable working conditions including a minimum of social security should be an entitlement backed by national legislation. For promoting livelihood, there should be a public program and an institutional mechanism to monitor, review, and further develop that program with a dedicated national fund to which the Common Minimum Programme of the United Progressive Alliance government is committed. In order to expand employment and improve the livelihood of those dependent on the unorganized sector, the commission has formulated an action program consisting of a number of immediate measures including a minimum wage, standards for working conditions, amelioration of gender disparities, social security, collective bargaining, and expansion of employment through enterprise development.

Basic principles of moral philosophy and human rights support the need to ensure socially acceptable conditions of work. Bodies like the ILO and others concerned with human rights and development have adopted such rights and principles as international covenants. In practice, progress in these areas has occurred at different paces in different countries dictated by, among other things, social norms and the resultant national ethos governing development and human dignity.

The Indian Constitution provides an overarching framework for regulating conditions of work as well as the protection and promotion of livelihoods. The fundamental rights guaranteed by the constitution prohibit the exploitation of labor in the forms of forced labor and child labor in factories and mines or in hazardous occupations (articles 13 and 14). It also guarantees nondiscrimination by the state and equality of opportunity in matters of public employment (articles 15 and 16). The right to form associations and unions is also a fundamental right under article 19.

The directive principles of the constitution (in Part IV) lay down goalposts and the direction of state policy. While the right to work is not a fundamental right for the citizens of India, it is included in the directive principles of state policy. The constitution states, "The state shall within the limits of its economic capacity and development, make effective provision for securing the right to work." The directive principles also include provision for just and human conditions of work and maternity relief. Further, "The state shall Endeavour to secure by suitable legislation, or economic organization or any other way, to all workers, agricultural, industrial or otherwise, work, a living wage, and conditions of work ensuring a decent standard of life."

Extralegality

Hernando De Soto in his 1986 book describes the phenomenon of informality based on his empirical observations. He finds that "individuals are not informal; their actions and activities are. Nor do those who operate informally comprise a precise or static sector of society; they live within a gray area which has a long frontier with the legal world and in which individuals take refuge when the cost of obeying the law outweighs the benefit. Only rarely does informality mean breaking all the laws; most individuals disobey specific legal provisions."[55]

De Soto further observes that such illegality is not antisocial in intent like drug trafficking, theft, or abduction but is designed to achieve such essentially legal objectives as building a house, providing a service, or developing a business. It seems to him that people are better off when they violate the laws than when they respect them. He concludes that informal activities expand when the legal system imposes rules that exceed the socially accepted

---

[55]   H. De Soto, *The Other Path* (1986).

legal framework and when the state does not have sufficient coercive authority.

In order to deal with the phenomenon of people in the informal sector who are not pursuing fully illegal activities but also are not operating fully within the provisions of the law, De Soto introduces the concept of extralegality, which he defines as what happens when people in the informal sector, "rather than surrender to anarchy, developed their own laws and institutions, which we call the 'system of extralegal norms,' to make up for the shortcomings of the official legal system. They created an alternative order to that of the formal sector."[56]

Case Study: Extralegality in Tanzania[57]

In the last four decades, Tanzania has thoroughly reengineered and modernized its written law. Nevertheless, poverty still prevails. Citizens are not using the tools created to allow them to cooperate on a nationwide basis. Assets cannot be fixed in a way that makes them economically useful, and they cannot be pulled together from their dispersed local arrangements into one consistent network of systematized representations. In contractual obligations, no one holds people accountable for their commitments. Assets primarily tend not to be liquid and cannot be used to create credit or capital. People are not interconnected, and transactions cannot be tracked from owner

---

[56]   *Ibid.*

[57]   Adapted from H. De Soto, "The Challenge of Connecting Informal and Formal Property Systems: Some Reflections on the Case of Tanzania," in De Soto and Cheneval, *Realizing Property Rights*, www.swisshumanrightsbook.com.

to owner. Business organizations do not have statutes that allow members to work under one point of control; they do not have the means to divide labor and control risks through limited liability and asset partitioning or associate in standard forms like corporations, cooperatives, and other collectives. There is no way to identify people with certainty, and contracts cannot reach a market outside the limited confines of family and acquaintances. Under these conditions of widespread extralegality, wealth continues to elude the majority of the nation's people; women especially have yet to be empowered.

Extralegal Traps

In the process of creating solutions for operating outside the law, people in Tanzania have built their own economic model. Seventeen solid and well-documented archetypes of social interaction underpin this model, whose further development is fundamental to the creation of a legal economic order rooted in Tanzania's indigenous culture. However, there are several important legal bottlenecks. Tanzania has designed most of the policies and laws that are required to build a market economy. Norms are in place to allow Tanzanian entrepreneurs to register and incorporate businesses, establish guarantees (using movable or immovable assets), obtain credit (at micro finance institutions or commercial banks), carry out international trade, participate in public procurement tenders, advertise, take out insurance, resolve disputes, and withdraw businesses from the market voluntarily or through bankruptcy. On the property front, citizens have legal access to rights over land and buildings in urban areas as well as access to occupancy rights in rural areas. In addition, the law provides that they can inherit these rights and resolve disputes through appropriate institutions. In short, the legal mechanisms needed to start up, operate, expand, and eventually close a business appear to be in place. Unfortunately, most Tanzanians do not use this legal system: 98 percent of all businesses (a total of 1,482,000) operate extralegally; 89 percent of all properties (1,447,000 urban properties and 60,200,000 rural hectares, of which only 10 percent—mainly Massai pastoral land—is under clan control) are held extralegally, and the rest are privately held.

The Tanzanian extralegal economy has assets worth US$29 billion, which is ten times all foreign direct investments since independence. It is virtually impossible for 90 percent of Tanzanians to enter the legal economy because of insurmountable financial and administrative barriers. "If a poor entrepreneur throughout a 50 year business life obeys the law, it will require him/her to make cash payments of US$91,000 to the State for the requisite licenses, permits, and approvals, and to spend 1,118 days in government offices petitioning for them (during which he could have earned US$ 9,350). The same entrepreneur would have to wait another 32,216 days for administrators to resolve all his/her requests, and during that time lose another US$79,600 in potential income. The grand total of these costs: almost US$ 180,000—enough money for 31 additional small enterprises."[58]

Tanzanians in the extralegal economy have actually created a self-organized system of documented institutions that allows them to govern their actions. The extralegal economy is the result of the local interactions of millions of Tanzanians who, in spite of only being able to deal among themselves at local levels, have nevertheless

---

[58]   *Ibid.*, 26.

created an abstract order to govern the way they relate to each other. This illustrates the important point that the informal sector is a complex adaptive system and not a mere collection of individual economic agents. Work in the informal sector will therefore demand a systems approach—we will take this up in chapter 4.

Spontaneously created tools of organization include references that testify to the trustworthiness of economic agents; consensuses that recognize the rights of people to their land, businesses, and chattel; informal mechanisms that store and retrieve information; authorizations that empower enterprises to operate in certain areas; titles that assign responsibilities and rights to business organizations; mechanisms that establish prices; and extrajudicial mechanisms that settle disputes. The authors identify seventeen archetypes of extralegal instruments in use. They then point out the limitations of these instruments compared to those required in a modern market economy based on the rule of law. The three examples below illustrate these archetypes and their limitations.

The archetypes of property. In the extralegal economy, property rights have only local validity. To build an effective bottom-up property system that all Tanzanians and foreigners can recognize, these dispersed mechanisms for ensuring property rights must be pulled together into one consistent network of systematized representations. These mechanisms also lack the low-cost legal connecting devices that would allow people to use their property to access credit, capital, services, and insurance as well as to secure inheritance.

The archetypes of business organizations. Business organizations still lack an enforceable law that allows each enterprise to function unwaveringly under one point of control where the division of labor; the combination of assets; and the interconnection of contracts between suppliers, clients, creditors, and investors can take place. The extralegal system does not fully separate the legal personality of the enterprise from its owners; nor does it allow the partition of assets so that all parties—including workers, owners, suppliers, and creditors—can feel that their rights are protected. Businesses lack the legal provisions that can give entrepreneurs limited liability in order to reduce risk and increase information about property committed to transactions; also lacking are perpetual succession rules that allow a collective to live beyond the death or departure of its initiators. Missing, too, are clear provisions for statutes and standard organizational forms so that all enterprises can have similar structures and can capture information about each other easily and thereby avoid exploitation.

The archetypes of the expanded market. The extralegal system does not equally provide the extralegal sector with enforceable rights and obligations throughout the whole nation. It does not protect trading names and the trademarks of products, or protect imports and exports at national and international levels, or allow enterprises to advertise freely, or give them the means to demonstrate cash flow to outsiders using official accounting standards, or allow them to issue shares to raise capital and guarantees to obtain credit outside their local circles.

Living in Slums

One billion people live in slums. That's one in seven of us. Without urgent action, 1.4 billion people will live in slums by 2020.[59]

---

[59]   Homeless International, www.homeless-international.org.

What are slums? The United Nations characterizes slums or informal settlements as places without the following:[60]

- durable housing of a permanent nature that protects against extreme climate conditions;
- sufficient living space, which means not more than three people sharing the same room;
- easy access to safe water in sufficient amounts at an affordable price;
- access to adequate sanitation in the form of a private or public toilet shared by a reasonable number of people; and
- security of tenure that prevents forced evictions.

Poor quality and overcrowded housing in slums has a significant impact on people's lives. Poor housing means diseases spread more easily, the effect of disasters like flooding are amplified, and people lack privacy and safety. Those living beside busy city roads and railways, on shorelines or riverbanks, and on and around rubbish dumps feel the constant dangers of these unsafe environments. With no legal rights to land, slum dwellers face the threat of eviction and can find it difficult to secure jobs and access credit and finance. Not having a formal, legal address can prevent slum dwellers from accessing services including health care, education, water, and electricity. Gaining secure tenure of safe land is the first step toward building a permanent home and accessing other opportunities.

Poor sanitation and unsafe water claim the lives of many slum dwellers every year. Contaminated water supplies, poor hygiene,

---

[60] UN-Habitat, www.unhabitat.org.SOWC/06/07/B/Slum2.

and a lack of decent toilets and sewers increase the spread of deadly diseases in slums. Diarrhea kills 1.5 million children under five each year. Without toilets, women suffer from the lack of privacy and dignity, and the burden of getting water (often from far away) usually falls on women and girls. The price of available water and sanitation facilities is often unaffordable.[61]

Case Studies of Slums: Dharavi and Kibera

This section will describe two important slums as case studies. As the case studies show, these slums have some core characteristics but also some major differences. It is important to bear this in mind so that we do not think of all slums as identical. One slum is India's largest and the other Africa's largest. These two slums have their own specific problems associated with empowering the poor and are at different stages of informal development. Slums like these and the differences between them are the primary reason a bottom-up approach is necessary, one in which the poor empower themselves.

Dharavi

It is home to more than a million people. Many are second-generation residents whose parents moved in years ago. Dharavi today bears no resemblance to the fishing village it once was. A city within a city, it is one unending stretch of narrow, dirty lanes; open sewers; and cramped huts.

----
[61] *Ibid.*

Social situation. In a city where house rents are among the highest in the world, Dharavi provides a cheap and affordable option to those who move to Mumbai to earn their living. Rents here can be as low as INR 185 (US$4) per month. As Dharavi is located between Mumbai's two main suburban rail lines, most people find it convenient for work. Even in the smallest of rooms, there is usually a cooking gas stove and continuous electricity. Many residents have a small color television with a cable connection that ensures they can catch up with their favorite soaps. Some of them even have a video player.

More than a million people live here, on a 427-acre stretch of land. To an outsider, Dharavi seems horrific. There are open sewers everywhere; ramshackle houses put together in tiny spaces create a huge risk of fire; the monsoons that come threaten to destroy the entire city within a city each year; and there is only one toilet for every 1,440 people. Only a third of people have access to clean drinking water. There is a complete lack of privacy and hygiene; wages are low; working conditions are terrible; and living between two railway lines is neither pleasant nor safe.[62] One commentator describes the community as follows: "The heat, the smells, the horrid living conditions are all incredibly appalling. However, it was hard not to notice that despite the misery, there was also *life*. Adults had jobs, and children went to school and played cricket amongst the garbage and goats. Whenever I would take a photo of a group of children, they would erupt in screams of joy and laughter. In my extremely sheltered

---

[62] D. Benson, Dharavi, Mumbai: The Pros and Cons of Living in a Slum, 2013, danielbenson.hubpages.com.

view of the world, I see these conditions as repulsive. But for the people of Dharavi, this is life."[63]

The economic situation. The Brihanmumbai Municipal Corporation owns most of the land in Dharavi, with private landholders and the central government controlling the rest. An informal real-estate market operates in the area, with prices varying by location and building quality. While some residents live in structures with tin walls and plastic sheeting, many have moved up to brick or concrete and have added lofts, upper stories, and decorative elements. Some owners lease spaces to tenants, having purchased more than one property or moved out of Dharavi.[64]

Dharavi also has a large number of thriving small-scale industries that produce embroidered garments, export-quality leather goods, pottery, and plastic. Most of these products are made in tiny manufacturing units spread across the slum and are sold in domestic as well as international markets.[65] Nothing is considered garbage in the slums. Men and women work from eight in the morning to eleven at night in the blistering heat, sorting bits of plastic to be cut into smaller pieces and eventually melted down. In addition to recycling, clothing manufacturing is also firmly established, along with other industries.

As the hub of the informal economy, the slum is the location of most residents' jobs. The self-created economic zone, running on cheap labor and encroached land, boasts an annual output

[63]   *Ibid.*

[64]   K. Savchuk and M. Echanove, Dharavi: Urban Typhoon, 2008.

[65]   BBC, http://news.bbc.co.uk/2/shared/spl/hi/world/o6/ dharavi_slum/html/ dharavi_slum_ intro.stm.

near US$1 billion. Banks have been trying to tap this productivity for decades now, hoping to move money from the huge parallel cash economy into the banking system. They have been opening branches and use novel methods to expand their presence. But taking basic banking to the urban poor has proved easier than convincing them to use the facilities.[66]

Bank branches are always overcrowded with migrant laborers and small entrepreneurs. They believe in paper currency and are unwilling to use automated teller machines, and since most of them are illiterate, bank staff must help them fill out the forms to protect them from fraud.

Many banks in the area are working with nongovernmental organizations to target women, going door to door and explaining the benefits of saving and investing. The idea is that once the women are convinced, it is easier to acquire business from the household.

Financial literacy is the only way to beat the banks' main competition, moneylenders and chit funds. These lenders charge usurious interest rates and give out loans without seeking documents, mainly for consumption.

But the banks don't seem to have relevant products for these people. For example, they do not encourage consumption loans in Dharavi, because the people don't have any documents to show their repayment capability. Yet providing loans to the flourishing small- and medium-scale businesses is a lucrative practice. These loans, in most cases, provide necessary working capital, as businesses here are predominantly engaged in small jobs for bigger firms.

---

[66]   M. Mandavia, 2013.

Lack of legal or adequate title deeds or papers makes it very difficult to disburse term loans for factory expansion. The issue with land rights also dampens the potential to give out home loans. Remittances remain the most popular banking products in Dharavi and attract the highest volume.

Kibera[67]

There are approximately 2.5 million slum dwellers in about two hundred settlements in Nairobi. This number represents 60 percent of the Nairobi population, which occupies just 6 percent of the land. Kibera houses almost a million of these people. Kibera is the biggest slum in Africa and one of the biggest in the world.

Kibera's slums assault the senses like a barbeque in a hot toilet. Raw waste carves gullies along the ragged ribbons of bare earth that serve as side streets and alleys, where children crawl and play in dirt you wouldn't step in unless you had to; for all my cringing, nobody seemed to mind much. Forests of twisted aerials sprout from the roves of shacks raised up from the mud and topped with sheets of metal. The main streets are full of the hustle and bustle of the ultimate free market, the sort of anarchic community libertarians beg for, but would beg to be rescued from. AirTel signs and M-PESA logos compete with butchers and charcoal-sellers, bombarding the senses with a barrage of color that still can't quite match that smell.[68]

---

[67] Facts and Information about Kibera, www. kibera.org.uk/facts.

[68] Robbens.

Social situation. The government owns all the land, but it offers the residents (regarded as squatters) no services, opens no schools, operates no hospitals, paves no roads, connects no power lines, and pumps no water into homes. In the slum, 10 percent of people are shack owners, and many of these people own many other shacks and sublet them. All the rest are tenants with no rights. The average size of a shack in this area is twelve feet by twelve feet; a typical shack has mud walls screened with concrete, a corrugated tin roof, and a dirt or concrete floor. The cost is about KES 700 (US$7.90) per month. These shacks often house eight or more people, many sleeping on the floor.

There are many tensions in Kibera, particularly tribal tensions but also between landlords and tenants and between those with and those without jobs. Until recently, Kibera had no water, and it had to be collected from the Nairobi dam. The dam water is not clean and causes typhoid and cholera. Currently, there are two main water pipes into Kibera, one from the municipal council and one from the World Bank. Residents collect water at KES 3 per 20 liters.

A cheap, illicit, strong, and sometimes toxic brew, *changaa*, is widely available; and with unemployment over 50 percent in Kibera, many start drinking early in the morning, leading to violence, crime, and rape. Many young girls become pregnant; at any one time, about 50 percent of sixteen-to-twenty-five-year-old girls are pregnant. Most of these pregnancies are unwanted, resulting in many cases of unsafe abortion.

Kibera needs land and tenancy rights, housing, water, electricity, health clinics, education, employment, security, and much more. Many donors and charitable organizations including churches are attempting to address all of these issues to a greater or lesser extent.[69]

The economic situation. A recent article in *The Economist* describes the situation in Kibera:

> Kibera is a thriving economic machine. Local residents provide most of the goods and services. Tailors are hunched over pedal-powered sewing machines. Accountants and lawyers share trestle tables in open-air offices. Carpenters carve frames for double beds along a railway line. Whole skinned cows hang in spotless butcher shops. "Give me 30 bob," says a customer to a paraffin seller, who has just taken delivery of several jerry cans from a porter with a steel-frame wheelbarrow. All day long, sweaty porters cart supplies along filthy lanes, hissing to shoo people out of the way.
>
> The key to making it in Kibera is access to capital. A market of one million potential customers crowds in on entrepreneurs, but raising the money to start a business is hard. Most banks won't lend to them because they have no collateral, perhaps not even a fixed address. Those who manage to borrow face high interest rates. Moses Mwega pays 25% a year and considers himself lucky. Over the years he has built up a cosmetics shop selling creams, wigs and shampoos. The bank recently accepted his stock, a television set and a second-hand sofa, including lace doilies, as collateral. He got 350,000 shillings ($4,000) to expand his business.[70]

---

[69]   Facts and Information about Kibera, www.kibera.org.un/facts.

[70]   "Upwardly Mobile Africa: Boomtown Slum," *The Economist*, December 22, 2012, www.economist.com/news.

The transformer, like all power in Kibera, is run by shady types who tap into the city grid. They are less than scrupulous when it comes to safety, and they charge heavily. But at least Kibera has power, unlike many other parts of Africa. Soft drinks sold in shops are chilled. Rooftops are awash with TV aerials, and mobile phones are as ubiquitous as in the West.

The foregoing section on slums describes deplorable living conditions on the one hand but thriving economic activity on the other. There are many poor people as well as slum millionaires. These are only two examples of the many paradoxes in these systems. Such extreme forms of informality and extralegality constitute a huge challenge for those hoping to help people living in informal systems enjoy legal rights. Land and property rights, labor and business rights, children's rights, and rights to health and education are nonexistent in this setting. Not only are the residents not usually aware of these rights, but they are unlikely to be persuaded that net benefits will flow from such rights.

These slums are complex, adaptive, self-organizing systems. Emergent creativity is evident everywhere. The linear thinking typical of development projects designed using logical frameworks is therefore likely to fail. Housing upgrade projects either have failed or have had limited impact. Only holistic approaches designed using complex, adaptive systems thinking are likely to succeed. Later chapters will address pathways to systemic change drawing from legal empowerment and sustainable livelihood approaches that bring together access to justice and business, labor, and property rights and build on existing assets, but below is a brief description of how Slum

Dwellers International (SDI) seeks to improve the lot of slum dwellers.

SDI argues that they work within the system in order to change it. "Achieving scale in urban development policy and practice begins at the individual settlement level. When local authorities engage with informal settlement communities, residents become active partners in upgrading their built environment. When communities and authorities learn together and produce developmental outcomes together, they are able to reach many more communities than the top-down initiatives that some countries attempt. Further, when communities own the process of upgrading, they are able to ensure that it is sustainable and continues to grow over time."[71] SDI praxis of house building reflects their realization that top-down pressure from international financial institutions on developing countries' housing delivery need to be matched by an opposite force from below:

---

[71]   Slum Dwellers International, http://www.sdinet.org/method-inclusive-cities/.

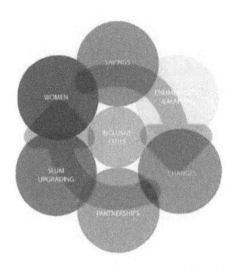

From: Slum Dwellers International

These authorities would have to feel the pressure from the homeless poor, and for this pressure to have any lasting effect, it had to be from organized communities ready to drive their own autonomous Development. If these organized communities were federated and were able to replicate people-driven housing development on a large scale supported by transnational alliances of shack/slum dwellers, then the pressure on government would intensify. SDI understood this process would generally oblige the state to participate in dialogue. SDI's house building praxis appears in this light to be an understanding that what countries in the South need is not participation by the people in a government process, but government's participation in a people's process. It seems that the social movement soon recognized that in this regard the local federations of homeless people would play a vital, pioneering role.[72]

This represents a paradigm shift in the way economics and politics are understood in industrial society: for the first time, slum dwellers can have the power and capacity to be a profound influence on the dialectics of their survival.

This is an interesting approach to self-empowerment, and while some of SDI's premises might be debatable, the principle of

---

[72]   *Ibid.*

bottom-up self-empowerment is crucial. However, the bottom-up process need not replace top-down pressure from powers that be; we might also seek ways in which the bottom-up approach might work in sync with top-down strategies to find positive reinforcement. To do this, we will need to adopt a win-win approach demonstrating that power can be a positive-sum game.

Refugees and Internally Displaced Persons (IDPs)

The largest numbers of people without ESCR live in the informal or extralegal sectors of their societies and, indeed, constitute the majority of the population in most developing countries—and thus the majority of the world's people. A subset of these live in the socially brutal but sometimes economically vibrant systems called slums. There are two other special groups who also deal with conditions as bad as or even worse than slums. These people usually have had to flee their homes for various reasons or have been driven off their land. Now they live in camps or in special situations far from home, where their children cannot attend school with their far-away friends and where they have little access to sanitation, education, health services, or justice. They have few or no property, business, and labor rights. Those in the first of these groups, known as *refugees,* have moved from their country of citizenship and now live in another country, usually without documentation. Those in the other group live in their own country but have left their habitual surroundings, services, property, and livelihoods and are termed *internally displaced persons* (IDPs). Helping them realize their ESCR poses special problems, and special provisions have sometimes been made to help them. We will briefly review these special provisions here.

Refugees

According to the UN, a refugee is a person who, "owing to a well-founded fear of being persecuted for reasons of race, religion, nationality, membership of a particular social group or political opinion, is outside the country of his nationality and is unable or, owing to such fear, is unwilling to avail himself of the protection of that country, or who, not having a nationality and being outside the country of his former residence, is unable or, owing to such fear, is unwilling to return to it."[73]

Most of the provisions relating to employment, self-employment, and welfare under the UN Refugee Convention provide that refugees should be given "the most favorable treatment" accorded to other noncitizens "in the same circumstances." Restrictions on the employment of noncitizens are not to be applied to refugees who have been in the country of refuge for more than three years, who are married to a national of the country of refuge, or who have children possessing the nationality of the country of refuge. Refugees seeking self-employment are in a slightly better position. They are to be accorded "treatment as favorable as possible and, in any event, not less favorable than that accorded to aliens generally in the same circumstances." Refugees who seek to practice a profession and whose qualifications the host country recognizes are to be treated in the same way as those seeking self-employment. In addition, refugees who do manage to obtain employment are to benefit from "the same treatment as nationals" with respect

---

[73] United Nations, Convention Relating to the Status of Refugees, Geneva, 1951, www.untreaty.un.org.

to pay and employment, and refugees are to have "the same treatment as nationals" with respect to social security, subject to the restrictions set out under article 24.[74]

When it comes to publicly controlled housing and education, other than elementary education, refugees are again to be granted "treatment as favorable as possible and, in any event, not less favorable than that accorded to aliens generally in the same circumstances." In relation to elementary education, public relief, and assistance and the rationing of products in short supply (where a rationing system exists), refugees are to get better treatment. The UN Refugee Convention provides that refugees are to get "the same treatment as nationals" in these areas.[75]

According to a recent report of the United Nations High Commissioner for Refugees (UNHCR), a majority of the 10.5 million refugees under its mandate fled from conflicts, more than half of them from Afghanistan, Iraq, and Somalia. Some 27.5 million people were internally displaced by conflict in 2011, and many of them needed protection.[76]

The 1951 Convention[77] and its 1967 Protocol[78] equally reflect the recognition that refugee issues are of international concern—

---

[74]   Ibid.

[75]   University of Minnesota, Human Rights Resource Center, Circle of Rights, ESCR Activism, www1.umn.edu/humanrts/edumat.

[76]   UNHCR, *Global Report: State of the Worlds' Refugees,* 2012, www.unhcr.org/gr.

[77]   United Nations, Convention Relating to the Status of Refugees, Geneva, 1951, www.untreaty.un.org.

[78]   United Nations, Protocol Relating to the Status of Refugees, 1967, New York, www.intreaty.un.org.

that they involve international responsibilities and make international cooperation a necessity. States are required not to return refugees to danger; not to discriminate against refugees; to ensure that refugees enjoy a minimum standard of treatment including freedom of movement and basic health, social, and economic rights; and to recognize refugees' identity and legal status, which is particularly important in a world that is so reliant on legal identity.

The discrepancies between refugees recognized under the 1951 convention and the broader group of persons in need of international protection arise in part from how some states have interpreted the definition of *refugee* in the 1951 convention and in part from limitations inherent in the instrument itself. Over time, the adoption of subsequent global and regional refugee instruments have helped to address these discrepancies; so have international human rights advocates and state practice and jurisprudence.[79]

According to the report, today's conflicts frequently involve different ethnic or religious groups, combining political, communitarian, and criminal violence. Violence that appears indiscriminate may also deliberately target certain groups of civilians and may include the use of sexual and gender-based violence. These armed conflicts may be aimed at securing social or economic power and usually affect areas in repeated cycles. Instead of uniformed forces and non-state actors who exercise de facto control over territory and people, today's conflicts often involve a myriad of private actors who may feel

---

[79] V. Turk, Protection Gaps in Europe? Persons Fleeing from the Indiscriminate Effects of Generalised Violence, Brussels, www.refworld.org/cgi-bin/textis.

little sense of responsibility toward local populations. Some include violent criminal organizations who seek to take control of land and territory for economic purposes or individuals associated with violent international ideological movements that seek to exploit local grievances. Today's conflicts blur the distinction between combatant and civilian—a cornerstone of international humanitarian law.

The *Economist*'s "The World in 2011" has noted that of 163 states covered by an index of state capability devised by the Economist Intelligence Unit, only 34 are classified as highly capable. State capabilities are rated as moderate in 38 countries, while the majority of countries have either weak (38) or very weak (58) capabilities. The *Economist*'s indicators of a state's ability to deliver its essential functions included its recent history of stability, the security of its citizens, its corruption levels, the size of its gray economy, the extent of the rule of law, the quality of its bureaucracy, whether the government controls all its territory, the extent of foreign influence, the degree of ethnic fragmentation, the degree of social cohesion, and trust in public institutions. In these weak or very weak states, the work of international organizations like UNHCR and nongovernmental human-rights organizations are of great importance in assisting refugees and IDPs achieve their ECSR and in bringing about an reintegration process that would help return them to normal life in mainstream society[80].

Fortunately, there is now also broad agreement that persecution within the meaning of the 1951 convention may emanate not only from the state but also from de facto authorities or groups or even

---

[80] *The Economist.* 2010. The World in 2011.

individuals in situations where the authorities are either unwilling or unable to provide protection that would enable displaced persons safely to remain within or to return to their countries.[81]

Some asylum states maintain, however, that persons fleeing armed conflict or large-scale violence cannot qualify as refugees under the 1951 convention unless they are "singled out" for treatment different from that experienced by other members of their communities. As a result, refugees fleeing ethnic or religious persecution by nonstate actors in a civil war have been rejected as refugees under the convention in certain countries. However, once admitted, they are often authorized to remain on humanitarian grounds. In other countries, war refugees in identical circumstances have been accepted as 1951 convention refugees.

In addition to international treaty obligations, regional refugee instruments have great value in defining standards for the treatment of all people in need of international protection while taking into account the specificities of various regions. Such instruments thus complement global refugee instruments. These regional instruments include the 1984 OAU Refugee Convention in Africa, the 1984 Cartagena Convention in Latin America, and the 2001 Revised Bangkok Principles in Asia.[82]

IDPs

There is no legal definition of IDPs as there is for refugees. However, a United Nations report, *The Guiding Principles on Internal Displacement*, uses this definition: "Internally displaced

---

[81]   *Ibid.*

[82]   *Ibid.*

persons are persons or groups of persons who have been forced or obliged to flee or to leave their homes or places of habitual residence, in particular as a result of, or in order to avoid, the effects of armed conflict, situations of generalized violence, violations of human rights or natural or human-made disasters, and who have not crossed an internationally recognized State border."[83] At the end of 2006, there were an estimated 24.5 million IDPs in some fifty-two countries. The region with the largest IDP population is Africa, with some 11.8 million IDPs in twenty-one countries.[84]

There is no international treaty that applies specifically to IDPs. *The Guiding Principles on Internal Displacement* lays out the responsibilities of states before displacement—that is, to prevent displacement—as well as during and after displacement. The UN General Assembly, the African Commission on Human and People's Rights (ACHPR), and the signatories to the 2006 Pact on Security, Stability, and Development in the Great Lakes Region (which include Sudan, the Democratic Republic of the Congo, and Uganda) all have endorsed the guiding principles. The guiding principles, however, are nonbinding, leading to the observation that "The UN Principles for Housing and Property Restitution for Refugees and IDPs, otherwise known as the Pinheiro Principles, provides guidance on the management of the technical and legal aspects of housing, land and property (HLP) restitution."[85]

---

[83]   F. Deng, *The Guiding Principles on Internally Displaced Persons* (New York: United Nations, 1998), E/CN.4/1998/53/Add1.

[84]   Wikipedia, https//:en.wikipedia.org/wiki/internally_displaced_person.

[85]   *Ibid.*

Restitution rights are of great importance to IDPs and refugees around the world and provide a way to prevent aggressors from benefiting from conflict. However, without a clear understanding of each local context, full restitution rights can fail to protect the people they are designed to protect for a number of reasons:

- Refugees and IDPs may never have had property (as in Afghanistan).
- They may be unable to access what property they have (as in Colombia, Guatemala, South Africa, and Sudan).
- Ownership may be unclear, as families may have expanded or split, making division of the land an issue.
- The death of a property owner may leave dependents without a clear claim to the land.
- People may have settled on land that once belonged to refugees or IDPs. Even if they know it is not theirs, they may have nowhere else to go (as in Colombia, Rwanda, and Timor-Leste).
- Refugees and IDPs' claims may compete with those of others including the state and its foreign or local business partners (as in Aceh, Angola, Colombia, Liberia, and Sudan).

In the absence of an international treaty on IDPs, the legal framework for the protection of displaced persons in Africa offers a good illustration of a regional approach: "In a general way, displaced persons are primarily protected by national laws. To this end, they have the right to full protection by national laws and enjoy the rights that they confer, without any distinction that may result from their displaced situation. Displaced persons are also protected by international human rights law, and should they find themselves in a state involved in an internal or international armed conflict they shall be protected by international Humanitarian law."[86]

A few specific instruments have been endorsed for the protection of displaced persons: "Guidelines of the HCR ... concerning persons displaced within their countries constitute a normative framework applicable to persons displaced within their country. It constitutes the first international norms expressly conceived to address the needs of displaced persons. Although these principles are based on existing international norms, they do not have binding obligations as treaties."[87]

In Africa, a specific convention on the internally displaced, the Convention on the Protection of Internally Displaced Persons in Africa, was adopted on October 23, 2009. This convention, also known as the Kampala Convention, constitutes a positive development and is without doubt the first instrument of its kind in the world. It provides a regional framework for the protection and assistance of displaced persons before, during, and after displacement. The convention is a major benchmark. It is the first legal instrument of its kind in the world to impose on states the obligation to protect and assist their displaced citizens.

At the African subregional level, there exist specific documents on internal displacement, notably the Great Lakes Convention on the protection and assistance to internally displaced persons and the 2006 Protocol on the Property Rights of Returning Persons.

---

[86] M. Sahli-Fadel, *Report of the Mechanism of the Special Rapporteur on the Rights of Refugees, Asylum Seekers, Migrants and Internally Displaced Persons in Africa Since Its Creation*, African Commission on Human and People's Rights, www.achpr.org/sessions/52nd/intercession-activity-reports.

[87] *Ibid.*, section 2.2.10.

These two documents are applicable in all the countries of the subregion that have ratified them.

Conclusion

Helping marginalized people to enjoy ESCR or even to become aware of the existence of these rights requires an understanding of the systems in which these people live and the rules associated with these systems. As described here, people are sometimes forced into informality and extralegality and at other times chose to live in these systems because the perceived benefits are greater.

Informal systems include mainstream informality but also the special situations of slums, refugees, and internally displaced peoples, who often live in even more deplorable conditions. When the majority of the population of a country lives outside the rule of law, does not pay taxes, and so forth, it is difficult to see how their governments can provide basic public goods and services. These elementary obligations are required for their general well-being and provide the opportunity to become even more productive and so reinforce a virtuous upward cycle of development. Many of these informal social systems have become self-organizing complex systems. Advocating change will require a deep understanding of the rules people have devised to survive in these contexts. Otherwise, we risk creating more poverty as well as resistance to change. Yet the majority of the people in developing countries will not improve, and their rights as human beings will not be realized, unless we support their self-rise out of the systems in which they are trapped.

3

Economic, Social, and Cultural Rights as Legal Rights

Legal rights are those bestowed on a person by a legal system, whether at a national or international level. These are claim rights, implying they entail responsibilities, obligations, or duties on other parties. Economic, social, and cultural rights are socioeconomic human rights, such as the right to housing and an adequate standard of living and the rights to health and education. The provision of legal rights to the poor, indeed to everyone, is not only desirable for the greater good of all humanity but also is a commitment made by state parties to the Universal Declaration of Human Rights (UDHR).[88] Over the years, the commitment has been translated into law in the form of treaties, customary international law, general principles, regional agreements, and domestic law. These laws express and guarantee human rights. Founded on the UDHR, the International Covenant on Civil and Political Rights and the International Covenant on Economic, Social, and Cultural Rights (ICESCR) entered into force in 1976. The World Conference on Human Rights in Vienna in 1993 established some new consensus agreements on human rights including the indivisibility and interdependence of human rights; for example, it established the interdependence of economic development, democracy, and human rights.

Human rights are sometimes described as having three generations. The first is civil and political; the second is

---

[88]   United Nations, Universal Declaration of Human Rights, 1948.

economic, social, and cultural; and the third includes more recent international agreements on intergenerational equity and sustainability, natural resources, a healthy environment, and economic and social development. These third-generation rights are generally seen as aspirational soft law, and sovereign states do not always accept them as binding. We must find innovative ways to help the poor, marginalized people of the world realize these rights, which are central to their achievement of sustainable livelihoods. This book will seek to describe some practical strategies toward this end that hopefully will be attractive to both states and citizens.

Among the rights enshrined in the UDHR and of special relevance to people living in poverty are the rights to life, liberty, and security of person; the right to recognition everywhere as a person before the law; the right to equality before the law and to equal protection of the law; the right to a nationality; the right to own property alone as well as in association with others and not to be arbitrarily deprived of property; the right of equal access to public services in one's own country; the right to social security and the economic, social, and cultural rights indispensable for dignity and the free development of personality; the rights to work, to just and favorable conditions of work, and to protection against unemployment; the right to a standard of living adequate for health and well-being; and the right to education. Member states have a legal obligation to respect, protect, and fulfill economic, social, and cultural rights and are expected to take progressive action toward their fulfillment.[89]

---

[89] Ibid.

Poor people everywhere are generally unable to claim these rights because of lack of awareness, capability, or organization; state incapacity or unwillingness to meet obligations; or deliberate and systematic exclusion of the poor in order to serve the interests of the elite. This has led to the widespread perception that ESCR are paper rights and to cynicism among the poor when they hear that they are entitled to these rights. The test of whether these rights are legal rights or just moral rights is the degree of justiciability. In other words, can poor people go to the courts or similar institutions and win enforceable legal remedies when their ESCR are denied?

This chapter therefore first reviews the justiciability of ESCR in general and, in so doing, makes the case that a growing body of evidence confirms the justiciability of ESCR but with various limitations, caveats, and lessons learned about how to proceed. The discussion below is based on the comprehensive Centre of Housing Rights and Evictions 2003 Report,[90] which contains case studies from the Asia Pacific, the Americas, Africa, Europe, and international mechanisms. The second half of this chapter illustrates the applications of the principles of ESCR to a major social system, the health system, in order to show how ECSR can be given expression in a systemic manner. Subsequent chapters will address the issue of economic rights. People need to play a much larger role in the realization of economic rights, in making a sustainable livelihood, and to do this, an even more self-empowering approach is necessary.

---

[90] M. Langford, *Litigating Economic, Social, and Cultural Rights* (Centre for Housing Rights and Evictions: 2008).

ESCR as Legal Rights: Are They Justiciable?[91]

If an individual or community is legally empowered to claim in a court or similar institution a remedy for a violation of a right, then the right is justiciable in the strict sense. Establishing this right remains a major struggle in many places where ESCR are not enshrined in the constitution or laws or where international law is not incorporated within domestic law. The principal strategy in such circumstances has often been to ask courts to acknowledge the socioeconomic dimensions of civil and political rights, since these are more likely to be actionable. But the critical issue is what legal protections the courts will provide if a right is taken away. Are there concrete entitlements to essential goods and services, or is there only an obligation for governments to pursue policy goals? If it is only an obligation to pursue a policy, how closely will courts scrutinize government performance?

Courts find it difficult to order the implementation of novel and detailed policies with specific resource consequences (for example, to produce and provide a vaccine for a particular disease). They are reluctant to intervene if governments have a number of different policy options available for addressing an economic, social, or cultural right or if their orders will have significant budgetary consequences. When confronted with difficult choices, courts often defer to the principle of the separation of powers, claiming that the democratically elected branches of government and not the courts should decide such

---

[91] This section is adapted from M. Langford, *Litigating Economic, Social, and Cultural Rights* (Centre for Housing Rights and Evictions: 2008).

issues.[92] Such dilemmas are surmountable, particularly if the violation is serious, if policy or legislative decisions have already been made, or if orders can be crafted to allow governments the necessary flexibility to make policy decisions. In the treatment action campaign (TAC) against HIV/AIDS cases in South Africa, for example, the judge poignantly asked the government how it could claim it lacked the resources to provide a medicine when it had not developed a plan to determine the cost of a provision program or assessed the different means at its disposal to access the resources.

Matthew Craven identifies the biggest constraint to justiciability: "justiciability depends not upon the generality of the norm concerned, but rather on the authority of the body making the decision."[93] If courts have the authority to decide on the entitlements of rights bearers, they are capable of developing reasonable principles and judgments. Yet the issue in many cases is not only the lack of express judicial authority but also excessive judicial restraint (reluctance to enforce ESCR). Courts and similar bodies have often made conservative interpretations of their own authority. This is a major factor in the slow pace of development in jurisprudence in many jurisdictions.

---

[92] C. Fabre, "Constitutionalising Social Rights," *Journal of Political Philosophy* 6, no. 3 (1998): 263–284 (quoted in Langford).

[93] M. Craven, "The Domestic Application of ICESCR," *Netherlands Law Review* 40 (quoted in Langford).

Naresh Singh

The Duties to Respect, Protect, and Fulfill and the Overarching Obligation Not to Discriminate

The duty to respect. The duty to respect means that states must refrain from interfering directly or indirectly with the enjoyment of rights, such as by denying people access to essential resources or entitlements necessary to the enjoyment of ESCR. Violations of this obligation arise in most case studies, particularly in traditionally litigated areas, such as labor rights (in the form of dismissal from employment and restrictions on trade union freedom) and housing rights (in the form of forced evictions). Recent cases have concerned contamination of water supplies, restrictions on the provision of medicines by medical practitioners, and police interference in the ability of the homeless to access food, shelter, and medicines. The Indian *Olga Tellis* case is notable for drawing on US due process jurisprudence to require the Bombay authorities to provide adequate notice before the eviction of pavement dwellers and recommending that alternative accommodation be provided.[94] The duty to respect is certainly a type of obligation that most judicial authorities are comfortable enforcing. It often serves as the most obvious example of justiciability. There is a clearly identifiable government action that a court can examine and censure.

However, governments in default will usually justify their actions by reference to broader public-policy purposes, such as national security, economic development, or even environmental protection, and contend that the remedies, such as resettlement, are too expensive. Courts can be overly deferential to these arguments.

---

[94] M. Langford, *Litigating Economic, Social, and Cultural Rights* (Centre for Housing Rights and Evictions: 2008).

The duty to protect. Some cases therefore invoke a duty to protect that requires governments to prevent private actors (individuals, corporations, or international organizations) from interfering with the enjoyment of a right. The number of cases relating to the obligation to protect is not large. In particular, government duties in the context of privatization to ensure access to and affordability of services have not received significant judicial attention. While employers, landlords, and potential polluters are likely to be regulated by legislation, other actors, such as private water and food vendors and other service providers, are not.

The duty to fulfill. The duty to fulfill—or, more accurately, the obligation to take steps progressively to realize ESCR within the constraints of available resources[95]—is presumed to be the most difficult to litigate. Some have argued that the various programs and policies needed to ensure everyone's economic and social rights to the maximum extent possible given available resources require the balancing of too many variables. The idea is that the myriad policy choices and budgetary decisions involved in implementing social and economic rights are too complex for courts and that courts cannot (or should not) access all the expertise necessary to make such decisions.

Nonetheless, courts have played a role in supervising these positive obligations, particularly when government action is woefully inadequate; when the state fails to implement existing programs; or when legislation, policies, and programs discriminate on prohibited grounds.

---

[95]   See, for example, *The International Covenant on Economic, Social, and Cultural Rights*, article 2.

Cases concerning the obligation to use maximum available resources are perhaps the rarest and most challenging. Courts have been willing to intervene more forcefully to order governments to take action where government programs are nonexistent or patently flawed.

The implementation or review of existing legislation and policies is the area where the most significant litigation has occurred. Much of the jurisprudence in India has involved forcing governments to implement programs already designed and funded. The Indian Supreme Court, for example, recently ordered and supervised the implementation of a raft of programs designed to prevent malnutrition and starvation.[96] In Argentina, the highest court ordered that a program to produce a vaccine, which already had received funding, be implemented more swiftly because a certain region of the country faced an epidemic.[97]

The proscription on retrogressive measures is, on its face, amenable to adjudication. Governments should be required to justify the removal of any program that benefits a vulnerable group. Admittedly, this aspect has not been the subject of extensive litigation. For example, the Hungarian Constitutional Court struck down massive rollbacks in social security, maternal benefits, and education subsidies even though international financial institutions strongly supported the cuts. However, this decision relied more on the principle of legal certainty than on constitutional rights to minimum subsistence or fully fledged

---

[96]   M. Langford, *Litigating Economic, Social, and Cultural Rights* (Centre for Housing Rights and Evictions: 2008). page 35

[97]   M. Langford, *Litigating Economic, Social, and Cultural Rights* (Centre for Housing Rights and Evictions: 2008)., page 60.

social and economic rights, thus leaving it open to attack.[98] In Canada, the court found rollbacks to protections of the right to organize and bargain collectively unconstitutional, because they denied vulnerable agricultural workers protection of the right to freedom of association enjoyed by other workers.[99]

Nondiscrimination and equality. The right to nondiscrimination runs like a thread through the duties outlined above. Rights to nondiscrimination and equality have been the basis for extensive litigation on ESCR in relation to personal characteristics, such as race, sex, age, and marital status. Recently, courts have applied the right to nondiscrimination to accrued characteristics, such as health status, poverty, or the reliance on social security. The advantage of using discrimination norms is that the party accused of discriminatory action must show that it would be too costly or unreasonable to refrain from the discriminatory act. The disadvantage is that it is often difficult to challenge the inadequacy of social rights unless courts take a substantive and not a formal view of equality. Not only does a formal approach ignore the difficulties that marginalized groups face (for example, if university places are simply allocated on the basis of merit, then minorities who cannot access primary and secondary education of sufficient quality are less likely to access higher education), but it can lead to unintended consequences. In one case, litigation for equal heating subsidies for men and women led to the removal of the subsidy. This "equalizing down" may lead to formal equality—what

---

[98]   A. Sajo, "How the Rule of Law Killed Hungarian Welfare Reform," *East European Constitutional Review,* Winter 1996: 31–34.

[99]   Dunmore v.Ontario, 3 S.C.R. 1016.

the Supreme Court of Canada has termed "equality with a vengeance"—but, with it, the loss of social rights.[100]

The rights to nondiscrimination and equality have played three important roles in ESCR advocacy: (a) poverty is often a result of *direct* societal exclusion and marginalization; (b) poverty means that otherwise reasonable measures place the most burden on vulnerable groups, resulting in indirect discrimination; and (c) *positive measures* or affirmative action to assist vulnerable groups is necessary to remove discrimination in practice and ensure substantive equality.

Courts have frequently struck down direct discrimination in social legislation and policy. The most famous case in the socioeconomic arena is *Brown v. Board of Education,* in which the segregation of black and white schoolchildren and university students was ruled a contravention of the constitutional right to equal treatment before the law.[101]

Effectiveness

It is common to hear people ask whether litigation has accomplished its ends. Was it effective? Did human rights beneficiaries gain from legal action? Many judicial decisions have a direct or indirect beneficial impact on reducing poverty and social exclusion. But the results are not uniform, largely due to variable implementation of court orders, which may be the

---

[100] Schachter v. Canada, [1992] 2 S.C.R. 679.

[101] M. Langford, 2003. *Litigating Economic, Social, and Cultural Rights* (Centre for Housing Rights and Evictions:). 177.

most necessary but most difficult task to ensure that litigation is effective[102].

In many cases, a litigation strategy is the only strategy available, all other avenues having been exhausted. In India, the court is considered the last bastion for the poor, the only official institution that would listen to them. Furthermore, courts are sometimes better placed to protect the rights of minorities than are the majorities who control governments.

Many claimants believe that the right to a hearing is as important as the remedy itself. Litigation has been critical in demonstrating that ESCR are legal rights and not just policy objectives. In other words, litigation is a long-term strategy to demonstrate the indivisibility of all human rights and thereby compel policy makers to take ESCR more seriously[103].

While many litigation cases have led to an increased observance of social and economic rights, an equal number of cases have made no direct impact. Evictions proceeded. Retrogressive measures were allowed. Social programs were not progressively improved. The pollution of water sources continued. Compensation was not paid.

We also need to be wary of the pitfalls represented by the failure to obtain a favorable decision and the failure to ensure implementation. For example, an unfavorable decision may set an unhelpful legal precedent, the broader social movement may experience a setback, vulnerable parties may forfeit opportunities for direct action, and communities may be given false hope. Therefore, careful case selection is imperative.

---

[102]   *Ibid*. case studies.

[103]   *Ibid* 66, 79.

Obstacles

ESCR litigation faces a formidable array of obstacles. Sometimes, these may be insurmountable (such as political repression or the bribery of community leaders), but many may be overcome with sufficient resources, awareness of ESCR, social mobilization, and so on. Rather than seeing obstacles as reasons not to claim and enforce ESCR and achieve effective remedies, the obstacles themselves increasingly are being seen as violations of rights. Access to effective legal remedies is part of economic, social, and cultural rights just as it is part of civil and political rights. The removal of these obstacles has become part of the process of claiming and enforcing and mobilizing around ESCR. Below, we will describe some common obstacles.

Inadequate law. ESCR are fully justiciable in an increasing number of countries, but the number is not large.

Western and common-law countries, where courts are open to broad interpretations of the right to life and rights against torture or discrimination, have often relied on civil and political rights. An important component of promoting more expansive interpretations of these rights is to draw on the interdependence of all rights and to urge the judiciary to interpret constitutions and legislation to be consistent with international human-rights law.[104] But there are clear limitations. In the US, some advocates believe there is no significant scope for further advances in the law,

---

[104] C. Dionko, The Philippines: Confronting Privatisation of Essential Services, chapter 4, 2003, in M. Langford, 2003. *Litigating Economic, Social, and Cultural Rights* (Centre for Housing Rights and Evictions:...

particularly in a country that has adamantly refused to recognize ESCR in international law.

The incorporation of ESCR within a domestic legal system is clearly an advantage as the experiences in Latin America and South Africa demonstrate. However, such incorporation means that vulnerable populations must exhaust local remedies before seeking international remedies. If the judiciary is conservative and slow to resolve issues domestically, this can mean long delays in achieving a successful decision at the international level.[105]

Most judges are skeptical of ESCR and have little awareness of international law: "Getting the judges, even senior judges, to see there is no 'in principle' difference between the various rights, I think, is the hardest part in the courts."[106] Many interviewees noted the importance of judicial education, emphasizing that it is most effective when conducted by fellow judges. Irrespective of legal interpretation, many judges are hostile to the poor and to minorities. Even investigations by human-rights commissions into issues of poverty and homelessness in Canada have been "riddled with discriminatory stereotypes about people in welfare."[107]

Lack of legal resources. Both lawyers and advocates note the difficulty of accessing useful and appropriate legal resources on

---

[105] M. Scheinin, Protecting Indigenous Livelihoods and Cultural Rights, chapter 17, 2003, in M. Langford, 2003. *Litigating Economic, Social, and Cultural Rights* (Centre for Housing Rights and Evictions:)...

[106] G. Budlender et al., South Africa: Positive Obligations and the Right to Housing, chapter 10, 2003, in M. Langford, 2003. *Litigating Economic, Social, and Cultural Rights* (Centre for Housing Rights and Evictions:)...

[107] B. Porter, Canada: Substantive Equality Rights for the Poor, chapter 7, 2003, footnote 2.

ESCR. This applies particularly to those legal groups handling many cases or operating independently of academic institutions and the ESCR movement. Full-text judgments from other countries or forums are often difficult to find. The use of comparative law is also a particular challenge, as courts tend to be selective about the other jurisdictions from which they will draw guidance. For example, South African judges will look to Indian jurisprudence, but the Philippines judiciary prefers the Supreme Court of the United States. Some interviewees noted that the legal profession itself can be an obstacle and that lawyers needed to be better trained in and sensitized to ESCR so that they can make better use of this area of law and make arguments that are more confident.

Lack of financial resources. Litigation invariably requires significant financial resources. The burden is more pronounced for cases that (a) are legally or factually ambitious, thereby requiring significant interdisciplinary sociological, health, economic, and environmental evidence; (b) involve large numbers of victims; or (c) involve a strong opponent that uses delaying and procedural tactics. The active involvement of academic lawyers, international nongovernmental organizations, union volunteers, community members; the free donation of services by lawyers and experts; or the contingent levying of legal fees can lessen the cost of litigation. Attracting lawyers is sometimes difficult if the applicants are an unpopular minority. There is a clear need for increased funding for legal centers and nongovernmental organizations so that they can conduct ESCR litigation.

The power of the opposition. The ESCR framework challenges the dominant discourses and practices around liberalization, privatization, and diminished roles for governments. Attempts to increase government spending on social programs are often not politically popular. In many cases, advocates have had to justify programs as purely instrumental or economically justifiable rather than arguing based on issues of dignity or rights.

The power of the opposing forces extends not only to governments and the private sector but to citizens as well. The powerful middle class is not always sympathetic and is sometimes openly antagonistic toward the poor. Some environmental movements display this bias. Housing-rights advocates in Argentina, India, and Europe say that this animosity has provided governments with support in cases involving evictions.

Advocates have also sometimes faced harassment by governments or corporations. For example, in Bangladesh, the police swamped the courts and lawyers' homes with slum dwellers. In cases against multinational companies, community leaders have been offered money to stop the litigation.

Social mobilization. Social awareness and high-profile campaigns are often the best way to sensitize the judiciary about ESCR and to ensure the implementation of court decisions. However, the ability to mobilize public opinion is dependent on networks, organizations dedicated to particular issues, community leadership and public awareness, and the acceptance of ESCR. Many of these factors are outside the control of legally oriented organizations. Ensuring that legal and non-legal strategies are complementary carries an additional resource burden. Furthermore, reaching the public often requires that issues be framed in a sensational manner and with a public face. The media are more likely to cover torture or extrajudicial killings than the closure of a school. This partly explains why many successful ESCR cases concern a threat to life or some element of violence (as, for example, in the case of evictions).

Remedies and procedures. Not all courts are accustomed to making orders regarding ESCR, particularly when this involves large numbers of applicants or the supervision of government compliance with the implementation of programs. Furthermore, adjudication bodies are often overly deferential to governments and only make recommendations, although, in the case of international and regional human-rights adjudication bodies, this is the sole remedial power available.

The reasons behind this are complex. On the one hand, this deference is sometimes related to concerns about the appropriateness of judicial intervention in policy making or the capacity of courts to supervise orders. On the other hand, courts seem reluctant to issue orders that governments would disobey, since the refusal of authorities to comply with the orders could diminish the authority of the court. ESCR are a new and evolving area, and it is perhaps understandable that courts are cautious and are feeling their way out to some extent. Advocates have emphasized that at the early stages of the development of domestic jurisprudence, it is important to choose cases that will allow the courts, the legal profession, and the public to become more comfortable with the idea of courts adjudicating and enforcing ESCR.[108]

Strategies

A human-rights approach. The experiences above show that it has been the adoption of a human-rights approach as much

---

[108] M. Langford, 2003, *Litigating Economic, Social, and Cultural Rights* (Centre for Housing Rights and Evictions: 2003)...

as reliance on human-rights law that had made a difference in litigation. By starting from human-rights principles—such as nondiscrimination, participation, and accountability—and selecting cases based on actual violations of internationally recognized ESCR, advocates have been able eventually to access or develop the required relevant law.

Case selection. Three categories of case selection tend to be successful. First is litigation that starts with claims related to civil and political rights, such as the contamination of water or forced evictions or discrimination. These actions tend to make the judiciary or the public more comfortable with ESCR. Second are cases involving large, egregious violations or clear failures of governments to implement their own programs. Third are modest claims that leave open the possibility for future development of jurisprudence. For example, Canadian advocates have worked hard over two decades to lay the foundations for broader interpretations of equality rights and the right to security of persons in future cases.[109]

The involvement of rights claimants. Successful strategies tend to assign an important role to the claimants, to those people suffering because of ESCR violations. This not only improves the evidentiary basis of the claim but also is crucial in the long-term empowerment of communities and in following up on orders. In Canada, the Charter Committee on Poverty Issues developed a model of "accountable litigation" in which low-income representatives are part of the project team for each case, advising and assisting in the development of the written argument. Often

---

[109] , B. Porter, 2003 in M. Langford, 2003. *Litigating Economic, Social, and Cultural Rights* (Centre for Housing Rights and Evictions:...

this meant ESCR arguments were given greater prominence than lawyers might have been inclined to give them.[110] In India, one lawyer, after two decades of public-interest litigation (in which any citizen can petition the Supreme Court), now refuses to take any case unless a community is directly involved.[111] In cases covering large and remote groups (for example, those suffering from a disease), public-awareness campaigns and the development of localized leadership and initiatives are necessary.

Other nonlitigation strategies. Complementary nonlitigation strategies, such as social mobilization, awareness and media campaigns, and political lobbying, are frequently viewed as indispensable for successful litigation. Such strategies are important in sensitizing the judiciary and showing them that ESCR claimants have public support and that all other avenues for remedying the violations have been exhausted.

Furthermore and most critically, these strategies place pressure on the opposing party—the government, corporations, or other organizations involved—to comply with any decision of the adjudication body. The involvement of high-profile moral or technical voices, such as those of unions, religious institutions, or intellectuals, creates vast supportive networks and provides the litigation with added legitimacy.

Evidence. A number of the cases, particularly those involving positive obligations, have obliged advocates to rely on experts

---

[110] M. Langford, 2003 2003 *Litigating Economic, Social, and Cultural Rights* (Centre for Housing Rights and Evictions:).

[111] M.C. Mehta, interview in chapter 3 on India, M. Langford, 2003 *Litigating Economic, Social, and Cultural Rights* (Centre for Housing Rights and Evictions:).n

in a wide range of disciplines. These have included sociology, economics, environmental science, and health. Properly defined and measured statistics showing the effect of a policy, the lack of reasonable policy implementation, or the damage to victims have sometimes been the deciding factor in a case. Evidence is compelling in health cases if advocates are able to show the efficacy of certain medicines and in environmental cases if they are able to show the existence of contamination. In the Canadian minimum-income criteria cases, advocates were able to demonstrate that widely held prejudices and assumptions about poor people in the rental industry were flawed.[112] In the Indian food rights cases, experts provided detailed evidence of the food supplies and financial resources needed to reach the population at risk of malnutrition and starvation. However, while experts are useful, it is imperative not to overburden the courts with incomprehensible statistics, and advocates emphasized the need to be clear at the outset about what the evidence is meant to establish.

Remedies. While courts appear willing to provide remedies that redress the violations of ESCR, ensuring court supervision of court orders can be critical in guaranteeing their effectiveness. Decisions in environment cases in India and school segregation cases in the US have taken twenty years to implement and have required constant recourse to the courts in the follow-up phase. This may require the careful preparation of arguments and additional sensitization of the judiciary in terms of comparable experiences.

---

[112]   *Ibid*, B. Porter, 2003 M. Langford, 2003*Litigating Economic, Social, and Cultural Rights* (Centre for Housing Rights and Evictions). in.

Advocates stress that it is important to adopt a flexible approach to remedies, adapting them to the issue and the context of the case. Sometimes, a declaratory order is all that is required, and it may be unwise to scare the court away from a finding of a violation by demanding large or complex damage awards or judicially imposed policy changes. Other times, it is better to give the government the responsibility of designing the appropriate remedy and reporting to the court after a period of time with its plan for compliance. In other cases, however, it is important to ensure that victims receive proper compensation for rights violations and that the court sets out very precise orders for governmental compliance.

A Human-Rights Approach to Health[113]

This section describes a human-rights-based approach to health. This example illustrates the systems approach to social and cultural rights in general. The systems approach is quite distinct from the litigation approach discussed above, which it complements. It also illustrates the responsibility the ICESCR puts on states to build the necessary systems capacity to meet stated ECSR obligations to their citizens. It should be noted that the emphasis is on provision of health services, while the approach described in the next chapter focuses on realization of economic rights, which requires a legal-empowerment approach.

What is the right to health? The UN Committee on ESCR (CESCR) has interpreted the right to health as the right to the highest attainable standard of health, encompassing medical

---

[113] This section adapted from G. Backman et al., *Lancet* 372 (2008): 2047–85.

care, access to safe drinking water, adequate sanitation, education, health-related information, and other underlying determinants of health.[114] It includes freedoms like the right to be free from discrimination and involuntary medical treatment and entitlements like the right to essential primary health care. Like other human rights, the right to health has particular concern for disadvantaged people and populations including those living in poverty. The right to health requires an effective, responsive, integrated health system of good quality that is accessible to all. International human-rights law recognizes that the right to the highest attainable standard of health cannot be realized overnight; it is expressly subject to both progressive realization and resource availability.[115] Put simply, progressive realization means that a country has to improve its human-rights performance steadily; if there is no progress, the government of that country has to provide a rational and objective explanation. Because of their greater resources, more is expected of high-income than of low-income countries. However, the right to health also imposes some obligations effective immediately, such as nondiscrimination and the requirement that a state at least prepare a national plan for health care and protection. Furthermore, there are indicators and benchmarks to monitor progressive realization of the right to health and to ensure individuals and communities have opportunities for active and informed participation in health decisions that affect them. Under international human-rights law, developed countries have some responsibilities for the realization

---

[114] Quoted from CESCR, 2000, by Backman et al., 2008.

[115] United Nations, International Covenant on Economic, Social and Cultural Rights, 1966.

of the right to health in developing countries.[116] Because the right to health gives rise to legal entitlements and obligations, effective mechanisms of monitoring and accountability are necessary.

Although the right to health adds power to campaigning and advocacy, it is not just a slogan; it has a concise and constructive contribution to make to health policy and practice. Health workers can use the right to devise equitable policies and programs that strengthen health systems and place important health issues higher up national and international agendas.[117]

Medicine, public health, and human rights have much common ground. To one degree or another, each field stresses the importance of the underlying determinants of health and quality medical care, each reaches beyond the health sector in scope, each struggles against discrimination and disadvantage, each demands respect for cultural diversity, and each attaches importance to public information and education. The right to health cannot be realized without the interventions and insights of health workers; and the classic, long-established objectives of public health and medicine can benefit from the newer and more dynamic discipline of human rights. A few enlightened people understood the relationships between these fields when the WHO Constitution was drafted in 1946 and when the Alma-Ata Declaration was adopted in 1978, affirming the right to the highest attainable standard of health.[118]

---

[116] Quoted from CESCR, 2000 by Backman et al., 2008.

[117] P. Hunt and G. Backman, "Health Systems and the Right to the Highest Attainable Standard of Health," *Health and Human Rights* 10 (2008): 81–92.

[118] WHO, Alma-Ata Declaration, 1978.

Until recently, the right to health attracted limited support from civil society or any other sector. The understanding and practice of health and human rights has improved since the Alma-Ata Conference. One vital part of this process has been a deepening understanding of the right to health. However, it was not until 2000 that an authoritative statement of the right to health emerged when the CESCR, working in close collaboration with the WHO and many others, drafted and adopted General Comment 14. Although it is not complete, perfect, or binding, General Comment 14 is compelling and groundbreaking. The comment shows a substantive understanding of the right to health that can develop and improve in the light of practical experience. The influence of Alma-Ata on General Comment 14 is explicit and clear.

Although much more work is needed to grasp all the implications of the right to the highest attainable standard of health, the general comment confirms that the right cannot be dismissed as a rhetorical device. General Comment 14 provides a common right-to-health language for talking about health issues and sets out a way of analyzing the right to health, making it easier for policy makers and practitioners to use. The next section summarizes General Comment 14 and highlights important elements including the requirement that health facilities and services be available, accessible, and culturally acceptable.

Health-related facilities and services can be available within a country but inaccessible to all those who need them. For example, access to essential medicines is an indispensable part of the right to health with several dimensions. First, medicines must be accessible in remote rural areas as well as in urban centers, which has major implications for the design of medicine supply systems. Second, medicines must be affordable to all including those living in poverty, which has obvious implications for funding and pricing arrangements. Third, given the fundamental human-rights principles of nondiscrimination and equality, a national medicines policy must ensure access for disadvantaged individuals and communities, such as women and girls, people living with HIV/AIDS, elderly people, and people with disabilities. Because equal treatment does not always secure equal access, a state must sometimes take measures in favor of disadvantaged people. As far as possible, the state must obtain data to identify marginalized groups and monitor their progress toward equal access. Fourth, reliable information about medicines must be accessible to patients and health workers so they can make well-informed decisions and use medicines safely.

Health-related facilities and services may be available and accessible but insensitive to culture and gender. For example, improving access to sexual and reproductive health care is not simply about scaling up.

Principles of General Comment 14

Article 12 of the International Covenant on Economic, Social, and Cultural Rights very briefly sets out the right to the highest attainable standard of health. General Comment 14 provides the UN Committee on Economic, Social, and Cultural Rights' interpretation of article 12. Although not legally binding, the comment is highly authoritative. Provided below is a summary of General Comment 14.

- Encompassing physical and mental health, the right to health places obligations on governments in relation to health care and the underlying determinants of health. These obligations include the provision of clean water, adequate sanitation, nutritious food, adequate shelter, education, a safe environment, health-related information, and freedom from discrimination.

- Governments have, for example, obligations regarding maternal, child, and reproductive health; healthy workplace environments; the prevention, treatment, and control of diseases; and the availability of health facilities, services, and goods.

- Governments have an obligation to give particular attention to marginal individuals, communities, and populations, creating a need for reliable and specific data.

- Within a country, health facilities, services, and goods must be accessible (and affordable) to everyone without discrimination; culturally acceptable (that is, respectful of medical ethics and sensitive to gender and culture); and of good quality.

- The right to health is subject to progressive realization and resource availability.

- Nonetheless, governments must take deliberate, concrete, and targeted steps to ensure the progressive realization of the right as expeditiously and effectively as possible.

- However, core obligations are subject neither to progressive realization nor to resource availability. Expressly taking into account the Alma-Ata Declaration, these obligations include the requirements to ensure access to health facilities, goods, and services for everyone including marginal groups without discrimination; to ensure everyone is free from hunger; to ensure access to basic shelter, housing, sanitation, and an adequate supply of safe and potable water; and to provide essential drugs as defined under the WHO action program on essential drugs. The obligations also include ensuring an equitable distribution of all health facilities, goods, and services as well as adoption and implementation of a national public-health strategy and plan of action by way of a participatory and transparent process.

- The right to health requires opportunities for as much participation as possible by individuals and communities in health-related decisions.
- Governments have an obligation to ensure that nonstate stakeholders are respectful of the right to health (for example, they must not discriminate).
- Developed states, and others in a position to assist, should provide international assistance and cooperation in health to developing countries (such as economic and technical assistance to help developing countries fulfill their core obligations). All states "have an obligation to ensure that their actions as members of international organizations take due account of the right to health."[119]
- Monitoring, accountability, and redress are essential. Given progressive realization, indicators and benchmarks are indispensable for holding governments to account.
- The right to health is closely related to and dependent upon numerous other human rights, such as the rights to life, education, and access to information.

---

[119]   Ibid., General Comment 14, paragraph 39.

- In narrowly defined circumstances and as a last resort, governments may interfere with the enjoyment of some human rights to achieve a public-health goal. For example, under certain circumstances, quarantine for a serious communicable disease, such as Ebola virus disease, may be necessary for the public good and lawful under human rights even though it limits an individual's freedom of movement.

The Application of General Comment 14 to Health Systems

The WHO identifies six essential building blocks that make up health systems: health services (medical and public health); a health workforce; a health information system; medical products, vaccines, and technologies; health financing; and leadership, governance, and stewardship.[120] Although debatable, these building blocks provide a useful way of looking at health systems and are essential steps toward the realization of the right to health. However, a health system might have all these building blocks but still not serve human rights. For example, the system might include both medical care and public health but might not secure fair access; or there might be a health information system, but important data might not be available. A major challenge for human rights is to apply or integrate the right to health across the six building blocks. The right-to-health analysis provided by General Comment 14 has to be systematically and consistently applied to health services, the health workforce, health information, medical products, financing, and stewardship—that

---

[120]   WHO, 2007, quoted by Backman et al., 2008.

is, all the elements that together constitute a functioning health system. Set out below are principles that help in the application of General Comment 14 to the health system as a whole.

Legal recognition. Countries should give recognition to the right to health in national law and by ratifying relevant human-rights treaties. Legal recognition is just one of the first steps on a long and difficult journey to realizing the right to health. Without follow-up from social movements, health workers, progressive government ministers and public officials, activist courts, and international support—in addition to governmental respect for the rule of law—legal recognition is likely to be an empty promise.

Standards. Although important, legal recognition of the right to health is usually confined to a general formulation that does not set out in any detail what is required of those with responsibilities for health. For this reason, countries must not only recognize the right to health in national law but also ensure that there are detailed provisions clarifying what society can expect by way of health-related services and facilities. For example, provisions should specify standards for the quality and quantity of drinking water, blood safety, essential medicines, the quality of medical care, and so on. Laws, regulations, protocols, guidelines, and codes of conduct may provide such clarifications. The WHO has published important standards on various health issues.

Participation. Health systems must also include institutional arrangements for the active and informed participation in strategy development, policy making, implementation, and accountability by all relevant stakeholders including disadvantaged individuals, communities, and populations.

Transparency. Tempered by the confidentiality of personal data, this requirement applies to all those working in health-related sectors including countries, international organizations, public-private partnerships, business enterprises, and civil-society organizations.

Equity, equality, and nondiscrimination. Health systems must be accessible to all including those living in poverty; minority groups; indigenous people; women; children; people living in slums and rural areas; people with disabilities; and other disadvantaged individuals, communities, and populations. Additionally, health systems must be responsive to the particular health needs of women, children, adolescents, elderly people, and so on. Outreach programs are necessary to ensure that disadvantaged people have the same access as people that are more privileged. The right-to-health principles of equality and nondiscrimination are akin to the health concept of equity.[121] All three concepts have a social-justice component. In some respects, equality and nondiscrimination, because they are reinforced by law, are more powerful than equity. For example, if a government or other body does not take effective steps to tackle discrimination, it can be held to account and required to take remedial measures.

Respect for cultural difference. From the right-to-health perspective, health systems must be respectful of cultural difference. Health workers must be sensitive to issues of culture, ethnicity, and sex; strategies must also be in place to enable indigenous people to study medicine and public health.

Quality. All health-related services and facilities must be of good quality. For example, regulations and standards consistent with the WHO guidelines for the quality of drinking water should be in place. The quality requirement also extends to the way

---

[121]   CESCR, 2000.

patients and others are treated: health workers must treat patients and others politely and with respect. Because medicines may be counterfeit, states must establish appropriate regulatory systems.[122]

Planning. Some important implications arise from the right to health being subject to progressive realization and resource availability. The Alma-Ata Declaration, General Comment 14, and other documents recognize the crucial importance of planning.[123] States must have comprehensive national health plans encompassing both the public and private sectors for the development of health systems; because the plans have to be based on evidence, a state must conduct a situational analysis with disaggregated data before drafting the plan. Health research and development should also inform the planning process. According to General Comment 14, the plan must include certain features, such as clear objectives and how these are to be achieved, timeframes, effective coordination mechanisms, reporting procedures, a detailed budget, financing arrangements (national and international), assessment arrangements, indicators and benchmarks to measure achievement, and one or more accountability devices. Indicators and benchmarks are already commonplace features of many health systems, but they rarely have all the elements that are important from a human-rights perspective, such as appropriate disaggregation.

A fair, transparent, participatory, and inclusive process for prioritizing competing health needs is required—one that takes

---

[122] P. Hunt and R. Khosla, "The Human Right to Medicines," *SUR* 5 (2008): 99–116.

[123] WHO, Alma-Ata Declaration, International Conference on Primary Health Care, 1978.

into account explicit criteria, such as the well-being of those living in poverty and not just the claims of powerful groups with vested interests.[124] The process of prioritization should give particular attention to the core obligations identified in General Comment 14, because they are required of all countries, whatever their stage of economic development. The list of core obligations is illustrative rather than exhaustive. One of the core obligations is to adopt and implement a national public health strategy and plan of action based on epidemiological evidence that addresses the health concerns of the whole population.

Before the finalization of the plan, key elements must undergo impact assessment to ensure that they are likely to be consistent with national and international legal obligations including those relating to the right to the highest attainable standard of health.[125] In addition, the plan must maintain the present realization of the right to health, although this might be waived in exceptional circumstances.

A low-income country might not be in a position to deliver universal access to health services, but a comprehensive national health plan should include a commitment to reach this aim.[126] Such a commitment is the minimum expected from all countries, whatever their stage of economic development. A developing country's commitment to universal access gives an

---

[124] P. Hunt et al., Neglected Diseases: A Human Rights Analysis, WHO: Geneva.

[125] P. Hunt and G. McNaughton, Impact Assessments, Poverty, and Human Rights: A Case Study Using the Highest Attainable Standard of Health, www2.essex.ac.uk/human_rights_centre.

[126] CESCR, Right to Attainment of the Highest Possible Standard of Health, WHO: Geneva, 2000.

important message to health workers, the public, and donors. When a country cannot provide universal access, it must have fair, transparent, rational, evidence-informed processes (such as protocols and guidelines) in place to ensure reasonable decisions about who has access to health-related facilities and services and on which terms.

Progressive realization. This does not mean that a government is free to choose whatever measures it wishes to take so long as they reflect some degree of progress. General Comment 14 requires that governments take deliberate, concrete, and targeted steps to ensure progressive realization as quickly and effectively as possible. Progressive realization, maximum available resources, and core obligations need closer conceptual and operational attention. Some courts have rejected the idea of core obligations and required that government policies be reasonable. Other courts have taken the same position as the CESCR in General Comment 14 and found that some health-related responsibilities are so fundamental that they are subject neither to progressive realization nor to resource availability. This position most closely matches the concept of the right to health: progressive realization is an important concept with a crucial role but only up to the boundaries of core obligations.

Referral systems. Health systems should have a mix of primary (community-based), secondary (district-based), and tertiary (specialized) facilities and services that provide a continuum of prevention and care. The system also needs an effective process by which health workers can assess whether patients will benefit from additional services and can refer patients from one facility or department to another. There must be a mechanism to refer patients between alternative health systems (such as traditional health practitioners) and mainstream health systems. The absence of an effective referral system is inconsistent with the right to health.

Coordination. Health systems and the right to health depend on effective coordination across a range of public and private stakeholders (including nongovernmental organizations) at the national and international levels. Effective coordination between various sectors and departments, such as health, environment, water, sanitation, education, food, shelter, finance, and transport, is important for health systems, which also require coordination within sectors and departments, such as ministries of health. The need for coordination extends to policy making and delivery of services. Uganda has recently added several interventions, such as deworming of children, supplementation with vitamin A, and health promotion information, to its Child Health Days. Now known as Child Health Days Plus, these days depend on and reinforce improved coordination between and within sectors and national and international partners including civil society.

International cooperation. Health systems have international dimensions including the control of infectious diseases, the dissemination of health research, and regulatory initiatives, such as the International Health Regulations[127] and the WHO Framework Convention on Tobacco Control. The international dimension of health systems is reflected in countries' human-rights responsibilities of international assistance and cooperation, which can be traced through the Charter of the United Nations, the Universal Declaration of Human Rights, and some more recent international human-rights declarations and binding

[127]   WHO, International Health Regulations 2005, second edition, 2008.

treaties. At least, all countries have a human-rights responsibility to cooperate on transboundary health issues and to do no harm to their neighbors.[128]

High-income countries have an additional responsibility to provide appropriate international assistance and cooperation in health for low-income countries. High-income countries should especially help others full their core obligations. The Swedish International Development Cooperation Agency (SIDA), for example, supports several stakeholders with crucial roles related to the right to health in Uganda. The agency has given funds to various organizations: the Ugandan Government; WHO for its human-rights work in Uganda; the Uganda Human Rights Commission; and civil-society organizations including Straight Talk, which aims to increase understanding of adolescence, sexuality, and reproductive health.[129] For their part, low-income countries have a responsibility to seek appropriate international assistance and cooperation to help them strengthen their health systems.[130] As members of international organizations, General Comment 14 confirms that the human-rights responsibility of international assistance and cooperation in health extends to all participating countries. Scandinavian countries, for example, have proposed a trust fund for justice and human rights in the World Bank.[131]

---

[128]   International Council on Human Rights Policy, 2003.

[129]   Straight Talk Foundation, 2008, www.straight-talk.org.ug.

[130]   P. Hunt, Report of the UN Special Rapporteur on the Right to Health to the UN Human Rights Council, 2008, UN Doc A/HRC/7/11.

[131]   M. Darrow, *Between Light and Shadow: the World Bank, the IMF, and International Human Rights Law* (Portland: Hart, 2003).

Legal obligation. Crucially, the right to the highest attainable standard of health gives rise to legally binding obligations. The health system must have, for example, a comprehensive national health plan; outreach programs for the disadvantaged; a minimum package of health-related services and facilities; effective referral systems; arrangements to ensure the participation of those affected by decision making in health; respect for cultural difference; and so on. One of the distinctive contributions of the right to the highest attainable standard of health is that it reinforces good health practices with legal obligation and accountability. States are legally obliged to take all appropriate steps to implement the right-to-health features of health systems. Of course, some governments implement these features without reference to the right to health. But many governments do not ensure that these features are in place, and in these cases, the right to health has an especially important role.

Monitoring and accountability. Individuals and communities should have the opportunity to understand how those with responsibilities have discharged their duties and provide those with responsibilities the opportunity to explain what they have done and why. Where a person or institution has made a mistake, accountability requires redress. Accountability is not a matter of blame and punishment but a fair and reasonable process to identify what works, so that it can be repeated, and what does not, so that it can be revised.

Something as complex and important as health systems needs effective, transparent, accessible, and independent accountability mechanisms—health commissioners, national human-rights institutions, democratically elected local health councils, public hearings, patients' committees, impact assessments, and judicial proceedings. The media and civil-society organizations also have crucial roles.

In many health systems, accountability is extremely weak. In some countries, the same body provides and regulates health services as well as holding those responsible to account. Accountability can also be little more than a device to check that health funds are going to the right places. Human-rights accountability is concerned with ensuring that health systems are improving and that the right to the highest attainable standard of health is being progressively realized for all including disadvantaged individuals, communities, and populations. In some countries, although it plays an important part, the private health sector is largely unregulated. The requirement of human-rights accountability extends to both the public and the private health sectors and to international bodies working on health-related issues.[132]

All bodies—public, private, national, and international—working on health-related issues urgently need accountability. The design of appropriate and independent accountability mechanisms requires creativity and leadership.

Monitoring and Reporting on ESCR

This chapter has outlined the two fundamental and complimentary approaches to analyzing, promoting, and providing ECSR to deprived people everywhere. In closing, it is useful to provide

---

[132] A. Clapham, *Human Rights Obligations of Non State Actors*, (Oxford University Press, 2006).

an introduction to the ways to monitor these rights and support accountability.

Several bodies monitor the extent to which those who have ratified the IESCR have met their obligations. These include UN bodies, especially the CESCR, which is a subcommittee of the General Assembly (UNGA) under the Economic and Social Council (ECOSOC). They also include national bodies (governmental, nongovernmental, or quasigovernmental), such as national human rights commissions; the US State Department, which produces regular reports on human-rights abuses internationally; and international nongovernmental organizations, such as Human Rights Watch.

Most of the monitoring work performed by these organizations is based on ad hoc surveys, anecdotes, media articles, or direct observation of particular events. The SESCR, to which states parties to the covenant are obliged to report, carries out the most systematic attempts at monitoring. This reporting is quite comprehensive as a quick review of the country reports to the CESR will reveal. The basic weakness of this system, of course, is that the state parties are themselves doing the reporting. Below are some sample questions and a few answers from the Peru 2011 report followed by an example from the China 2012 report so that the reader can see the kinds of information that might be included.

Reports to the CESCR[133]

The following example from the 2011 Peru report to the CESCR includes a sample of the questions the commission asked in the report and the state party responses. The report itself is broken

---

[133]   CESCR, Peru National Report to the CESCR, UNECOSOC, 2011.

down into fifteen articles with three to five questions per article. Some examples of the topics discussed include article 12 on the right to physical and mental health; article 7, which covers favorable work conditions; and the more general articles 1–5, which cover basic rights and nondiscrimination practices. Not included in the sample provided is a second document, which is a review of the responses authored by the CESCR.[134] This document, entitled "Concluding observations of the CESCR," makes recommendations based upon the actions, words, and situation of the state in question and provides some accountability to the self-reporting process.

---

[134] CESCR, Consideration of Reports Submitted by States Parties under Articles 16 and 17 of the Covenant, 2012, http://www.refworld.org/publisher

CESCR: *Please indicate whether there exist in your country distinctions, exclusions, restrictions or preferences in legislation, administrative practice or concrete relationships between individuals or groups of individuals, on grounds of race, color, sex, political opinion, nationality or social origin, which nullify or constitute obstacles to equality of opportunity or treatment in employment or occupation. What measures are being taken to eliminate such discrimination?*

36. **Peru Report:** As mentioned in response to question "1.d", Act No. 26772 and its regulations, approved by Supreme Decree No. 002-98-TR, provide that offers of employment and access to education facilities may not include requirements that constitute discrimination or the nullification or impairment of equality of opportunity. The Constitution likewise prohibits any kind of discrimination. In this respect, Peru has ratified ILO Conventions No. 100, on equal remuneration, and No. 111, on discrimination in respect of employment and occupation.

Article 13 of the Covenant

CESCR: *With a view to achieving full realization of the right of everyone to education: How does Peru comply with the obligation to provide compulsory primary education available free to all?*

252. **Peru Report:** Education in Peru is compulsory for pupils at the initial, primary and secondary levels121. Coverage in the educational system is currently nearly universal among those aged 6 to 11 (96.5%), with no great disparities by gender, area or poverty level. In 2007, the net coverage level in primary education reached 93.6 per cent122.

CESCR: *How far is access to higher education general in our country? What is the cost of this higher education? Has free education been established or is it being introduced?*

CESCR: *What measures has your country adopted or is intending to adopt to improve the living conditions of teachers?*

CESCR: *Please describe the legal, administrative and judicial system of your country aimed at respecting and protecting the freedom indispensable for scientific research and creative activity, in particular: Measures designed to promote enjoyment of this freedom including creation of all the conditions and facilities necessary for scientific research and creative activity.*

CESCR: *Please indicate whether Peru has a national health policy. Indicate whether it has adopted the WHO approach to primary health care as part of its health policy. If so, what measures have been adopted to provide primary health care?*

CESCR: *Is it possible to say from the breakdown of any of the indicators used or by any other means whether there are some groups in the country whose state of health is considerably worse than that of the majority of the population? Please define these groups as precisely as possible, giving details. Which geographical areas of Peru, if any, are in a worse situation with regard to the health of the population?*

Here is an excerpt of China's report to the CESCR:[135]

> **Article 2**
>
> **CESCR:** *Measures taken by the State party to guarantee the full realization of economic, social and cultural rights*
>
> 1. **China:** Each State party to the present Covenant undertakes to take steps, individually and through international assistance and cooperation, especially economic and technical, to the maximum of its available resources, with a view to achieving progressively the full realization of the rights recognized in the present Covenant by all appropriate means, including particularly the adoption of legislative measures.
>
> 2. **China:** The States parties to the present Covenant undertake to guarantee that the rights enunciated in the present Covenant will be exercised without discrimination of any kind as to race, color, sex, language, religion, political or other opinion, national or social origin, property, birth or other status.
>
> 3. **China:** Developing countries, with due regard to human rights and their national economy, may determine to what extent they would guarantee the economic rights recognized in the present Covenant to non-nationals.

In its initial implementation report, China addressed the promotion of a legal system to protect the economic, social, and cultural rights of citizens; the development of international economic and technical cooperation; and the safeguarding of the legitimate rights and interests of foreign nationals in China. Related content therefore will not be repeated unnecessarily here. Since China submitted its initial implementation report in 2003, it has adopted the following new legislation and measures.

---

[135]   CESCR, National Report of China to the CESCR, UNECOSOC, 2012, E/C,12/ CHN/2.

Most Recent Legislation, Programs, and Measures

On March 14, 2004, the second session of the Tenth National People's Congress adopted an amendment to the constitution, explicitly writing into the constitution the statement that "the State respects and protects human rights." The incorporation of human rights into the constitution had a long-term impact on the cause of human rights in China, signaling that the construction of a human-rights legal system in China had entered a new stage of historical development.

In order to implement this constitutional principle, the state has taken further steps to perfect a system to guarantee human rights, incorporating the development strategy for the cause of human rights into the national economic and social development strategy.

In March 2006, China's National People's Congress adopted the Eleventh Five-Year Plan for National Economic and Social Development, in which it laid out the development targets and roadmap for the economic, social, and cultural fields in China for 2006–2010. These included the building of a new socialist countryside, promotion of coordinated regional development, construction of a resource-conserving and environmentally friendly society, priority development of education, raising the level of people's health, and strengthening cultural construction.

In its observations on China's initial implementation report, adopted in 2005, the CESCR recommended that China formulate a "national human rights plan of action." In April 2009, China rolled out its first National Human Rights Plan of Action (2009–2010). This was the first national program in China focused specifically on human rights and covered various areas of civic, political, social, economic, and cultural rights. These included work targets and concrete measures for the two-year period related to guaranteeing the right to work, the right to a basic standard of living, the right to social security, the right to health, and the right to education. The program also addressed cultural rights, environmental rights, and the rights and interests of farmers, guaranteeing human rights during the reconstruction following the great Sichuan earthquake and guaranteeing the rights of ethnic minorities, women, children, the elderly, and the sick. Social organizations, nongovernmental organizations, news media, and the general public actively participated in the popularization and implementation of the plan of action. At the beginning of December 2009, the Chinese government carried out an interim appraisal of the plan's implementation, the results of which demonstrated that all the various target tasks of the plan were on schedule. Of the tasks designed to be implemented over the course of two years, most were around 50 percent complete, with some having reached 65 percent, providing an excellent basis for the full completion of the plan of action's target tasks.

In addition, since the submission of its initial implementation report, China has further perfected a legal system that guarantees economic, social, and cultural rights.

Conclusion

ESCR have their legal international origins in the UDHR, which almost all of the countries of the world have now ratified as member states of the UN. By doing so, they have legally committed themselves to the obligations set out in the UDHR and the attendant ICESCR. But getting these states to keep their commitments to their citizens is still a challenge. This chapter therefore reviewed the two principal strategies for getting states to act on their obligations. The first seeks to compel them to respect these obligations through litigation in the courts and discusses tactics, lessons learned, and approaches that have worked. The other, known as the human-rights-based approach to development, describes how capacity can be built in a systemic way to help states accelerate the so-called progressive realization of these rights. A description of the application of the right to the highest attainable standard of health and the health systems needed for its realization illustrates this approach. Finally, the sample reporting from Peru and China to the CESCR demonstrates the way countries are expected to report on their progress.

This chapter has focused mainly on the provision of social rights by states. In the next two chapters, we will examine the legal-empowerment approach to helping marginalized people realize their economic rights.

4

ECONOMIC RIGHTS THROUGH LEGAL EMPOWERMENT

Most development initiatives still tend to focus on the official economy, the formal legal system, and other established institutions and are implemented mostly at a national rather than a local level. For instance, programs promoting access to justice and the rule of law generally emphasize formal institutions, such as parliaments, the electoral system, the judiciary, and the executive branch of government. Economic assistance tends to focus on improving the investment climate for registered or foreign businesses. Yet most people in developing countries, particularly the poor, scarcely interact with national institutions and the formal legal system. Their lives are mostly shaped by informal local norms and institutions, such as the conditions of the slum in which they live or the degree of corruption of local officials. Big national reforms pass them by. The political and economic elites zealously guard the economic space, squeezing the less well-connected survival activities into the informal sector, which is itself controlled by the well connected. This chapter proposes a bottom-up, civil-society-driven agenda complemented by a top-down, state-sponsored agenda in which the poor themselves are central actors. We will describe this legal-empowerment approach below.

Legal Empowerment of the Poor

The Asian Development Bank (ADB) indicates that at the heart of their process of poverty reduction is the critical concept of empowering the poor to "participate in decisions that shape their lives."[136] They state that this requires citizens to have the knowledge and resources to interact in an informed manner with employers, the state, and other citizens as well as with private and public institutions regarding their legal rights and obligations. Legal empowerment, the ADB concludes, is impossible without the participation of the poor on issues that affect their livelihood, basic rights, and security.

The Commission on Legal Empowerment of the Poor (CLEP) examined the extent to which people globally were able to use the law to protect their assets and create new opportunities to improve their livelihoods. It found that around 4 billion people, the majority of the world's population, are excluded from the rule of law. This figure included the 2.6 billion people living on less than US$2 a day and another 1.4 billion slightly better off but not able to use the law to obtain their rights or improve their livelihoods. At best, they live with very modest, unprotected assets that they cannot leverage in the market due to cumulative mechanisms of exclusion.[137]

The CLEP declared that by design or by default, markets, laws, institutions, and politics often fail to serve the common good, excluding or discriminating against poor women and men.

---

[136] ADB, Legal Empowerment: Good Governance and Poverty Reduction, 2000, www.adb.org.

[137] CLEP, *Making the Law Work for Everyone* Vol. 1, 19, 2008.

Democracy is often more of a mantra than a reality; the rule of law in practice is often rule *by* law, arbitrarily and unequally applied. While people in poor countries may have rights on paper, that is often where they remain. Frequently, the only laws that people know are informal rules, some traditional, others more recent. Even the most developed countries are far from eradicating exclusion and legal disempowerment.

The commission's report is perhaps the most comprehensive global treatment of legal empowerment.[138]

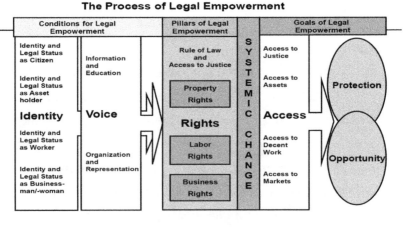

The Process of Legal Empowerment

The schema above illustrates the analytical framework for legal empowerment of the poor as developed by the commission.[139] It comprises four crucial pillars: access to justice and the rule of law, property rights, business rights, and labor rights. These pillars reinforce and rely on each other, and a lot depends on their convergence and synergy. Only systemic change aimed at

---

[138]   CLEP, *Making the Law Work for Everyone* Vols. 1 and 2, 2008.

[139]   *Ibid.*, 1, 27.

achieving the civic and economic potential of the poor can realize legal empowerment. However, legal empowerment is not merely about legal reform. For legal empowerment to take place, the poor must have identity and voice.

Legal identity is a cornerstone for access to justice. Despite the unequivocal provision in the Universal Declaration of Human Rights, tens of millions of people lack a formally documented legal identity. The United Nations Children's Fund estimates that more than seven in ten children in the world's least-developed countries do not have birth certificates or other registration documents.[140] This prevents many of them from accessing education and health care. It leaves them more vulnerable to exploitation, such as child labor and human trafficking. And without documentary proof of their existence, their parents may find it hard to interact politically, economically, and even socially outside their local communities. Formal institutions may use their lack of documents to block them from taking advantage of antipoverty programs specifically intended for them.

Identity corresponds to proof of their civic and economic agency as citizens, asset holders, workers, and businesspeople. Without a voice, they will not be able to demand their rights and hold their governments accountable for their obligations. Crucially, this voice requires education, information, and awareness on one hand and on organization and representation on the other.

As a reform process, legal empowerment requires parallel and coordinated interventions. The whole process is iterative, and the relationship between the legal empowerment process and

---

[140] UNICEF, The Rights Start to Life: A Statistical Analysis of Birth Registration, 2008, www.childinfo.org/birthregistration.

systemic change is mutually reinforcing. Poor people who are legally empowered will have increased voice and identity; they will have more influence on institutional and legal reforms and social policies, which, in turn, will improve the realization of their rights as citizens, asset holders, workers, and businesspeople. It is an advantage in practice and in principle that legal empowerment is less prescriptive than other approaches. By having as its aim the increased capacity of the poor including in the public sphere, legal empowerment takes responsibility for development away from outside forces and transfers it to the poor themselves. Development depends on more than markets and economic policy; it also depends on how laws and institutions function and relate to citizens. That, in turn, reflects the distribution of power and influence in society. We will now consider some substantive examples of policy change and legal reform to provide legal rights to the poor.

Access to Justice and the Rule of Law

Laws that are vital to the poor are often unclear, contradictory, outdated, or discriminatory in their impact. In the Philippines, for instance, settlers must prove they lived on land before 1992 in order to obtain formal rights; informal settlers can rarely demonstrate such proof, while settlers since 1992 are excluded by the law altogether.[141]

The poor may be unable to access the justice system because they do not understand it or lack knowledge about it. They may be illiterate, which severely hampers their ability to interact with the justice system. In many countries, the law is drafted and administered

---

[141]   *Ibid.*, 1, 33.

only in the national language, which many poor people may be unable to speak or read. In almost all African countries, for example, the justice system operates solely in English, French, or Portuguese, thereby excluding the majority of the population, which speaks only local languages. Courts may be far away and underfunded and may take years to decide cases. Bringing a case to court swiftly may require bribes. Judicial procedures may be inaccessible for those who lack legal representation, which is generally too expensive for the poor. Restrictions on who may practice law and provide legal services may block more accessible forms of legal services, such as legal clinics and paralegals. Difficulties in obtaining access to justice reinforce poverty and exclusion. As surveys of legal needs, crime, and victims demonstrate, the poor need better legal protection. Their personal security is often threatened. Many live in constant fear of eviction and expropriation.[142]

The most serious problems that the poor report in surveys of their legal needs surround changes in the major relationships that govern their lives and their assets. For example, since poor people usually live in family homes without formal documentation or registration, the death of the head of the family throws into question who owns the home and who has the right to live there. In addition, the poor often prepare land for farming and then use it without ever establishing formal rights. The absence of formal rights leaves the poor vulnerable to eviction if the legal landowner changes and makes due process and full compensation less likely during attempts at eviction by the public authorities. Similarly, if her rights have not been formalized, a woman who helps build a business with her husband is likely to lose everything in cases of

---

[142]   *Ibid.*

divorce. When communities jointly own pastures, share water, and use the same fishing grounds, it is almost impossible for people who move out to realize their assets, which effectively limits their freedom to change their way of life. At the same time, new arrivals may be denied access to collectively owned assets.

Despite their need for the legal system, many poor people steer clear of it and of state institutions in general. They believe, often correctly, that these institutions will not help solve their problems. Even if the system could conceivably provide adequate redress, it may take too long, cost too much, and require expertise or information that the poor lack. The principle of equality before the law is fundamentally important yet incredibly difficult to fulfill. Even full-fledged democracies with well-functioning state institutions struggle to do so. In countries where democracy is weak, elites are more likely to capture institutions. All too often, the law is a tool of the state and the ruling elites to use as they please—an option for the few, not an obligation that applies equally to all.

According to the commission's report, a number of far-reaching reforms will be required to address the challenge of giving the poor access to justice and the rule of law.[143]

So what is to be done? According to the CLEP,

First among rights is that which guarantees all others: access to justice and the rule of law. Legal empowerment is impossible when, de jure or de facto, poor people are denied access to a wellfunctioning justice system. Where just laws enshrine and enforce the rights and obligations of society, the benefits to all, especially the poor, are beyond measure. Ensuring equitable

---

[143] CLEP, *Making the Law Work for Everyone*, Vol. 1, 5–9, 2008.

access to justice, though fundamental to progress, is hard to achieve. Even if the legal system is technically inclusive and fair, equal access to justice can only be realized with the commitment of the state and public institutions. Legal empowerment measures in the domain of accessible institutions must: Ensure that everyone has the fundamental right to legal identity, and is registered at birth; Repeal or modify laws and regulations that are biased against the rights, interests, and livelihoods of poor people; Facilitate the creation of state and civil society organizations and coalitions, including paralegals who work in the interest of the excluded; Establish a legitimate state monopoly on the means of coercion, through, for example, effective and impartial policing; Make the formal judicial system, land administration systems, and relevant public institutions more accessible by recognizing and integrating customary and informal legal procedures with which the poor are already familiar; Encourage courts to give due consideration to the interests of the poor; Support mechanisms for alternative dispute resolution; Foster and institutionalize access to legal services so that the poor will know about laws and be able to take advantage of them; Support concrete measures for the legal empowerment of women, minorities, refugees and internally displaced persons, and indigenous peoples.[144]

Property Rights

The relevance of property rights goes far beyond their role as economic assets. Secure and accessible property rights provide

---

[144]   *Ibid.*

a sense of identity, dignity, and belonging. They create reliable ties of rights and obligations within a community and a system of mutual recognition of rights and responsibilities beyond it.

For many poor individuals and communities, land is more than just an aggregate of occupied and used plots. It is the expression of a way of life, which they should have the opportunity to improve by their own efforts. Starting out as ownership over parcels of nature, property arrangements have evolved enormously to cover land; other concrete assets; and abstractions like pollution quotas, financial products, inventions, and ideas. Overwhelming evidence from all over the world shows that functional property relationships are associated with stable growth and social contracts, whereas dysfunctional property relationships are associated with poor, unequal, and unstable societies. When property rights are out of reach or rights are subject to competing claims, people's assets are often not secure and their economic potential remains severely inhibited. Yet most of the world's poor lack effective property rights—they are without secure tenure, unaware of their legal rights, or unable to exercise them. This is true not only in the poorest states but also in more prosperous ones, such as Brazil, China, and Russia. The intrinsic economic power of their property remains untapped, and the poor unable, for example, to provide collateral on a loan to increase their incomes or improve their businesses. Insecurity hits the poor hard. They can be subject to arbitrary evictions, forced off their land at any time without compensation, and are powerless in disputes over assets with powerful actors. Their livelihoods are under constant threat, and there is little to encourage future investment in their land or small-scale businesses. In many countries, state institutions do not provide the protection the poor need and are entitled to.

The poor may document their assets through informal local arrangements that provide some protection and liquidity. But these are rarely recognized by national institutions and do not allow capital to be leveraged more widely. Whatever their economic assets, people have the right to remain underemployed. Owners cannot use their assets to get loans, enforce contracts, or expand beyond a personal network of familiar customers and partners. Their property is often vulnerable to seizure through force or law. Moreover, informal capital is invisible and unproductive for the national economy. And since the poor are unable to participate in the economy beyond their immediate vicinity, there are few possibilities for trade.

This is a huge opportunity wasted. In Peru, for instance, according to some estimates, informal capital amounts to more than US$74 billion. In Haiti, it's more than US$5.4 billion; in Honduras, nearly US$13 billion; in Albania, nearly US$16 billion; in Tanzania, more than US$29 billion; in the Philippines, more than US$132 billion; in Egypt, more than US$248 billion; and in Mexico, more than US$310 billion.[145] That this informal capital cannot be put to its full use is particularly galling because it is already where it is needed most—in the hands of poor people and their communities. External sources of capital, such as official aid and foreign investment, are less abundant and do not always reach the poor.

Vulnerable groups suffer most from a lack of property rights. Indigenous peoples are frequently victims of property discrimination; collectively held indigenous lands have often been declared public or unoccupied lands (and it is possible to retain collectivity when formalizing property rights). Women, who constitute half of the world's population, own very little of the

---

[145] www.ild.org.pe/en/whatwedo/diagnostics.

world's property—as little as 2 percent in some countries. Rarely do they own more than 15 percent of it.[146] Even when women do have legal property rights, their actual control of land may be tenuous, since men often mediate access.

So What Is to Be Done?

Ownership of property, alone or in association with others, is a human right. A fully functioning property system is composed of four building blocks: a system of rules that defines the bundle of rights and obligations between people and assets reflecting the multiplicity and diversity of property systems around the world, a system of governance, a functioning market for the exchange of assets, and an instrument of social policy.

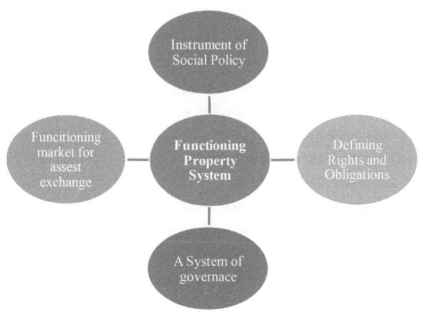

---

[146] www.icrw.org. See also FAO, Women's Rights to Land and Natural Resources: Implications for a Rights Based Approach, 1999.

Each of these components can be dysfunctional, operating against the poor. When the system fully functions, it becomes a vehicle for the inclusion of the poor in the formal economy and a mechanism for their upward social mobility. When the entire system or a single component is dysfunctional, it deprives the poor of opportunity or discriminates against them. Such a system operates in the following four ways:

1) *As a system of rules that defines the bundle of rights and obligations between people and assets.* Property ownership creates ties that bind individual citizens together through the formation of networks of economic and legal rights and corresponding obligations. The credible enforcement of these rights and obligations requires a judicial mechanism that allows for equitable, transparent, and efficient dispute resolution.

2) *As a system of governance.* Property systems are a central facet of state functionality and, as such, are an important measurement of fiduciary and administrative effectiveness. The institutional order of the state is based on technical rules and relationships that define interactions between stakeholders. These range from the direct ownership of land to the promulgation of rules that govern security of land and house tenure, land planning, zoning, taxing, and other aspects of property management. Technological innovation, which has radically reduced the cost of information, has generated the possibility for further transparency and accountability in property systems as an instrument of governance.

3) *As a functioning market for the exchange of assets.* A fully functional property system allows land, houses, moveable

property, equity shares, and ideas to be transformed into assets to be bought and sold at rates determined by market forces. This subjects the exchange of property to a level of transparency and accountability and allows for the development of financial mechanisms—including credit and insurance—to facilitate transactions and improve economic outcomes. The owners of land, houses, and moveable property can thus leverage their assets, transforming them from static investments into capital. However, property rights are a necessary but not sufficient precondition for the development of these financial mechanisms; they also develop through cooperation between the market, special funds targeted at access to finance, and the state.

4) *As an instrument of social policy.* In the absence or failure of the market, the state often plays a direct role in addressing the needs of the poor. The state has at its disposal instruments to endow its citizens with assets, such as public housing, low-interest loans, and the distribution of state land. Such instruments help to overcome natural competition for assets. The state also supports social cohesion through the development of co-ownership of infrastructure and services by government and the citizen, supporting the equilibrium between individual and collective interests. Provision of infrastructure by the state critically affects the value and desirability of assets and can therefore fundamentally affect opportunities for the poor.

As reforms of property rights are inherently risky, reformers should pay full attention to securing the rights of the poor.

Women, who constitute half the world's population, own only 10 percent of the world's property. Indigenous people and others also experience active discrimination. Ensuring group rights requires imaginative legal thinking. Providing the absolute poor with rights and access to assets means direct social interventions.

To be fully productive, assets need a system of formal recognition encompassing both individual and collective property rights. This includes recognition of customary rights. Embodying them in standard records, titles, and contracts in accordance with the law protects households and businesses. Evictions should only be an option in circumstances that threaten the physical safety of life and property, or when contract agreements have been breached, or under fair eminent-domain procedures. Eviction must follow due legal processes, which must be equally applicable, contestable, and independent, and those evicted must be fully compensated. Property rights including tenure security should not only be protected by law but also by connecting the property of the poor to wide societal interest (by increasing the range of validation of their tenure security). The poor must have the option to use property as collateral for obtaining credit, such as business loans or mortgages. Formal recognition of property rights encourages compliance by attaching owners to assets, assets to addresses, and addresses to enforcement; that is, it makes people accountable.

As such, property reform can strengthen access to legal identity and to justice. Property records unify dispersed arrangements into a single, legally compatible system. This integrates fragmented local markets, enabling businesses to seek out new opportunities outside their immediate vicinity and putting them in the context of the law, where they due process and association of cause will better protect them. Legal empowerment measures in this domain must do the following:

> Promote efficient governance of individual and collective property in order to integrate the extralegal economy into the formal economy and ensure it remains easily accessible to all citizens

> Ensure that all property recognised in each nation is legally enforceable by law and that all owners have access to the same rights and standards

> Create a functioning market for the exchange of assets that is accessible, transparent, and accountable

> Broaden the availability of property rights, including tenure security, through social and other public policies, such as access to housing, low interest loans, and the distribution of state land

> Promote an inclusive property-rights system that will automatically recognise real and immoveable property bought by men as the co-property of their wives or common-law partners.

Lessons Learned about Reforming Property Rights

Pitfalls litter the road of legal property-rights reform. Some lessons learned from experience can help, but we must realize the considerable burdens of judgment we bear as we try to measure the applicability of particular lessons to future reforms in very different contexts. Below are some mistakes that have hindered property-rights reform in the past.

Disregarding that effective property rights for the poor are the result of power relations and systemic interaction. Many efforts to give the poor effective and enforceable property rights have focused on necessary technical and legal issues. This has come at the expense of ignoring the high degree to which power relations have affected the property rights of the most vulnerable members of society. This has hindered effective realization of anticipated reform benefits for the poor. Associational power of the poor, more symmetric information, legal literacy, procedural assistance, and building institutional capacity are as important as the formal legal instruments of property rights.

Failing to assess the credit market environment of the property system and assuming that credit markets will evolve automatically from property rights. In general, rates of mortgaging remain very low in developing countries, partly due to low demand and partly due to the availability of less risky alternative sources of loans. In the past, this has been partly due to low home values in local markets. Given the reluctance of banks to destroy the entire livelihood of a poor family in the event of foreclosure and the likelihood of local resistance to attempts to take or sell off the collateralized property, there is limited access to mortgages and credit, especially in rural areas. Understanding the role of credit markets in relation to property-rights formalization has led to some important shifts in donor land policies in recent years. For markets to move land and real property to the poor in a sustainable manner, targeted credit must be provided.

Assuming that the state is strong and trustworthy and that therefore property titles and registries are reliable and corruption proof. In many countries, land administration is one of the most corrupt public services. The most egregious examples include irregularities and outright fraud in allocating and managing public lands. Even petty corruption in regular service delivery can involve large sums and have far-reaching economic consequences.

Failure to include moveable property and shareholder schemes of ownership and value addition in policies promoting property rights. Innovative forms of corporate shareholder ownership that do not rely on real estate or credit can extend the asset base of the poor. Unlike land and housing, the reproductive potential of intangible forms of property is potentially unlimited.

Repressing opportunities alongside risk. Even a moderate increase in the liberties and entitlements that come with private property can often create considerable benefits. Thin bundles of property rights that reduce the fungibility of property contribute to the exclusion of the poor from the chain of value addition in cases of land development, compensation payments, and general increase of property value. The risks of the land and financial market have invited special policy measures intended to protect the poor from predators and harmful market forces. Such practices mainly include placing conditions on forming collectives in order to register property under a single legal entity, restrictions on the right to transfer (moratoria) after land privatization or titling, quantitative ceilings of ownership, and special qualifications to profit from land and real estate redistribution. Incentives to form collectives are beneficial where they relate to and protect existing communal structures. They are often dysfunctional in contexts where a majority or a very active minority of people would prefer to act as individuals or small family groups and where the moratoria are too long.

Failure to conceive gender-equitable property-rights systems. In many countries, formal statutory law operates in conjunction with customary law and cultural norms and practices based on patriarchal attitudes that make it difficult to enforce women's legal rights to land as wives and daughters. Individualistic statutory law favoring the male household head and customary practices and hierarchies combine into a mix that is harmful for women. Where customary law and more gender-conscious statutory law conflict, the customary law often trumps. In some instances, statutory law has erased customary practices favoring widows or women in general. Legal reform does not improve the precarious property-rights situation of women if there are no enforcement mechanisms and if legal assistance and support services are not affordable or accessible for women.

Some Consequences of Property Reform

The area of property rights for the poor is as important as it is complicated. Some of the consequences of past attempts at reform are set out below to provide further guidance to action.

Enduring extralegality of the majority of asset holders. Imperfect implementation or a mismatch between official institutions and local practices can cause informal property arrangements to persist even after the establishment of titling programs.

Disruption of existing tenurial arrangements. Careless implementation of formal documentation may have the effect of inadvertently disrupting existing tenurial arrangements. There may be sound policy reasons for seeking to modify or eliminate some existing tenurial practices. It is important, however, that any such reforms are the result of informed and participatory decision making and not the inadvertent result of poorly designed or implemented titling processes.

Concentration and discrimination. In many countries including the countries of the former Soviet Union, some people may be less well positioned to participate effectively in the documentation and registration process than others, with the effect that their rights are poorly protected. Individuals who lose in such contexts are usually women, absentee right holders or mortgagees, and people with less education and limited access to information who fall victim to manipulation and fraud.

Increase in disputes. Registration of land should reduce the incidence of land disputes by clarifying boundaries; resolving ambiguities about rights over land; and putting in place a registration system that is transparent, reliable, and accessible. In the short term, however, the process of adjudication and formalization of rights may bring to the surface latent disputes that otherwise might have remained below the surface. The planning phase of a reform project needs to address this potential risk.

Failure of titling to result in capitalization in the absence of adequate land and capital markets. State-of-the art analysis reveals only a modest positive effect of land titling on access to mortgage credit and no impact on access to other forms of credit. It shows no effect on the labor income of the households holding new titles. However, moving a poor household from uncertain usufructuary rights to a more complete bundle of property rights substantially increases investment in family houses. Property registration and guarantee of the homes reduces the size of families, and these smaller families invest more in the education of their children. Another study finds that formal property rights lead to an increase in available time for productive activities for property holders who no longer need to defend their assets.[147]

Property rights bring increased economic benefits when linked to a functional credit system and market, but by themselves, they do not cause the emergence of a functional and pro poor credit system. Legal property rights effectively lead to credit and investment where robust financial markets exist and where there are further incentives for investment. Even when in possession of

---

[147] Field, 2004.

titles and registered property, small-scale farmers and the urban poor most often do not put their land or modest dwellings at risk by using them as collateral for credit. Tenure security and economic benefits other than capitalization via collateral of land property seem to be primordial for the poor. Although they are efficient producers, small-scale farmers and businesspeople tend to lose out in land and financial markets that are regulated with provisions that privilege consolidation. Market-based land reforms therefore now tend to operate in conjunction with targeted credit for the poor.

Costs and benefits of property-rights protection. From the perspective of the poor and the state, the costs of formal titles have to be weighed against the costs of insecurity of tenure or against informal costs (bribes) of obtaining titles that harm the poor and the state. In many unreformed contexts, few households can afford the cost of a title.[148] Adapting laws and procedures to the social context can considerably reduce the costs of titling and registration by reducing administrative inefficiencies and by the use of modern technology. Legally enforced property-rights systems are not necessarily ineffective and expensive.

Fees and taxes. The integration of irregular settlements into legal property-rights systems increases tax revenues to governments. On the other hand, it is obvious that inappropriate fees and taxes can push people back into extralegality. As far as the poor are concerned, registration fees and taxes have to be set at minimal levels. The following key elements have to be in place for property tax reform: existence of adequate technical expertise; appropriate land records and administration as the

---

[148] Augustinus, 2003, 25.

basis for property lists; and sufficient flexibility to allow the phasing in of major changes. Finally, political understanding and will are perhaps the most critical preconditions to meet the substantial challenges of implementing a highly visible, difficult-to-evade tax.

Labor Rights

Most of the world's poor scrape by doing insecure and poorly paid jobs in the informal economy. They are street vendors, rubbish collectors, construction workers, small-scale furniture makers, garment workers working from home, fishers, small farmers, and forest gatherers. Nearly all of the almost 500 million working poor who earn less than one dollar a day labor in the unofficial economy. Informal work accounts for more than half of total employment in developing countries and as much as 90 percent in some South Asian and African countries. Roughly half of all informal workers are self-employed, often in disguised wage relationships; informal enterprises or households employ another quarter; and the final quarter is employed informally by formal businesses.

However hard they work, these self-employed workers, casual day laborers, and industrial outworkers cannot escape poverty. They have basic rights and protections in theory but not in practice. They do not benefit from labor laws and collective bargaining arrangements, because their employment relationships are unclear. They suffer inferior working conditions and job insecurity. They typically do not have access to state or employer benefits and social security. Recognition and enforcement of the rights of individual workers and of their organizations is critical for breaking the cycle of poverty.[149] Informal employment often expands in upturns as well as downturns. While recession throws people into informal work to survive, recovery may also boost informal employment in entrepreneurial small firms and subcontracted and outsourced activities linked to the global production system.[150]

The last two decades have seen a marked increase in women's participation in the labor force. The pervasive segmentation of labor markets by gender suggests that women's labor has not simply replaced that of men. Rather, a parallel process has created low-paid and poor informal employment opportunities primarily for women.[151]

Indigenous peoples have also often have had to resort to into informal because of the loss of their traditional lands, relocation without compensation and basic support services, underinvestment in education and health, and ill-adapted educational systems and materials. More broadly, increasing global competition, ineffective labor regulations, and rising informality widen the gap between labor law enforcement and the reality of the workplace.

The poor may spend most of their waking hours at the workplace, barely surviving on what they take from it. But labor is not a commodity. In the same way that we must recognize the property and physical assets of the poor, we must recognize the greatest asset of the poor—their labor and human capital. The legitimacy, even the acceptability, of the economy depends

---

[149]   ILO, Working out of Poverty, 2003.

[150]   M. Chen, Men and Women in the Informal Economy: A Stastistical Picture, ILO, Geneva.

[151]   M. Chen, Progress World's Women: Women, Work, Poverty, UN, 2005.

upon basic labor rights, as does the development of human capital necessary for sustained growth. In turn, the continuous improvement of labor and social rights depends on a successfully functioning market economy. We must replace the typical and tired pattern of low productivity, low earnings, and high risks by fulfilling the Declaration of Fundamental Principles and Rights at Work and the Decent Work Agenda.[152], [153] To fulfill these agendas, an emerging global social contract is necessary to provide protection and opportunity to workers in the informal economy. The CLEP has suggested advancing simultaneously on labor rights, job creation, and social protection, focusing particularly on the working poor in the informal economy.

All workers in the informal economy should be covered at least by a minimum floor as explained in the ILO declaration. The declaration established the application of core human rights to the arena of labor or work; included in its provisions are calls for the elimination of forced labor, child labor, and employment discrimination as well as for freedoms of voice, organization, and bargaining.

The declaration also constitutes the foundations for implementing other labor rights and providing enabling conditions to exercise them, thus achieving the objective of providing employment opportunities while ensuring protection. This minimum floor could include three additional labor standards for determinants of working conditions: hours of work, diseases and accidents at work, and minimum wage. An enlarged minimum floor has already gained international acceptance, notably during

---

[152]   ILO, Declaration of Fundamental Principles and Rights at Work, 1998.

[153]   ILO, Decent Work Agenda, 1999.

the last generation of free-trade agreements between the United States and countries of Asia and Latin America. The adoption of such a minimum floor would ensure the rights to rest, to health coverage for work-related risks, and to fair remuneration— all according to standards established by national legislation. Enforcement of such rights and provisions should be required for all workers in the informal economy, independently of the size or form of the economic unit in which they work. This would justify reinforcement and, eventually, a redesign of labor-inspection institutions.

For informal workers outside formal enterprises, full compliance of labor rights as established by national legislation needs to be enforced. This should go beyond the minimum floor, eventually requiring reforms to labor legislation for the facilitation of compliance. Advances in this direction would lead to full achievement of the Decent Work Agenda objectives.

The situation of workers in informal enterprises poses additional challenges, since many informal enterprises lack the productivity and income to absorb the costs of compliance.[154] Because enforcement could destroy employment opportunities in such cases, we need a strategy for increasing compliance and promoting progressive enforcement without legally adopting a dual system. An expanded minimum floor should, however, be enforced even in these enterprises, since cost concerns cannot be accepted as an argument for noncompliance given the nature of the rights involved and the fact that compliance does not necessarily involve significant costs.

---

[154] V. Tokman, "Informality, Insecurity and Social Cohesion," *International Labor Review* 126 (2007), 1–2.

In summary, the CLEP has made the following recommendations for improving the labor rights of the poor:

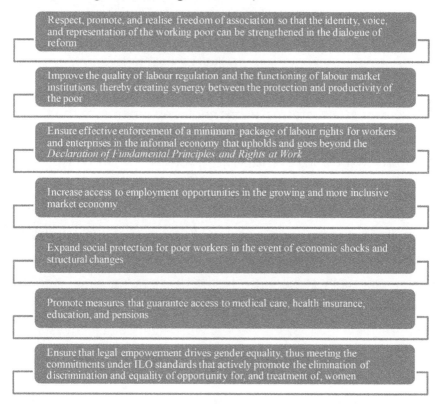

Respect, promote, and realise freedom of association so that the identity, voice, and representation of the working poor can be strengthened in the dialogue of reform

Improve the quality of labour regulation and the functioning of labour market institutions, thereby creating synergy between the protection and productivity of the poor

Ensure effective enforcement of a minimum package of labour rights for workers and enterprises in the informal economy that upholds and goes beyond the *Declaration of Fundamental Principles and Rights at Work*

Increase access to employment opportunities in the growing and more inclusive market economy

Expand social protection for poor workers in the event of economic shocks and structural changes

Promote measures that guarantee access to medical care, health insurance, education, and pensions

Ensure that legal empowerment drives gender equality, thus meeting the commitments under ILO standards that actively promote the elimination of discrimination and equality of opportunity for, and treatment of, women

Business Rights

Business rights is not yet a new term in law. Rather, it refers to a composite of the existing rights of individuals and groups of people to engage in economic activity and market transactions. The commission has bundled these rights together based on their vital instrumentality in the livelihoods and economic prospects of the poor. Business rights include the right to start a legally recognized business without arbitrarily applied regulations or discrimination in the application of norms and procedures. These rights focus on removing unnecessary barriers that limit economic opportunities and on protecting the investments that people make in their enterprises, however small they may be. Business rights derive from political and civil rights as well as economic and social ones. The right to organize and the freedom of association, for instance, underpin the right to form business cooperatives, other companies, and employers' and workers' associations. Business activities are an expression of an entire class of liberties, such as freedom of association, freedom of movement, freedom to develop one's own talents, and freedom to exchange legitimately acquired goods and services.

The rationale for promoting business rights is their connection to fundamental individual freedoms as well as the immense importance of small- and medium-sized enterprises in overcoming poverty. A large proportion of the poor work in such businesses (even more if we include farming), so reforms in this area have a large effect on the poor. As such enterprises grow, they provide increased labor and rising incomes. Even modest growth in income at this level makes a profound difference to security and quality of life. The more inclusive the formal market becomes, the better the opportunities for expanding the coverage and quality of labor rights, which in turn builds human capital.

The poor are entitled to rights not only when working for others but also in developing their own businesses. Access to basic financial services is indispensable for potential or emerging entrepreneurs. Just as important is access to protections and opportunities like the ability to contract; to make deals; to raise investment capital through shares, bonds, or other means; to contain personal financial risk through asset shielding and limited liability; and to pass ownership from one generation to another. These rights may not be equally relevant to every entrepreneur, but they are instrumental in poverty eradication and economic development. They must be accessible to all the many micro, small, and medium enterprises in the developing world—many operated by women—that employ a large portion of the labor force. The success or failure of this economic sector will often spell the difference between economic progress and stagnation, between increased employment and widespread joblessness, and between a broader society of stakeholders and deeper inequality leading to a weakened social contract.

Legal mechanisms or rights that would help empower informal businesses include the following:

1) Legal and bureaucratic procedures that allow informal operators or businesses to operate include simplified registration, licensing, and permit procedures; identification devices including ID cards for individual operators and business identification; and legislation—for example, in the form of municipal bylaws—that allows street vendors to operate in public spaces.

2) Appropriate legal frameworks that enshrine economic rights could include access to transport and communication infrastructure; improved skills and technology; business development services; and business incentive and trade promotion packages including tax deferrals, subsidies, and trade fairs.

3) User rights to public resources and appropriate zoning regulation could include rights to urban public land, pastures, forests, and waterways as well as appropriate zoning regulations governing where and under what conditions informal operators or businesses can operate in central business districts, suburban areas, and industrial zones.

4) Regulatory guidelines and standards could guide what goods and services informal operators and businesses may buy and sell. Such guidelines also could determine environmental standards and establish marketing licenses for products and services.

5) Appropriate legal tools to govern the transactions and contractual relationships of informal operators or businesses include bargaining and negotiating mechanisms, enforceable legal contracts, and grievance and conflict resolution mechanisms. Other business tools include the right to issue shares and the rights to advertise and protect brands and trademarks.

6) Legal protection mechanisms could provide informal operators and businesses various kinds of temporary unemployment relief insurance. These could include land insurance, home insurance, and equipment insurance; bankruptcy rules and default rules; limited liability, asset, and capital protection; and capital withdrawal and transfer rules.

7) Representational and associational rights should allow businesses to join or form recognized associations that can represent them in relevant policy-making and rule-setting institutions. These rights also should allow membership in mainstream business associations, guilds, or other associations of similar types.

8) Mechanisms should facilitate the ease of doing legal business in the small and micro business sector by drastically reducing the time and costs of starting, licensing, registering, hiring for, getting loans for, paying taxes for, and closing a business.

Legal empowerment measures in the domain of business rights must therefore perform the following functions:

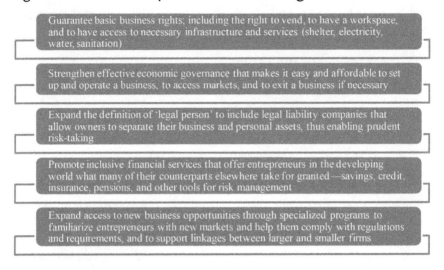

Guarantee basic business rights; including the right to vend, to have a workspace, and to have access to necessary infrastructure and services (shelter, electricity, water, sanitation)

Strengthen effective economic governance that makes it easy and affordable to set up and operate a business, to access markets, and to exit a business if necessary

Expand the definition of 'legal person' to include legal liability companies that allow owners to separate their business and personal assets, thus enabling prudent risk-taking

Promote inclusive financial services that offer entrepreneurs in the developing world what many of their counterparts elsewhere take for granted—savings, credit, insurance, pensions, and other tools for risk management

Expand access to new business opportunities through specialized programs to familiarize entrepreneurs with new markets and help them comply with regulations and requirements, and to support linkages between larger and smaller firms

Innovations for Informal Businesses

Past practices for dealing with informal businesses sought to formalize them; however, experience has shown that the transition from informal to formal is very complex and problematic. The process requires a careful transition that must meet the needs of various types of businesses and people from various regions of the world. Such a transition is likely to be much more productive if it builds on the existing strengths of the small, informal businesses. Through bold institutional innovations, this can be done. Some examples of such innovations are described below.[155]

Market-based institutions for the poor. The ability of informal businesses to operate on more nearly equal terms in the marketplace depends greatly on their capacity for collective

---

[155] R. Sobhan, A Macro Policy for Poverty Eradication through Structural Change, UNU WIDER, 2005.

action. The weakness of the poor in the marketplace originates in their isolation. Here, investments in institutions, whether through NGOs or collective action by the poor, remain crucial interventions. The challenge, therefore, is whether we will invest the poor and informal businesses with the capacity to develop the financial and organizational strength to sell products and services at a time and in a market that offers them the best terms, or simply watch as they continue to sell their goods out of distress or the need to subsist.

Taking up the challenge requires interventions in the macrocredit market. In order to underwrite such marketing ventures, we must design institutions to aggregate the market power of the poor, and we must deploy professionals with management skills who are especially trained to assist the poor in scaling up their participation in the market economy.

Adding value and supply chains to the labor of the poor and informal businesses. Many NGOs around the world provide marketing services to the poor for particular commodities in particular markets. The best service they can provide is to help poor and informal businesses add value to their labor by moving upmarket through either agricultural processing or providing inputs to the corporate sector. The pioneering roles of Amul Dairy in India and, more recently, BRAC are instructive model examples. They enable small dairy farmers or even poor households that own a cow bought through a micro credit loan to become part of a milk-processing chain, thus enabling the poor to share in the profits from selling pasteurized milk or cheese in the metropolitan market. There are opportunities to take such initiatives one step further—for example, by financially empowering the vast body of small farmers servicing the private agricultural processing sector or allowing handloom weavers to become equity stakeholders in upstream enterprises that could add value to their produce or labor.

Taking micro credit out of the ghetto.[156] Nowhere is there a greater need for developing a macro perspective for poverty eradication than in the area of monetary policy. The instruments of monetary policy appear exclusively to target macroeconomic stability, moderating inflation and meeting the credit needs of the corporate sector. The financial needs of the poor, once left to the informal sector, have now been segregated in the micro credit market. This apartheid within the monetary system remains a major anomaly. There is an argument that, by its very nature, micro credit can never aspire to eradicate poverty, because it only addresses one component of the various markets that condition the lives of the rural poor. Locking the poor into the micro credit system, which is based on the fiduciary responsibility of the household, excludes them from participating in the macro economy, isolates them from collective action, and condemns them to live on the fringes of the poverty line. Therefore, it is not surprising that those countries with the most extensive exposure to micro credit remain mired in poverty. However, it is not the aim to diminish the enormous contribution of micro credit in alleviating poverty and distress as well as enhancing the self-worth of the poor. There is, today, no reason such organizations as Grameen Bank should not graduate into the macro finance system. By accessing the deposits of the public and even marketing those assets at the global level through such financial instruments as

---

[156] From contribution by Rehman Sobhan to the CLEP Working Group on Informal Business.

securitization, the bank can utilize techniques that are already in widespread use in more advanced financial systems.

A number of commercial banks are already using NGOs and community-based organizations to provide banking services to the poor. Other examples include Scotia Bank in the Caribbean and ANZ Bank in the Pacific Islands, which have launched the programs Banking for the Poor and Mobile Banking for Villages, respectively. In Egypt, the Social Fund, Credit Guarantee Company, and micro finance NGOs are not only successful providers of credit to informal businesses but also organizers of permanent exhibitions for Micro Small and Medium Enterprises (MSMEs)' products, offering entrepreneurial training and outreach services to poor enterprises.

Mutual funds for the poor. Apart from the issue of redesigning monetary policy to deliver credit to the poor, the monetary system also needs to design special financial instruments to attract these micro savings into the corporate sector, particularly where doing so can serve the poor. The mutual fund is but one institutional mechanism to link the poor to the corporate sector. The underlying premise of the mutual fund is the notion of creating possibilities for the poor to own corporate assets. Opportunities are therefore opening for linking farmers to the agricultural processing corporate sector by giving them an equity stake in such enterprises. At the same time, the agricultural corporations should be motivated to invest in improving the productivity and capacities of their rural partners. Bangladesh provides an interesting illustration of the possibility of enabling the poor to own corporate assets. Financial policy need not limit itself to ownership of corporate assets. All assets, from urban land to real estate development to banks and corporate trading houses, could be redesigned to accommodate the poor as equity partners. The two institutional instruments to make this possible remain the mutual fund and a way for private limited companies to transform themselves into public limited companies. Here monetary and fiscal policy can provide incentives to encourage the corporatization of private wealth along with the reservation of space for equity ownership of this wealth by the poor.

Institutionalizing the collective identity of poor and informal businesses. Suggestions about building a collective identity for the poor and informal businesses through specially constructed institutions derive from the need for the poor to claim a place in society that is more commensurate with their numbers. The poor remain disempowered because they are isolated; when brought together, they emerge as a major force in the economy, in society, and—eventually—in the political arena. Below, we will describe three institutional arrangements can add value to the reform agenda.

Corporations of the poor and informal businesses. Community-based or self-help organizations (CBOs), cooperatives, and activity-based organizations that bring groups of the poor together should aspire to forge an institutional identity. Corporatizing CBOs will provide the legal foundations for collective action to enable these bodies of the poor to access credit, enter into contractual relationships, and deal with international organizations. The precise legal personae of these corporations may include limited liability companies with the poor as equity owners and cooperatives with the poor as partner members. But the common feature of all such corporate entities of the poor is that they must operate in the marketplace and generate income rather than limiting themselves to surviving as savings-and-loan associations.

Corporatizing microenterprises. The prospect of large numbers of microenterprises that until now have lived precarious lives in the informal sector coming together to form large corporate entities that would compete in national and global markets provides a new perspective on the role of the informal sector in the national economy. These corporate entities made up of microenterprises can become the natural partners of larger corporate entities, which could outsource many operations and component inputs to them. The larger corporate entities of microenterprises would eliminate both the costs and the managerial problems associated with building this linkage and open up new opportunities for the informal sector to formally integrate with the macro economy.

Bangladesh provides technology upgrades, quality control, credit, and marketing services to large numbers of handicraft enterprises across the country. However, it still deals with these enterprises as clients in need of assistance in the form of access to credit, markets, and skill development. BRAC has to take the next step of aggregating these producers into a larger corporate entity where they acquire an equity stake in the final profits of the enterprise. In India, the *papad* cooperative has developed into such an entity. About 100,000 small household enterprises that produce the spicy snack condiment papad have joined to become the largest single supply source of quality papad to grocery stores across the country.

Micro insurance to protect informal businesses. Microcredit can help the poor rise above poverty. Micro insurance can help by providing protection against certain perils; micro insurance complements other financial and social services. Because they often live and do business in risky environments—such as urban shantytowns with unsanitary conditions or rural areas prone to droughts or floods—the poor and informal businesses are more vulnerable than the rest of the population to perils including illness, accidental death and disability, theft, fire, agricultural losses, and natural or manmade disasters. They are also the least able to cope with crisis when it occurs.

Technology has allowed micro insurance to work successfully in a number of countries. For example, in Uganda and Malawi, some insurance providers issue smart cards to poor policyholders to confirm that they are who they say they are and can instantly provide information on their level of coverage and whether the premium has been paid. In the Philippines, insurers have minimized the transaction costs of collecting many small premiums by allowing people to pay via their mobile phones. In India, a barcode system is being tested as a way of managing client information. The barcode stickers are especially useful for illiterate clients, who can attach them to preaddressed envelopes to identify themselves.

Conclusion

This chapter has laid out an action agenda on economic rights for the poor in some detail. It draws heavily but not exclusively on the Commission on Legal Empowerment of the Poor, which emphasizes four pillars: access to justice and the rule of law, property rights, labor rights, and business rights. However, successful implementation is likely only if we take a holistic approach and the poor seize a central role through a process of self-empowerment. Such a holistic and self-empowering process will be both difficult and dangerous. Therefore, the next chapter provides some roadmaps and guideposts to implementation.

5

ROADMAPS TO LEGAL EMPOWERMENT AND INCLUSION

This chapter is about the roadmaps to legal empowerment: the thinking, considerations, planning, and tools that may increase the chances of success along the difficult and potentially tortuous journey of legal inclusion of the poor and excluded. Some of the main roads, such as changing power relations, taking a systems approach, renewing the social contract between state and citizens, the sustainable-livelihoods approach, and local economic development, we will address later.

Legal Empowerment Realities

Obviously, what legally empowers the poor in one nation may be unsuitable in another where there is a different social structure, economic environment, and universe of stakeholder groups. The procedures for determining a suitable reform strategy might look alike in both countries, but the substance of the outcome would be sharply different. In all cases, the process is messy and imprecise, yielding only what appear to be the best fitting policies given political realities and the imperfect information available to policy makers.

Development professionals must creatively seek to capitalize on the specific situation at hand, placing poor people's perceptions front and center. The poor are the intended beneficiaries of legal-empowerment policies. A legal or organizational change that looks self-evidently beneficial from the outside may seem too risky or not worth doing from the perspective of someone inside the poor community. That is why the poor must have a hand in implementation. It may be best to move forward selectively and not dissipate energy on too many legal or regulatory initiatives at once. Empowerment policies seldom take effect quickly. Individual uncertainty about implementation encourages poor people to withhold support for reforms, which can create self-fulfilling prophecies of slippage. One should therefore look for interventions that promise short-term rewards for beneficiaries. Design simplicity should be a key consideration to minimize conflict, uncertainty, and other implementation problems arising from the procedural and technical traits of legal-empowerment activities.

Juxtaposed to the beneficiaries are the so-called challengers who may prove to be roadblocks to reform. Government officials who gain from current policies and legal instruments may sabotage reform. Where possible, reformers should give them positive incentives to support legal empowerment policies instead of resisting them—for example, by offering civil servants promotions, interesting new responsibilities, training opportunities, or other perquisites if they help with implementation. Instead of trying to block reforms outright, powerful economic actors may subtly manipulate them to their advantage—a phenomenon known as *elite capture*. The sequential and conditional release of funds is one strategy for countering the persistent problem of elite capture. Collective counteraction by the poor to secure their rights in the face of resistance is difficult. Even if potential policy losers are a minority, such as a handful of large landholders or government bureaucrats, they tend to organize effectively to defend their interests.[157]

Prospective winners may not be aware of what they might gain and may rightly fear that they will lose out if change does not happen quickly. Hence, mobilization of allies and supportive stakeholders is fundamental. Success is most likely when one delivers measurable and meaningful benefits to the beneficiaries.

In some cases, legal empowerment also creates policy losers. One example is the redistribution of a right or benefit from one group of stakeholders to another when there are mutually exclusive claims to a fixed resource, such as fertile land or minerals. Landlords, shopkeepers, moneylenders, and other local elites may see a threat from disenfranchised people exercising new rights or reviving latent ones. Policy makers may endeavor to minimize redistributive conflicts by expanding economic opportunities to meet the needs of every side, but plenty of potential for confrontation remains as long as important stakeholders believe others' gains come at their expense. The fact that the mutual payoff to legal empowerment comes in the future and not immediately may exacerbate the situation.

The realities of existing power structures prevent the poor and excluded from taking charge of their own lives and livelihoods. Existing political, administrative, and judicial institutions are not geared to protect the rights of the poor. However, this does not mean we have to start from scratch. At the international level, we have the Universal Declaration of Human Rights and other legal covenants to which all governments are committed. What

---

[157]   Platteau, "Monitoring Elite Capture in Community Driven Development," *Development and Change* 35 (2004): 2.

is lacking are the myriad national and local rules of the game and policies that give substance to those grand declarations in the everyday lives of the poor. Putting the necessary reforms into effect requires sober analysis of what is feasible, but it also requires a readiness to take chances when the timing looks right. Pragmatic policy makers look for policy windows that open and use them to create a space for solving the particular problems facing the poor. At the national level, we have constitutions and laws, some aspects of which can be helpful and others harmful. Some capacity for positive change might exist, and we can build on this.

Contextual Analysis

Before proceeding very far with legal-empowerment activities, a contextual analysis must establish what reforms are most in demand and which have the greatest likelihood of success. Such an analysis also guides the implementation process and tells reformers which risks and which challenges to address. This improves the likelihood of success. The focus should be on social and cultural factors that could potentially affect implementation; on the economic context, which can both help and hinder; and on the openness and capacity of the state. A careful analysis of the reach and hold that informal institutions have on the poor should supplement the inventory of the above concerns. The full contextual analysis is the basis for a feasibility review of various empowerment scenarios. The most important elements of such an analysis are as follows:

The domestic social structure, especially its gender, class, and ethnic makeup, plus cultural attitudes toward participation and equality;

The economic context – including the distribution of wealth and income, and the level and rate of economic growth;

The characteristics of the state – both the political and the administrative system

The extent of economic and political informality and tensions with the formal and officially recognized systems.

Contextual analysis and knowledge of the policy environment are essential to estimate whether conditions appear ripe for extensive or modest legal-empowerment reforms, which implementation options seem most probable, what sequencing and timelines for reform are best, how the reforms should be designed, what tradeoffs need to be considered, which risk-mitigating mechanisms are worth trying, and what variables need special monitoring during implementation.

In some cases, the informal system is neither efficient nor fair. Context is critical. The distribution of power and wealth also matters for legal empowerment. If ownership of land, capital, and other productive assets is highly concentrated, reformers have to be cautious about regularizing the system of economic rights. Entrenching existing inequalities in ownership will negate the value of reform for the poor and can even lead to further marginalization. On the other hand, perpetuating exclusion from formal ownership due to unequal distribution of land and other assets may be an even worse option. Judgment must be married to context. We will discuss factors that affect the context of the legal-empowerment environment, such as stakeholders, allies, and beneficiaries, in more detail later on in this chapter.

The effectiveness of state institutions is another contextual factor. How capable is public administration in relation to corruption, capacity to deliver, and ability to protect citizens and their assets? In many countries, laws favorable to the poor exist but are not implemented. Where the state is not effective, its residents must protect assets and resolve disputes pragmatically— by aligning with a political patron, for instance. This will often hamper legal empowerment. In fragile states, the capacity is even weaker. The legal system is particularly ineffective in such societies. The good news is that once people understand the importance of legal reforms and governance functions for legal empowerment, it is often possible to mobilize the investment required to strengthen these functions. The intensity required may be one of effort rather than money.

Practitioners and policy makers can use the tool of contextual analysis within a country to determine the following: 1) if conditions appear ripe for legal-empowerment reforms; 2) which implementation options seem most probable; 3) what sequencing and timelines for reform look possible; 4) how the reforms should be designed; 5) what tradeoffs need to be considered; 6) which risk-mitigating mechanisms are worth trying, and 7) what contextual variables need careful monitoring during implementation.

Stakeholder Analysis

A second important early task in implementation is stakeholder analysis. Following the contextual analysis—or perhaps simultaneously with it, since implementation steps are never discrete—local activists and external change agents should undertake a stakeholder analysis of the constituencies concerned with the legal empowerment of the poor.

Stakeholders are interested parties with the capacity to advance or hinder a policy change. Their perceived interests determine their position, and they may or may not be formally or self-consciously organized. The objective is to differentiate among the superficially homogeneous beneficiaries and better to understand the divisions, alliances, and particular needs that exist among the poor. Other stakeholders who might oppose or assist the target group or groups also need to be scrutinized to see what motivates their behavior and to reflect on how they could be brought into the process. The purpose is to get a firmer grasp of the probability of succeeding with legal-empowerment reforms, managing the stakeholders, and establishing what it takes to build a minimum winning coalition for legal empowerment in the country.

Stakeholders act out of regard for their own advantage as they define it. Poor people are the target beneficiaries of legal empowerment and need to have as big a hand as possible in initiating and designing the relevant policies. Even though they lack physical, financial, and organizational resources and even social capital in many locales, the poor always have a passive capacity to derail legal reforms aimed at them. Because poor stakeholders are diverse, legal-empowerment policies may have surprisingly uneven impact if officials are inattentive to the needs and preferences of the intended beneficiaries.

Reforming Policy for Legal Empowerment and Inclusion

Policy context. As mentioned in the above overview, the policy context includes social, economic, political, and administrative structures and the nature and levels of informality. Because of the crucial importance of the local context for successful reforms, we will discuss each of these in more detail.

Social structure. A country with fewer poor people relative to its population will likely find it easier to integrate them into the legal and economic system compared to a country with more poor people (though the poor also may be easier to ignore when their numbers are lower). Similarly, a homogeneous country will find that empowering people at the bottom takes less effort compared to a country where the population is deeply divided by language, religion, or national origin. The absolute gap between rich and poor also matters, with a smaller gap facilitating implementation of policies that legally empower the poor. A society where women have considerable legal recognition will have less ground to make up with empowering poor women than another society. It also is important whether social and economic gaps are cumulative or cut across one another—that is, to what extent membership in a particular religious community or ethnic group correlates with discrimination, low income, exclusion from power, and other negative attributes. These social facts are a given at any point in time, though they can change in a country due to economic growth, human migration, mass education, and exposure to media, among other factors. Policy makers must tailor their empowerment strategies to the structures of particular societies.

Cultural factors are crucial to social structure as well. Assorted traditions and customary practices color the systems of property rights, contract enforcement, and dispute resolution that the poor typically use. Indigenous people are particularly likely to have elaborate but officially nonexistent systems in place for organizing economic life. A large gap may exist between the shared norms and values of the beneficiaries of legal empowerment and those of their stakeholder allies (not to mention their rivals or opponents). That cultural distance makes it harder to come up with workable and effective empowerment instruments and activities (see the additional discussion of informal institutions below). Another important social structure consideration is that many societies and subcultures reflect hierarchical and patriarchal power structures that may interfere with the implementation of legal empowerment, which requires the broad participation of the beneficiaries in decisions and the leveling effects of economic rights. Great tact may be needed to find socially acceptable yet effective means of involving, say, women or members of historically excluded minorities in choosing and implementing policies that expand the ambit of empowerment. Development practitioners need to pay close attention to these cultural factors when they consider how to carry out the legal empowerment of the poor.

Economic arrangements. A country's social structure cannot be isolated in practice from who holds the country's wealth and exercises economic power. The distribution pattern may reflect historical injustice whereby a privileged few used their political influence and access to the justice system to legitimize unfair claims to property. The more unequal the initial pattern of ownership of land, capital, and other productive assets, the more cautious reformers have to be about regularizing the system of economic rights. There is no advantage to the poor from locking in place preexisting inequities in proprietorship—though to correct those inequities, it is usually necessary to compensate current asset holders, which may be both financially costly and politically risky due to the resistance it is likely to spark. It is important that the proposed reforms establish the claims of the poor to assets without amplifying the existing skewed allocation of property.

Land is probably the most difficult economic resource to manage both because its supply is limited and because so many poor people depend directly on land for their survival. Indigenous peoples and subsistence farmers must assure their use of forests, pastures, and arable fields, but as mentioned earlier, that brings them into head-on conflict with wealthier claimants to the same limited resources. Land reforms have proven a conundrum in many countries due to the expense and complexity of managing overlapping claims to identical resources. In addition to the makeup of a nation's economic pie, the overall size of the pie influences the extent of absolute poverty and hence the urgency of poor people's empowerment and the scale of the effort needed to confront that social problem. Economic growth makes it easier to redistribute assets to the poor, but ironically, growth is also an unsettling force for the poor. A case in point is the redevelopment of the vast squatter settlement of Dharavi in Mumbai, India, described in some detail in chapter 1. As the land has soared in value, the city and state have advanced plans to replace the informal township with upscale development. Because Dharavi's residents lack ownership rights, their ability to defend their homes and shops is limited.

Fortunately, direct action and advocacy from civil society have gotten the government to agree to provide small apartments to the residents who will be displaced. That is not the end of the story, however. State and private developers have drawn up their plans without any consultation, and it is unclear who within Dharavi's population will get the new living units and work sites. Mumbai has sky-high real estate prices, and the state and private developers still stand to earn huge amounts over and above the cost of this mitigation effort.[158] On the other hand, mitigation may not have been forthcoming at all were it not for the dynamic economic conditions in Mumbai.

With the clear exception of many programs involving the transfer of land and property, the financial cost of empowerment programs may be modest. Since some elements of the legal empowerment of the poor are revenue neutral, it is possible to pick first those that require little or no expenditure of resources. Reformers should pay special attention to low-cost ways to enforce property rights, guarantee contracts, and provide fair resolution of business and commercial disputes. Still, even these activities will slow to a crawl if the country does not find enough funds to pay for them. Empowering the poor is a long-term endeavor, so ongoing budget support is problematic. Take many of the emerging market economies in Asia. They still frequently underpay their judges and allow their courts to languish with inadequate facilities. Many of these legal systems are swamped with a backlog of cases and are widely accused of corruption. Hence, fast economic growth does not necessarily put an end to resource scarcities if change is not a high priority.

The Political System

Political system variables (i.e., factors affecting the demand side of government) are crucial for implementation and need to be taken apart and looked at carefully. To combat legal disempowerment, there is no substitute for collective action by poor men and women

---

[158]   Patel, Toward Legal Empowerment of the Poor, 2007, www.undo.org/ legalempowermentofthepoor/docs.

to push for rights and protections as in the Mumbai case cited above. Therefore, when doing contextual analysis, practitioners must consider whether farmers, residents, workers, consumers, and other constituencies have legal protection to organize and petition the government or bargain with private entities to redress their grievances. In countries where these basic rights are neglected or suppressed, the legal empowerment of the poor will be harder to carry out. The right to organize does not exist in a vacuum separated from actual organizations, and thus the level of development of civil society is another important influence on the diagnosis for policy implementation. It is easier to carry out the legal empowerment of the poor in countries with strong community organizations, occupational membership groups, or pro-poor political parties than where such social capital is absent.

As we have stressed, implementation of the legal empowerment of the poor usually involves community participation, sometimes through formal venues set up for the purpose or else through the established mechanisms of local government. Simply making participatory procedures available, however, is not sufficient, because the better-off and more connected members of communities tend to take advantage of them. Two related forms of social exclusion are common: formal exclusion, which is when the poor and disadvantaged do not show up at meetings, and substantive exclusion, which is when they do not speak up in these venues.[159] In India, for example,

---

[159] B. Pozzoni and N. Kumar, "A Review of the Literature on Participatory Approaches to Local Development for an Evaluation of the Effectiveness of World Bank Support to Community Based and Driven Development Approaches," (working paper, Operations Evaluation Department, 2005).

local self-government appears to be working reasonably well, but some community members report being too intimidated to contradict local leaders and government administrators.[160] Social mobilization of the poor can help make participatory procedures in government more effective.

Democratic competition and free discussion of policy issues at the national level also sometimes facilitate the legal empowerment of the poor as leaders seek majority support with policy proposals favorable to disadvantaged citizens. But these are not panaceas. Procedural democratic rule is now quite common in the world, yet empirical studies show countries experiencing democratic reform do not have systematically better poverty outcomes.[161] For example, democratic countries are just as capable as dictatorships of carrying out government austerity programs that fall most heavily on the poor.[162]

The procedural democracies are not at all consistent in the extent to which they protect minorities, root out political corruption, and prevent state-sponsored violence against citizens. Often, the leadership positions in these countries are dominated by the same social stratum that was in charge before the advent of procedural democracy and competitive politics.

[160] S. Vishwanathan and R. Srivastava, Learning from the Poor, Asian Development Bank, Manila, 2007.

[161] M. Ross, "Is Democracy Good for the Poor?" *American Journal of Political Science* 50, no. 4 (2006): 860–874.

[162] M. Lindenberg and S. Devarajan, "Prescribing Strong Economic Medicine: Revisiting the Myths about Structural Adjustment, Democracy and Economic Performance in Developing Countries," *Comparative Politics* 25, no. 2 (1993): 169–182.

In some societies, religion or tradition legitimate this group's role, and deferential attitudes on the part of the poor may add another stumbling block to empowerment. One explanation for the economic disparities that persist under democracy is the holdover of identity politics that divide the poor.[163] There may also be deep-rooted patron-client networks that push down the poor (more on this topic later).

Take the example of the Philippines. Its government is chosen in contested elections. Thousands of community-based organizations exist in Manila and elsewhere, so there is a strong civil society. The Philippines has a national housing finance program to regularize the capital city's vast informal settlements. The implementation of the program relies on partnerships between community groups, local governments, and the private sector. Local governments are also required to set aside land for relocation of informal settlers and to compile lists of informal settlers who are eligible for relocation. Yet even in this relatively benign political environment, the community groups tend to have limited influence, and evictions and conversion of land to commercial use continue apace.[164]

Honduras and Nicaragua have analogous problems in rural areas. Land and forestry laws favor the poor on paper, but practice is different. In Nicaragua, constitutional and legislative provisions exist for the demarcation and titling of indigenous territories. Yet

---

[163]   A. Varshney, "Democracy and Poverty" in *Measuring Empowerment*, ed. Deepa Narayan-Parker (Oxford University Press, 2005).

[164]   G. Shatkin, "Obstacles to Empowerment: Local Politics and Civil Society in Metro Manila, Philippines," *Urban Studies*, 37, no. 12 (2000): 2357–2375.

the government continues to grant industrial logging concessions on community lands without fulfilling these requirements.

In Honduras, small-scale forest producers have use rights but seldom can meet the transaction costs of securing permits and other approvals owing to regulatory complexity and bureaucratic corruption. This forces them to rely on timber traders to secure permits and other approvals, which in turn fuels collusion between traders and public officials and elite capture of community forest-management rights.[165] Again, the quality of democratic institutions in these two countries appears to vary according to the class and income of the citizens using them.

These anecdotes obviously do not mean dictatorships are consistently better at confronting poverty than democracies. There are examples throughout history of authoritarian regimes that have carried out successful land reforms and other pro poor policies, but a far greater number of authoritarian regimes have done little or nothing to improve the health and well-being of ordinary citizens. We need to look beyond political labels when designing implementation strategies for the legal empowerment of the poor. It is important to think of political systems as merely different shades of gray when it comes to empowering the poor. At one end of the scale are systems of arbitrary personal rule, which typically are closed to grassroots participation in policy making but may be open to pro poor policies if the regime is a populist one that depends on mass support.

---

[165]   A. Wells et al., "Rural Livelihoods, Forest Law and the Illegal Trade in Timber in Honduras and Nicaragua," research paper for CIFOR, Bogor, Barat, 2004.

In more open and competitive systems, the poor may have progressively greater scope to sway public policy, but the rich may still exercise hegemony on key political economy issues. Happily, there are fewer political systems today where poor people cannot organize at all to have some countervailing influence on government decisions; but in a number of countries, freedom of association is still denied.[166] And even in the most receptive political systems, the influence of the poor is difficult to transform into extensive power. Development practitioners should be careful not to let preconceptions about regimes blind them to these possibilities.

Administrative State

One must also consider the supply side of political systems to understand implementation probabilities. How capable is the public administration? Does the state have the capacity to provide physical safety, to secure personal belongings, to settle disputes fairly, and to provide other public goods to society? Does it possess the personnel, skills, systems, and infrastructure to carry out these core functions? Even political will cannot drive reform in the face of binding constraints on the capacity of institutions charged with delivering empowerment. High-capacity states are ones that implement policies efficiently, predictably, and in the manner intended. High-capacity states may or may not be democratic, but they can carry out the legal empowerment of the poor if that is what the leadership wants. In very low-capacity states, on the other hand, supportive leadership is still beneficial, but the follow-through capability is missing. Residents must therefore improvise

[166] ILO, Organizing for Social Justice, 2004, www.ilo.org/public/eng/.

and figure out how to protect assets and resolve disputes through pragmatic means, such as aligning with a political patron (see the discussion of informal governance below).

Administrative weakness is usually rooted in a lack of human and financial resources, but a vicious cycle reinforces the problem. Burdensome or extraneous business and labor market regulations drive people into the shadow economy, while a collective perception of the ineffectiveness of the state gives rise to a social norm of noncompliance with taxes and regulations that further undermines the state's capacity to enforce the law and to provide public services.[167] However, the methodology underlying such studies has come under serious technical criticism.[168] Bureaucratic corruption can also be a major weakening factor, especially for the poor, who lack the wherewithal to pay bribes to make things happen within the bureaucracy. For people with means, on the other hand, the civil service may seem capable enough, because, unlike the poor, they can pay for individualized special treatment. Thus, bureaucratic corruption tends to reinforce the existing configuration of wealth and power. In cases where public-sector wages are low and virtually everything the civil service does is for sale, it may be almost impossible for the poor to get the public administration to work in their favor. Reformers in these contexts would have to address corruption before taking on implementation or choose to work in sectors where government employees are more professional and trustworthy.

---

[167]   G. Perry, Informality: Exit and Exclusion, World Bank, 2007.

[168]   J. Berg and S. Cazes, The Doing Business Indicators: Measurement Issues and Political Implications, ILO, Economic and Labor Market Papers, 2007/6, Geneva.

Attitudes of public servants are also significant. Receptivity of state institutions to the agenda of legal empowerment is as much about changing the bureaucratic mind-set as it is about new processes or additional resources. Too often, public functionaries, for a variety of reasons, lack a service orientation and see their job as an entitlement. This attitude must be changed to implement the legal empowerment of the poor. Again, we are talking about shades of capacity, not stark, monochromatic differences. Among developing and transitional countries, those with higher national incomes tend to have stronger administrative capabilities, though there are certainly exceptions to this pattern. The least developed countries, especially small island nations and land-locked countries, tend to have lower capacities, as a rule. The legal empowerment of the poor is obviously easiest to carry out on a national scale in countries with better capacity.

State capacity is at its nadir in countries where central authority is so ineffective that it has lost or is losing practical control over much of its territory. The legal empowerment of the poor in these political systems must happen entirely from the bottom up or the outside in, because the national government is too dysfunctional to work from the top down. Consider the extreme case of Somalia, with four overlapping judicial structures: a formal one in regional administrations and central governments created at international peace processes, a traditional, clan-based system, a growing number of Muslim *shari'a* courts in urban areas, and ad hoc mechanisms established by militias.[169] A nationwide implementation strategy for legal empowerment is currently

---

[169] A. Le Sage, Stateless Justice in Somalia: Formal and Informal Rule of Law Initiatives, Center for Humanitarian Dialogue, Geneva, 2005.

problematic in Somalia, though there may be local or regional space for reform.

Post-conflict states present a special situation for legal empowerment even if the central state has nominally reasserted its claim to authority. It is particularly vexing to figure out how to return property after its rightful owners have fled or been killed by one side or the other in a civil war. Often the disputes over homes and other assets are so intense they must be addressed at once to sustain peace. The international community has recognized that institutional reform of the legal infrastructure is essential for reconstruction and reconciliation. Yet a realistic timeframe for re-creating a justice system following serious armed conflict with formal courts, trained judges, and a retrained police force is close to twenty years.[170] That is a long period for implementation with many chances for administrative operation to deviate from initial policy intent.

Informality and the Policy Context

In chapter 1, we discussed informality and extralegality from the perspective of the local people. In this section, we discuss informality as a dimension of the policy environment in the economy, the polity, and the juridical system. The boundary between the informal and the formal economies is fluid, and poor people can push it in a direction that favors them. Cairo, to take an example, has an informal refuse-collection system that

---

[170]   K. Samuels, "Rule of Law Reform Initiatives in Post Conflict Countries: Operational Initiatives and Lessons Learnt," conflict prevention and reconstruction paper, 37, World Bank, 2006.

actually has a well-defined set of internal rights, responsibilities, and sanctions that evolved over several decades in response to a changing external environment. The city tried to bring refuse collection under municipal control by issuing licenses to large corporate contractors. Refuse collection is a major enterprise for poor people, so the city was threatening their livelihood. After negotiation and mutual adjustment, a new arrangement emerged in which small-scale service providers selectively adopted institutional forms recognized by the municipal authorities while hanging on to the personalized and adaptable practices that marked their informal system.[171] The second element of informality that concerns the legal empowerment of the poor is found in the political system. Informality here is based on implicit and unwritten understandings. In effect, it is a coping method for the poor. The terms used to describe this gray government zone are *patrimonialism* and *clientelism*. Its dimensions are hard to measure, but the informal patron-client political system is widespread in many countries and may crowd out the official state system of rule, along with that system's broad policies that guarantee rights and distribute privileges according to objective criteria.

Patron-client politics emerge from webs of personal bonds that develop between patrons and their individual clients or followers. These bonds are founded on mutual material advantage: the patron furnishes excludable resources (money, jobs) in return for support and cooperation (votes, attendance at rallies). Typically,

---

[171] R. Assaad, "Formalizing the Informal? The Transformation of Cairo's Waste Collection System," *Journal of Planning Education and Research,* 16, no. 2 (1996): 115–126.

marginalized members of society are drawn to patron-client arrangements as a more reliable means than the state to take care of their everyday concerns.[172] Clientelism is widely seen as a barrier to more transparent governance and professional public administration. It lives on, however, because it provides something of value to people. No society is so "advanced" that it relies exclusively on de jure institutions to run its common affairs. For all their drawbacks, informal patron-client exchanges are expedient means to get things done.

Clientelism evolves and adapts to the formal governance system in a similar way to what happens in the economic sphere. In fact, individuals who hold the formal levers of power often also head up patronage networks. Political openness, widespread political participation, and the emergence of broad programs that help people regardless of their personal affiliations are ways clientelism can be pushed back to benefit the poor.[173] But this is a struggle. Patrons do not give up their position willingly, and they often have multiple additional claims to power—not just their control over material resources but also legitimacy derived from a high position in the local system of social stratification and privilege. There may be a religiously or historically derived convention of deference to authority that makes poor people less likely to stand up for their rights against the wishes of traditional patrons.

---

[172] D. Brinkerhoff and A. Goldsmith, "Good Governance, Clientelism and Patrimonialism: New Perspectives on Old Problems," *International Public Management Journal* 7, no. 2 (2004): 163–185.

[173] D. Brinkerhoff and A. Goldsmith, "Institutional Dualism and International Development: A Revisionist Interpretation of Good Governance," *Administration and Society* 37, no. 2 (2005): 199–224.

Informality turns up a third time in the legal system itself, where we again see overlapping statutory and nonstate systems of law (including mafia-like self-regulating systems) in every country. As with economic informality and political clientelism, the informal legal structures exist partly because they are more accessible and user-friendly to people of limited means. Sometimes, private or mixed arrangements for rule enforcement and settlement are efficient because they enjoy the confidence of the participants and encourage flexibility and compromise within community norms. Other times, however, the non-state system is neither efficient nor fair.

There are obvious advantages to exercising rights through personalized and traditional authority, because it is less expensive, more familiar, and locally available. Yet just because de facto or relationship-based authority is embedded in poor communities does not mean they will be constructive in fighting poverty and injustice. A patron-client network, or clique, may provide a safe haven for society's most vulnerable, but it also limits their options. Long-established rules for allocating resources may work when the population is small, but they might buckle under population pressure. Additionally, a private legal mechanism may be accessible, but it could easily play favorites depending on a plaintiff's personal connections.

A bottom-line concern is that development professionals must creatively seek to capitalize on the available mix of de facto or traditional modes of authority. There is no reason to assume that the informal institutions, rules, and arrangements are either superior or inferior to their de jure or "modern" counterparts. Context is critical. India is a possible model for how to integrate representative and legal institutions, having extended official recognition to a system of village councils and people's courts.

Drawing on traditional norms, the councils are reported to be seeking out new roles and to be adapting to the democratic factor in India's formal political institutions.[174]

Several West African countries use decentralized local councils to administer land laws. These tend to be based on customary power structures, though thus far they appear upwardly accountable to the central state rather than downwardly accountable to local populations.[175] The box below entitled :Authority Systems : Land Rights "discusses how the integration of formality and informality may help the poor with land rights generally.[176]

Box 5.5 **Authority Systems: Land Rights**

Regarding the critical asset of land, there exists an internationally well recognized spectrum of rights, as shown in the figure below. Starting with the floor of freedom from eviction, security of tenure progressively improves as one follows the arrow. Land rights begin with the perception that one will not be evicted, based often on political statements to that effect. The right becomes stronger through customary law, temporary occupancy certificates, through anti-eviction legislation and adverse possession (otherwise known as squatters' rights) and group tenure. Long-term leases and individual freehold tenure represent the most secure forms of tenure. The noteworthy feature of the continuum of land rights is that it accommodates and reflects the diverse reality of land rights and social land tenures that exist in the world today (for example, family and group rights). It also demonstrates the potential for an incremental path to greater security consistent with the way the poor accumulate their resources over time. This approach may be a solid foundation for achieving consensus on the issue of land and property rights. It is also a good starting point

for developing an innovative spectrum of protection and opportunities in this area, where parallel opportunities-protection/security spectrums can also be linked (e.g. labour, justice, entrepreneurship).

---

[174] K. Pur and M. Moore, "Ambiguous Institutions: Traditional Governance and Local Democracy in Rural India," IDS Working Paper, 82, 2007.

[175] J. Ribbot, "Decentralization, Participation and Accountability and Sahelian Forestry: Legal Instruments of Political-Administrative Control," *Africa: Journal of the International African Institute* 69, no. 1 (1999): 23–65.

[176] CLEP. 2008.

In all instances, poor people's perceptions should remain front and center. Legal or organizational reforms that look self-evidently empowering to experts from outside the poor community may look dangerous from the perspective of someone on the inside. This could detract from the local support needed for implementation.

Policy makers have to come to grips with the national environment of public policy—that is, with the domestic social structure, the economic context, the nature of the political and administrative systems, and the scale of economic and legal informality. While a country's environment for reform has to be unpacked and probed on its own terms, this chapter offers useful questions to ask. Practitioners and policy makers can make good use of the tool of contextual analysis to determine if conditions appear ripe for reforms aimed at the legal empowerment of the poor. These policy makers must look to see which implementation scenarios seem most probable, what sequencing and timelines for reform look doable and how they should be designed, what tradeoffs need to be considered, what risk-mitigating mechanisms are worth trying, and what contextual variables need careful monitoring during implementation. Adhering to this general set of guidelines will increase the chances of successfully carrying out empowerment policies.

Policy Initiation

Where a public policy originates is an important factor to consider in its implementation.

There is also the question of who proposes such a policy and who formulates the approach. Although external donors and international agencies are a useful source of ideas for policy reform, the degree of domestic enthusiasm and support is what matters most for implementation. Often, a crisis, such as a natural disaster or warfare, may act as a powerful stimulus for introducing new policies; but it is neither a necessary nor a sufficient condition for implementation. In the wake of the Asian financial meltdown in the second half of the 1990s, for instance, Indonesia enacted a series of important labor-law reforms that began with guaranteeing the fundamental right of freedom of association. The first set of legislative changes repealed provisions that limited representation to a single, government-controlled national federation of trade unions and put into place a framework offering workers the chance to form federations as they wished. These reforms certainly would not have occurred under normal conditions.

Some grassroots groups, social movements, or membership-based groups of workers or small-business owners may mobilize and demand change. Some decision makers in the government may respond favorably. Such an option can provide motivation for insiders who can potentially champion change. When country actors choose policies and actions based on their own assessments of the likely benefits, the alternatives and options, and the costs, then one can credibly speak of independently derived preferences and a willingness to act. To the extent that country decision makers reveal their policy preferences publicly and assign resources to achieve announced policy and program goals, such actions indicate a commitment to change. When countries commit to changes funded by outside donor resources, the presence of political will becomes unclear. Commitment is questionable when the initiative for reform comes largely from external actors. Some degree of initiative from country decision makers must exist in order to talk meaningfully of political will.

It shows a level of commitment when country actors establish a system for tracking progress toward the legal empowerment of the poor and actively manage implementation by adapting to emerging circumstances over time. However, decision makers who have been able to observe policies, practices, and programs aimed at the legal empowerment of the poor in other countries can selectively adopt them for their own use.

Donors can come together to create a joint program strategy or a multi-donor group. This option provides another possibility for outsiders to assess the possibility for change. While external support can be a strong catalyst for change, external micromanagement can also easily render the process too burdensome for reformers and policy champions within a government. It is important that the donor role in the legal empowerment of the poor be supportive and not self-defeating.

Before adopting or initiating any of these options, reformers should think about whether to engage in several strategies for the legal empowerment of the poor at once or to proceed with one and then transition to others. Also, one must be on guard to ensure that a policy does not simply increase state power and patronage in ways inconsistent with pro poor objectives. Agrarian reform has often gone wrong, with the supposed beneficiaries becoming victims. The best guarantee against such perverse developments is to bring the poor themselves into the policy-initiation process. But community engagement and decentralized structures are not always the best choice. In some cases, central authorities may be the best allies for the poor, because they can potentially sidestep local spheres of interest in support of marginalized and disadvantaged communities. They may serve as counterweight for the poor and minorities against entrenched control of a local government by anti-poor factions. A concrete example is the key role played by the federal government of Brazil in combating forced labor in remote, rural areas of the country.[177] The next few sections discuss more factors that determine the policy context.

Policy Champions

The degree of initial government support for any policy derives from domestic leaders who share a perception of a problem and have agreed on how to solve it. One or a few of these people may emerge as policy champions, or entrepreneurs, who make a policy their signature issue and drive it forward over time. Securing political will for any new course of action requires champions to bring other government actors on board and prevent policy spoilers from blocking introduction of the policy. Having strong advocates at high levels of government is vital to getting the legislative and executive arms to cooperate and follow through on policy reform. Policy champions within government may be emboldened by backing and pressure from civil society within the country. A policy champion can come forward at any level of government. Many policies aimed at the legal empowerment of the poor do not start out at the national center but emerge from the periphery via local or regional governments. A mayor or town council, for example, may want to take care of problems at an irregular housing settlement, an open-air market, or a

---

[177]   ILO, Stopping Forced Labor, 2001, www.ilo.org./dyn/declaris.

waste-disposal site. Acting proactively, the local government may try to include the people who live or work in these areas in finding the solutions. Perhaps more commonly, the local government may simply go ahead with reforms devoid of popular participation, sometimes triggering an empowering reaction as poor men and women move to legally to protect themselves from the harm caused by the policy. In either scenario, the national government may be on the sidelines of implementation.

Protagonists dedicated to the task of implementation may emerge out of other stakeholder groups (see below) as well, not just from the public sector. Any individual with leadership skills, initiative, and commitment can play the role of policy champion, though champions may be most effective if they also have technical knowledge about the subject at hand. Having several policy champions is generally better for implementation.

Policy Stakeholders

The important thing to bear in mind when looking at stakeholders is that they act in response to economic and political incentives. At its core, legal empowerment is about changing incentives to induce poor people to be more creative and productive by allowing them greater autonomy and freedom. Change agents nevertheless must be on guard against perverse incentives that could lead some constituencies to act in ways detrimental to poverty reduction.

Accordingly, it is advisable to conduct a stakeholder analysis and to plot stakeholder interests and intentions regarding the problem that a particular policy seeks to address. There are many possible formats to use with stakeholder analysis, but the usual practice is to start by enumerating the possible constituencies. Examples from the land sector might include the following:

Individuals	• landowners, landlords, tenants, shareholders, squatters, refugees, as well as beneficiaries of specific programs
Private sector	• land developers, estate agents, notaries, lawyers, surveyors, planners, bankers, media
Public sector	• politicians, line ministries, provincial/municipal/district departments
Civil society	• business associations, NGOs, CBOs, CSOs, faith-based groups, public policy research institutes, universities
Traditional authorities	• chiefs, elders, and political figures
International partners	• multilateral institutions, bilateral agencies, private foundations, international NGOs

The next step, typically, is to estimate each constituency's position on an issue, the intensity of its interest in the outcome (or policy salience), and the group's relative power to affect the outcome. This may be tricky, because any given set of stakeholders need not have monolithic interests. Policy cleavages are important, because they affect the possibility of building alliances across groups. In addition, any one member of these groups may belong to several stakeholder categories, and this may present opportunities for communication, bargaining, and building coalitions among the groups. In general, it is must be remembered that the configuration of stakeholder interests and policy positions is not static. Sometimes it is helpful to rate the importance of the issue to the group and its potential influence on implementation on a rough scale from zero (no importance) to ten (vital). The priority to be accorded the group could also be quantified. Two generic strategies to contend with stakeholders are top-down, adversarial strategies and participatory collaboration.[178] Building alliances across stakeholder groups is vital and will activate the networks and coalitions to which the stakeholders belong.

Support for the legal empowerment of the poor will arise from stakeholders who view it as good politics and a means to build political support and legitimacy. Donors can assist, but the driving forces for change must come from within the country. National leadership in debating the difficult issues is crucial. With regard to participatory collaboration, there may not be agreement about who should be involved in decisions. Some stakeholders will not have a prearranged structure. Also, there may be no approved inter-stakeholder process for developing common policy positions. Such an institutional arrangement will therefore need to be created to implement the legal empowerment of the poor. Those working for the legal empowerment of the poor must overcome the challenges of establishing commonly agreed-upon definitions of problem situations and identifying the relevant stakeholders as a first step. Adversarial situations are even riskier for the poor.

Most of the time, disfavored, disenfranchised stakeholders stand to lose in confrontations with groups that have more resources. Resolution of the conflicting interests ranges along a continuum from negotiation to mediation to third-party adjudication or arbitration to refusal to compromise at all. Adversarial stakeholders ordinarily enter into negotiation when

---

[178]   A. Fung and E. Wright, "Countervailing Power in Empowered Participatory Governance," in *Deepening Democracy: Institutional Innovations in Empowered Participatory Governance* eds. Fung and Wright (London: Verso, 2003).

they see that it compares favorably to what they could obtain away from the bargaining table. Where conflict already exists, a strategic starting point for development professionals is to understand stakeholder preferences for how to deal with the clash of interests. In thinking about stakeholder preferences, there are four stylized stakeholders to consider: the policy's beneficiaries, obviously; its allies (who support the policy even though they may not benefit directly); practitioners responsible for the policy; and challengers of the policy. Below, we will sketch out some of the possibilities; these are illustrative categories, and the descriptions may not accurately depict any actual group in any given country. As noted, real groups may straddle the generic categories or switch back and forth among them. For example, a group may flip from being challengers to the legal empowerment of the poor at one time to being allies at another.

Beneficiaries	Allies	Practioners	Challengers
• Intended Targets of Legal Empowerment • Diverse Group of people • Women and Indigenous peoples present biggest challenge	• Pro-poor community associations and Civil Society Activist • Possibly professionals, politicians • Willing to sacrifice for the poor	• Government and Court Officials • Retain sources of power and influence • Chance for enhancing success of Legal Empowerment	• Foreign and domestic businesses, and lawyers • Prefer the status quo • Subtle manipulation of policies to their advantage

Beneficiaries. The intended beneficiaries are the 4 billion people who are unable to use the law to improve their livelihoods. Poor people are the target beneficiaries of policies directed at the legal empowerment of the poor. They are the majority of the population in many countries. The term the *poor* is a convenience, of course, for this multitude is far from a monolithic constituency—despite sharing hunger, ill health, inadequate housing, and other common pathologies of poverty. They live in remote rural villages and in urban shantytowns. They work as subsistence farmers, agricultural laborers, domestic workers, street vendors, and trash recyclers. They are members of underrepresented ethnic minorities—often internal or external migrants seeking improved opportunities in a new area where they lack a clear legal status. They have been displaced by war and civil unrest, and they are indigenous people who have been left out and left behind by the dominant society. A lopsided number of the poor are women, who usually have home and family responsibilities on top of any work they have found outside the home. It is useful to have a segmented census of the poor as a starting point for work on the legal empowerment of the poor in any country—to know who they are, where they are located, and to what extent their interests align.

Poor women present a particular challenge for the legal empowerment of the poor, because in some cases their gains can be to the disadvantage of the male half of the poor population. In East Africa, for instance, women tend to enjoy use rights to land (see the further discussion of the spectrum of land rights below) as wives and mothers but lack transfer rights due to customs that reserve these for men. Women therefore are without a secure claim to a natural resource they use for daily supplies of fuel, water, and food. Legal insecurity inhibits economic progress, because women cannot make decisions on expanding or developing land.[179] Their fathers, husbands, and sons are likely to balk at efforts to implement expanded women's rights in this important economic realm, because they would compromise

---

[179] UNEP, Women and the Environment, Nairobi, 2004.

men's rights to the same assets. Women's community-based organizations may be the answer. These have proven somewhat effective in preserving women's land access in Mexico, though effective land control does not necessarily follow.[180]

Poor indigenous people, who represent 15 percent of the world's poor but only 5 percent of its population, are another special test for the legal empowerment of the poor.[181] This is due to physical or social isolation from any influence on governing the nation-state. Some indigenous people are nomadic, and some have been dispossessed de jure or de facto of their ancestral lands. They may speak a separate language. Indigenous people often live in remote sites with high economic potential based on water, timber, or medicinal plants but lack legal instruments to prevent over extraction of natural resources by outsiders. All these characteristics make it all the more important for governments to reach these would-be beneficiaries.

Allies. The main allied stakeholders of policies aimed at the legal empowerment of the poor are pro poor community associations and activists in civil society. Some of these stakeholders will be local action or advocacy groups, such as the Indonesian Legal Aid Foundation, whose mission is to defend poor people in court and expand their rights. Allies may also include professional associations sympathetic to the plight of the excluded. For example, Ecuador's Association of Law School Deans supports

---

[180] C. Radel, "Women's Community-based Organisations, Conservation Projects and Effective Land Control in Southern Mexico," *Journal of Latin American Geography* 4, no. 2 (2005): 7–34.

[181] ILO, *Equality at Work: Tackling the Challenges*, Geneva, 2007.

legal assistance for the indigent in that country. National bar associations are engaged in similar activities in many nations.

Certain politicians may come out as allies. It is common, for example, to find even somewhat disreputable politicians offering to use public land to woo voters' support in slum areas. However, such persons may not be reliable allies. More dependable are the genuine policy champions who have emerged from among the national or local political leadership to make a progressive name for themselves as friends of legal empowerment.

Some commercial enterprises, and particularly larger companies and multinational corporations, may be policy allies on certain occasions. More than three thousand corporations in more than a hundred countries have joined the UN's Global Compact, which commits them to support high standards in the areas of the environment, human rights, and labor rights.[182] These firms often say they would like to forge partnerships with poor communities in the developing world to create business models that are sustainable, equitable, and embedded in the local culture.[183] Some signatories are turning to the poor as business partners, suppliers, or distributors.

Nairobi, for example, has a productive alliance between informal entrepreneurs and larger businesses. Two business associations joined with the street vendors' organization in a dialogue with local authorities to improve the status of street vending. Street vendors in Kenya's capital city are subject to harassment and demands for

---

[182] UN Global Compact Office, *UN Global Compact Annual Review*, New York, 2007.

[183] S. Hart, *Capitalism at the Crossroads: The Unlimited Business Opportunities in Solving the World's Most Difficult Problems* (Wharton School: 2005).

bribes from city inspectors. The uncertainty forces the vendors to limit their stock and hinders their productivity and income. The two conventional associations originally wanted to drive out street vending because of litter and crowding. However, they later came around because of a growing realization that the outdoor presence of vendors limits crime and thus is good for everyone's business, among other factors. Interestingly, the vendors' group wants its members to pay licensing fees based on the argument that paying gives the members legal cover and provides leverage for government services.[184]

It should go without saying that these observations do not mean every self-described ally of the poor is a true friend of the legal-empowerment agenda. The reality is far more subtle and complex than that. Some grassroots groups may feel threatened by the legal empowerment of the poor if they do not have the lead in directing the movement. Mechanistically applying generic labels to predetermined groups of actors and assuming they will behave according to their category is no way to conduct stakeholder analysis.

Practitioners. A third important set of generic stakeholders are practitioners—mainly the government officials, court officers, and others who draft, interpret, and administer the land laws, labor statutes, and commercial regulations in a country. Despite sometimes having low positions in the bureaucratic hierarchy of government, these officials can and do wield considerable effective discretionary authority over implementation.

---

[184] S. Kamunyori, "Growing Space for Dialogue: The Case of Street Vending in Nairobi's Central Business District" (master's thesis, MIT, 2007).

One common problem is that permits, business licenses, tax assessments, and the like are sources of power and potential illegal income through bribes, kickbacks, and other rent-seeking behavior. Even the abstruse text describing many of these regulations provides low-level government employees with power, as citizens cannot decode legal jargon easily on their own. The interests and attitudes of government officials at all levels are therefore an important factor in the implementation process. In Beijing, for example, law enforcement officers and local authorities look the other way when rural-urban migrant entrepreneurs do not comply fully with license requirements and instead lease licenses illegally from local residents. This illicit license-leasing practice persists because bureaucrats profit from it.[185] Streamlining the business-registration process in an effort to legally empower the poor would threaten illegal but routine bureaucratic income in China's capital city.

These comments do not imply that bureaucrats are always spoilers of reform. A new program may also mean that staff members gain promotions, have interesting new responsibilities, or receive training opportunities or other perquisites. Within every government executive agency or judicial institution, there may be potential policy champions who come to identify with a particular solution to a social problem and make strenuous efforts to get it implemented. As noted, entrepreneurial effort by policy champions in elected and administrative office is a consistent theme in successful policy implementation around the world.

---

[185]   X. He, "Why Do They Not Comply with the Law: Illegality and Semi-Legality among Rural-Urban Migrant Entrepreneurs in Beijing," *Law and Society Review* 39, no. 3 (2005): 527–562.

Challengers. A final constituency to consider is rival stakeholders that challenge disenfranchised people exercising new rights or reviving latent ones. These competing or oppositional stakeholders may include foreign businesses and large domestic companies but also small-scale landlords, mine owners, shopkeepers, and moneylenders as well as some lawyers, engineers, and other specialized experts who prefer the status quo. We should be careful about painting any class of people with too broad a brush, but numerous local elites and professionals are likely to feel threatened by confident and forceful poor people and may try to prevent improvements in poor people's status and income. Lawyers, for example, may lose the upper hand with clients if laws are translated into everyday language or if inexpensive conflict-resolution forums become widely available.

A common and tricky problem of implementation—as mentioned earlier—is when contending stakeholders do not try to block reforms outright but subtly manipulate emerging policies (and especially donor-driven programs) to their advantage. This distortion is chronic in activities directed at the legal empowerment of the poor. In many Asian countries, for example, prospective titling programs often have the perverse effect of inducing speculators to buy up land ahead of time from squatters for slightly more than informal prices. The squatters come out ahead in the short term but pay the opportunity cost of not waiting long enough to get the main benefit of the titling program—which accrues to the people with deeper pockets. Low income and vulnerability lead to a safety-first calculation, so squatters reasonably prefer to have their cash immediately. As a result, contrary to the stated intention of the titling program, elites capture most of the gains from it.

The sequential and conditional release of funds is one strategy for countering the persistent problem of elite capture.

Conclusion

This chapter has provided a detailed guide to help the seasoned practitioner as well as those new to the field of legal empowerment navigate a complex and difficult terrain. The complexity arises because several different interacting groups of actors interconnected in multiple ways find themselves in apparent competition for a piece of the same resource pie. Difficulties arise for many reasons. For example, the economic pie is often shrinking rather than growing, while the demands on it might be increasing. Those who have positions of power and privilege are not equal before the law and are able to grab a disproportionate share of the pie. The process of empowerment—or, better, self-empowerment—is not about providing a few more goods or services for the poor, which is what most development programs, national or international, seek to do. It is about questioning how fair the rules of society are, who makes these rules, and how the deprived might gain greater control over their own lives and livelihoods. In other words, it is about changing power relations between those who have and those who have not. While we have so far only hinted in this book about the power issues, we have, like typical development practitioners, sought to find roadmaps around the power problem rather than dealing with it head on. In the next chapter, we seek to do just that—address the challenge of skewed power relations that keep the poor in poverty.

6

Introduction

We have seen in the previous chapter that the legal empowerment of the poor involves a wide range of stakeholders, some supportive and others opposed in various ways. When the elites and the powerful feel threatened, they are likely to derail any empowerment process. In most of recorded human history, power relations between those with power and those without changed only through violent revolution—until the intellectual revolution of the enlightenment. Subsequently, we have seen major successes in changing societal power relations through a mixture of social movements, charismatic leaders, and violent and nonviolent demonstrations. These empowerment strategies have resulted in the ongoing women's revolution for equality with men, the Gandhian movement of nonviolence to drive the British out of India, the civil rights movement of Martin Luther King and others for rights of African Americans, and the defeat of apartheid in South Africa, among others movements less celebrated but no less important. More recently, political power changed hands from dictators to the populations at large in several Arab countries through the events of the so-called Arab Spring. These processes of self-empowerment generally started out with peaceful mass demonstrations but in most cases turned violent as those in power resisted changes in the status quo. Many of these transitions are still actively underway, and some violence continues.

Reforms seeking to include the excluded and to empower the deprived may create winners and losers even among the most powerful elites. While it might not be possible to have win-win solutions in all cases, it would be of tremendous value to be able to identify scenarios in which this is possible. In other words, under what conditions can power be a positive-sum game, and how might we create such conditions? This question is at the heart of all possible peaceful self-empowerment processes in which the poor can have a chance to become better off. Is the realization of ESCR for all a win-win situation in which all of humanity is better off? Or do some persons have to be deprived so that a few, through manipulation of the systems in place, can have all they want and more than they need? The common thread throughout all shifts in power relations seems to be that those with power never readily give it up to those without—unless, of course, we can make power into a positive-sum game.

Virtually all power analyses, whether in development or human-rights circles, tend to study the drivers of change through existing political, contextual, institutional, and stakeholder analyses as described in chapter 5. The underlying assumption is that power is a zero-sum game. Not much is available in the literature to help us find conditions and strategies to make power a positive-sum game. Yet this might be the key to the success of peaceful self-empowerment. We might need a new enlightenment, a new awakening, in which our individual humanity reveals its highest expression in our collective humanity and our spiritual realization of being supersedes our material drives to have more and more.

This chapter therefore seeks to sow the seeds of this new enlightenment by reviewing the literature on the nature of power in search of opportunities to recast the common zero-sum notion.

Next, it examines ways to analyze—and hopefully change—power relations. We will then assess the conditions under which power might become a positive-sum game so that the poor have a better chance of realizing their rights. The chapter also seeks, through revealing case studies, to illustrate practical approaches to achieving win-win situations in which power becomes a positive-sum game and the deprived gain greater control over their own lives.

Definitions of Power

Power has been defined in myriad ways; here are some of them:

- "The possibility of imposing one's will upon the behavior of others."[186]
- "The individual's capacity to move others, to entice others, to persuade and encourage others to attain specific goals or to engage in specific behavior."[187]
- "A potential for changing attitudes, beliefs, and behaviors of others."[188]
- The basic intuitive notion of A causing (or having the ability to cause) B to do something that B otherwise would not do (or, we might infer, to prevent B from doing something

[186] M. Weber, *Max Weber on Law in Economy and Society* (Cambridge: Harvard University Press, 1954).

[187] J. Cangemi, "Some Observations of Successful Leaders and Their Use of Power and Authority," *Education* 112 (1992): 499–505.

[188] R. F. Verderber and K. S. Verderber, Inter-Act Using Personal Communication Skills (Belmont: Wadsworth, 1992).

or achieving something that B would like if A feels it is not in A's best interest).[189]

The publication *Power and Society* by Laswell and Kaplan introduced a shift from the old power-as-resources approach to the new relational-power approach, which developed the idea of power as a type of causation.[190] This causal notion conceives of power as a relationship (actual or potential) in which the behavior of actor A at least partially causes a change in the behavior of actor B. *Behavior* in this context need not be defined narrowly but may include beliefs, attitudes, preferences, opinions, expectations, emotions, and predispositions to act. In this view, power is an actual or potential relationship between two or more actors (persons, states, groups, and so on) rather than a property of any one of them. For example, using this approach, you would not necessarily declare that A is powerful but rather that A has power over B.

Typologies of power

Galbraith refers to three types and three sources of power as follows:

Condign power "wins submission by the ability to impose an alternative to the preferences of the individual or group that is sufficiently unpleasant or painful so that these preferences are abandoned. There is an overtone of punishment. The expected

---

[189] R. Dahl, 1957.

[190] H. Lasswell and A. Kaplan, *Power and Society: A Framework for Political Inquiry* (New Haven: Yale University Press, 1950).

rebuke is usually too harsh, so the individual will endure, submit, or give into the power from fear or threat. The individual is aware of the submission via compulsion."[191] This form of power is the most vicious and coercive of the three.

Compensatory power "wins submission by the offer of affirmative reward—by the giving of something of value to the individual so submitting. Payments, share, praise, money for services. The individual is aware of the submission for a reward."[192] Of the three forms of power defined by Galbraith, the compensatory form is the closest to a voluntary or win-win exchange.

Conditioned power "wins submission by changing beliefs. Persuasion, education, habituation, social commitment to what seems natural, proper, right causes the individual to submit to the will of another or others. Submission reflects the preferred course; the fact of submission is not recognized. Conditioned power is central to the functioning of the modern economy and polity, and in capitalist and socialist countries alike."[193] This form of power develops more slowly but is the most potent in use.

His three sources of power are personality, property, and organization. *Personality* is "leadership in the common reference, a quality of mind, physique, speech, moral certainty or personal trait that gives access to instruments of power. The ability to persuade or create a belief." *Property* is "wealth, an aspect of authority, a certainty of purpose inviting conditioned submission. Property, income, wealth provides the wherewithal to purchase submission." *Organization* is "the most important source of power

---

[191]   J. K. Galbraith, *Anatomy of Power* (Boston: Houghton Mifflin, 1983).

[192]   *Ibid.*

[193]   *Ibid.*

in modern society, taken for granted, and required. Persuasion and submission to the purposes of the organization." [194]

French and Ravetz, on the other hand, describe five common types of power: coercive, reward, legitimate, expert, and referent.[195] Although their terminology and number of types are different, the ideas are quite similar to those of Galbraith. Coercive power bases its effectiveness on the ability to administer punishment or give negative reinforcements. The second type, reward power, rests on the ability to deliver something valued by the receiver. People who can deliver money, jobs, or political support have something other people want and therefore become extremely powerful in organizations. Legitimate power, the third type, resides in a person's position rather than the actual person. This type of formal power relies on position in a hierarchy of authority. Occasionally, people with legitimate power fail to recognize they have it, and then they may begin to notice others going around them to accomplish their goals. The fourth type, expert power, relies on a person's special knowledge and expertise in a given area. Anyone can have it if he or she formally and informally prepares sufficiently. The last type, referent power, includes admiration of a leader, which usually produces influence and acceptance by subordinates. Referent power acts a little like role-model power. It depends on respecting, liking, and holding another individual in high esteem. It usually develops over a long period of time.[196]

---

[194]   Ibid.

[195]   J. R. P. French and B. Ravetz, "The Social Basis of Power" in *Group Dynamics*, ed. D. Cartwright and A. Zander (New York: Harper and Row).

[196]   H. E. Fukua Jr., K. E. Payne, and J. P. Cangemi, "Leadership and the Effective Use of Power," www.Nationalforum.com/electronicjournalsvolumes.

One can create a win-win situation through a positive operating climate by choosing the most appropriate compliance-gaining tactics, which tend to lead to greater life or job satisfaction. It seems as though expert, reward, and referent power produce the greatest satisfaction, while coercive and legitimate power have the opposite effect.[197]

Analyzing Power Relations

There is an important distinction in power analysis between "power to" and "power over."[198] In power to, an agent or set of agents has the capacity to achieve an outcome, so this has also been called outcome power.[199] In power over, an agent or set of agents can use coercive power or, more broadly, an incentive structure to get another agent or set of agents to change their beliefs or their preferences or to achieve some outcome. This has been called social power. The incentive structure could employ the full range of costs and benefits of behaving in one way over another. Typically, actors have social power over others to the extent that they can manipulate the incentive structures of others. Incentives include opportunities and constraints that operate on actors given their extant beliefs and desires—that is, given their preferences.[200]

---

[197] *Ibid.*

[198] P. Pamsardi, "Power Over and Power To," in *The Encyclopedia of Power,* ed. Keith Dowding, 521–524.

[199] K. Dowding, "Power and Persuasion: Is Debate Zero Sum?" paper presented to the American Political Science Association, Seattle, 2011.

[200] *Ibid.*

Some have suggested that actors who can exercise power more cheaply than others therefore have more net power.[201] If A can get B to do something that is costly for B, some would contend that this is indicative of A having more power than if A could only get B to do something that is cheap for B. Even if A is unable to get B to comply with its demands, it may be able to impose costs on B for noncompliance. Both the costs to A and the costs to B are relevant to assessing influence. Is it costly or cheap for A to influence B? Is it costly or cheap for B to comply with A's demands?

Some describe power as having three faces. The three faces are decision-making power,[202] agenda-setting power (the power to keep things off the agenda and so prevent a decision from being made, for example),[203] and ideological power (the capacity to influence another's preferences, wants, or thoughts and beliefs).[204]

---

[201] J. C. Harsyani, "Measurement of Social Power, Opportunity Costs, and the Theory of Two-Person Bargaining Games," *Behavioural Science* 7 (1962): 67–80.

[202] R. Dahl, *Who Governs?* (New Haven, 1961).

[203] P. Bachrach and S. Baratz, "Two Faces of Power," *American Political Science Review* 56 (1962): 947–52.

[204] S. Lukes, *Power: A Radical View*, second edition (London: Palgrave MacMillan, 2005).

Soft Power

Nye introduced and developed the term *soft power*.[205], [206], [207] He used it to call attention to the ability to get others to want what you want. Noting that this ability to affect the preferences of others tends to be associated with intangible power resources, such as culture, ideology, and institutions, he distinguished it from the hard command power usually associated with tangible resources like military and economic strength. It is the ability to get what you want through attraction rather than coercion or payment. Fully defined, soft power is the ability to affect others through the co-optive means of framing the agenda, persuading, and eliciting positive attraction in order to obtain preferred outcomes.

Soft power provides a solid basis for us to think about how power can be a positive-sum game when it includes social relations of joint action through mutual agreement in which one actor is able to convince another actor to alter its beliefs, interests, or actions voluntarily and freely.

Finally, Foucault's observations on the nature of power are important to bear in mind, as they provide a useful way to understand the relations between human rights and

---

[205]   J. S. Nye, *Bound to Lead: The Changing Nature of American Power* (New York: Basic Books, 1990).

[206]   J. S. Nye, *Soft Power: The Means to Success in World Politics* (New York: Public Affairs, 2004).

[207]   J. S. Nye, *The Future of Power* (New York: Public Affairs, 2011).

power.[208, 209, 210] Souther summarizes some of the relevant observations of Foucault as follows:[211]

that power is ubiquitous and not centered in the state nor limited to it, indeed; modernity has seen the rise of 'disciplinary power' which operates through techniques such as hierarchical observation, normalizing judgment and examination;

power is active and productive in that it induces pleasure, forms knowledge, produces discourse and is not merely negative, prohibitive and repressive;

power lacks a single center it is always 'part of a chain,' operating 'through networks' and 'exercised from innumerable points, it is transitory and heterogeneous;

it is not a fixed entity but a fluid process so it is more important to consider how it works than what it is;

particular forms of power are emergent from a set of historical and social conditions that converge at a particular time and place, 'attracting and propagating one another' until they form' comprehensive systems.'

There is no conspiracy of power, even though particular operations of power may end up serving the interests of certain groups.

The exercise of power can be seen as action upon the actions of others;

which affirms, rather than negates, individual agency and thus rejects liberalism's implicit assumption of a mutually exclusive relation between power and freedom

208 Michel Foucault, *A Foucault Reader,* ed. Paul Rabinow (Pantheon, 1984).

209 Michel Foucault, "The Subject and Power," in Power: Essential Works of Foucault, Vol. 3, ed. James D. Faubion (London: Penguin, 2002).

210 Michel Foucault, *Society Must Be Defended* (London: Penguin, 2003).

211 J. Souter, "Emancipation and Domination: Human Rights and Power," *In-Spire Journal of Law, Politics and Societies* 3, no. 2.

Power and Human Rights

Neither metaphysical nor ontological justifications for human rights are compelling according to some liberal pragmatists. Metaphysics fail because "they confuse what we wish [humans] to be with what we empirically know them to be."[212] Nor can rights be grounded in a shared view of human nature in view of today's pluralistic societies. Similarly, ontological arguments for human rights are unclear, because they often presume to justify rights that exist independently of the political institutions that are responsible for creating them. The well-known difficulties of reconciling individual and collective rights compound the problem. This leads us into controversy regarding the proper ordering of rights. Either way, those who attempt to ground human rights in metaphysical and ontological arguments unwittingly undermine our commitment to the responsibilities that human rights entail.[213]

The liberal pragmatists argue that consensus for human rights may be found in a common fear of the abuse of power and in recognition of human rights' capacity to curb it.[214] Rather than relying upon a priori considerations for or against human rights, this "liberalism of fear" is historically rooted since it models itself upon the declarations of "never again" that followed the atrocities of the Second World War. Although abuses have obviously continued, increasingly powerful international human-

---

[212]   M. Ignatieff, *Human Rights as Politics and Idolatry* (Princeton University Press, 2001).

[213]   *Ibid.*

[214]   J. Shklar, "The Liberalism of Fear" in *Political Thought and Political Thinkers*, ed. Shklar and Hoffman.

rights institutions and nongovernmental organizations have successfully pressured abusive governments, and the ideals of human rights have fuelled many emancipatory campaigns, such as the civil rights movement and the antiapartheid struggle. The justification of human rights, the argument goes, lies in their practical ability to reduce suffering by keeping power in check.[215]

Although it may initially seem obvious, given their content, that human rights provide an emancipatory barrier against power, radical political theorists have argued that they are actually an instrument of power, regulation, or even domination. Souter summarizes the reasons for this line of thinking as follows:

1. Given the tension between the categorical and generic idiom of morality and the particularity and partiality of politics, when human rights descend from their moral pedestal and enter the political realm, they are liable to be co-opted, devalued, or contaminated by partisan political interests. Lip service to human rights frequently masks their continued violation.

2. Human rights are culturally insensitive and reflect Western individualist values rather than possessing any true universality. The *human* in human rights is fundamentally the Westerner who, in a movement analogous to the imperialism of the past, seeks to impose his rights on the other.

3. The rights of man, as Marx contends, can never provide the emancipation they promise. Their declarations of freedom and equality depoliticize and privatize inequalities of class,

---

215 J. Souter, "Emancipation and Domination: Human Rights and Power," *In-Spire Journal of Law, Politics and Societies* 3, no. 2.

race, and gender, which are left to operate unchecked in civil society. While offering narrow political emancipation, they cannot provide full human emancipation.[216]

4. Human rights, as a political project, will always have unintended side effects in excess of their stated aims. Despite their apolitical pretensions, human rights are ideological in the sense that they compete with and may preclude other emancipatory programs.[217]

5. The idea that human rights are intrinsically emancipatory derives from an unrealistic and narrow understanding of power. Once this is swept away, we can appreciate that they are inextricably bound up with its operation. Human rights act as conduits for relations of power, regulation, or even domination.[218]

Souter's article makes some further interesting links between human rights and power. He considers both the potential of human rights to curb the unchecked habits of power and the reverse situation, in which the application of human rights itself is an exercise of power that could be harmful. Here are his conclusions:

*   Human rights may indeed limit the use of power but only by exercising it themselves.

---

[216]   Karl Marx, "On the Jewish Question" in *Karl Marx: Selected Writings*, ed. D. McLennan (Oxford: Oxford University Press, 1987).

[217]   W. Brown, "The Most We Can Hope For: Human Rights and the Politics of Fatalism," *South Atlantic Quarterly* 103, no. 2/3 (451–463).

[218]   D. Ivison, *Rights* (Stocksfield: Acumen).

- We can reconceptualize the aim of human rights as ending harmful operations of power and rework emancipation as the process of freeing oneself from domination, not power.
- Since human rights do not take account of identities, they mask the powers that produced such identities by depoliticizing and privatizing them. Human rights can at one moment emancipate, as in the civil rights movement, but at another dominate, as through property rights that privilege the dominant economic class. Given this paradox, it is practically impossible to say anything generic about the emancipatory capacity of human rights.
- Although human rights have a potential to dominate, we must stress the capacity of human rights to reduce suffering over their capacity to emancipate. Secondly, one could argue that human rights are merely one part of a broader struggle for emancipation, and that other political programs are necessary to mitigate or offset their potentially harmful or dominating effects.
- The right to property may entrench the dominant power of the most affluent. However, if the government, say, also introduces redistributive measures, then this may limit the regulative effects of human rights. (Refer to discussion of a property rights system that can work for the poor in chapter 4.)

We therefore find ourselves in a paradoxical situation in which existing power structures often hinder the realization of human rights by the poor; under some conditions, human rights might help to change these structures in favor of the poor, but they sometimes also worsen the situation for specific groups. Part of this dilemma would be resolved if we could make power a positive-sum game.

Under What Conditions Can Power Be Positive-Sum?

The terms *zero-sum*, *positive-sum*, and *variable-sum* are drawn from game theory based on rational choice, which is increasingly used in various disciplines to help analyze power relationships. In rational-choice theory, human individuals or groups can be modeled as actors who choose from a choice set of possible actions in order to try to achieve desired outcomes. An actor's incentive structure comprises (its beliefs about) the costs associated with different actions in the choice set and the likelihoods that different actions will lead to desired outcomes.

In this setting, we can differentiate between *outcome power*, the ability of an actor to bring about or help bring about outcomes, and *social power*, the ability of an actor to change the incentive structures of other actors in order to bring about outcomes. This framework can model a wide range of social interactions where actors have the ability to exert power over others. For example, a powerful actor can take options away from another actor's choice set, can change the relative costs of actions, can change the likelihood that a given action will lead to a given outcome, or can change the other actor's beliefs about its incentive structure.

As with other models of power, this framework is neutral as to the use of coercion. For example, a threat of violence can change the likely costs and benefits of different actions; so can a financial penalty in a voluntarily agreed contract or, indeed, a friendly offer.[219]

While the terms *zero-sum* and *variable-sum* come from contemporary game theory, the ideas behind those terms are

---

[219] En.wikipedia.org/wiki/rational_choice_framework

much older, even thousands of years old, and can be described equally well, though perhaps less succinctly, in nontechnical language.

In a recent paper, James Read provides a summary of the conditions that he believes need to be met for a theory that will show persuasively that power can be variable-sum as well as the challenges such a theory will face because of nearly three thousand years of human civilization thinking of power as zero-sum.[220] Such a theory is important, however, because "we use the idea of power both to describe the social and political world, and to orient our action within it. To change our understanding of power is thus, to a certain degree, to change the political and social world itself."[221] According to Read,

> The most extensive and richly-detailed descriptions of power have assumed, explicitly or implicitly, that increased power for one necessarily entails an equivalent loss of power for another. There is no question that some important and enduring phenomena of the social and political world lend support to this assumption. But the zero-sum assumption cannot easily account for the peculiar blend of conflicting and shared interest, of competition and cooperation, which characterizes most important social and political relationships. (Of course the same is true in reverse for attempts to ground power on pure cooperation.) The zero-sum approach to

---

[220] J. H. Read, "Is Power Zero Sum or Variable Sum? Old Arguments and New Beginnings," paper prepared for the American Political Association Meeting, 2011.

[221] *Ibid.*

power may acknowledge the fact of cooperation and shared interest, but treats them as phenomena essentially different from power—even when they are inseparable components of relationships admittedly involving power. This artificial dichotomy in practice treats conflict as the active and dynamic element and relegates cooperation to a passive, taken-for-granted background.[222]

The principal argument in favor of a variable-sum understanding of power (whereby power can be collectively gained and collectively lost but also sometimes gained at another's expense) is that such an approach promises to be more faithful to the entire range of phenomena and to the complexity of relationships. However, to date, no adequate, fully worked out variable-sum treatment of power has appeared. Most theorists of power who challenge the zero-sum view do so briefly, identifying flaws in the zero-sum logic rather than offering an alternative theory. Any improved variable-sum theory of power must be able to do the following:

Account for conflictual and cooperative elements in power relations. Merely establishing that parties in conflict share limited common interests does not, by itself, demonstrate a cooperative exercise of power. These interests may fail to be realized, or they may be realized entirely through the action of one party on that party's terms—as when a victor in war offers generous terms to the defeated rival or when a slaveholder feeds his slaves well. Benefits received entirely through the act of another do not demonstrate that the recipient possesses much power.

---

[222]   *Ibid.*

Properly describe highly unequal, exploitive, or violent relations of power. Although it would explain them differently than a zero-sum theory, it cannot restrict its theorizing to relatively equal or cooperative instances of power. Nor should it present itself as more optimistic in its outlook or predictions than the zero-sum approach. Within the framework of a variable-sum understanding of power, zero-sum outcomes remain real possibilities in particular contexts. The negative-sum outcome—all sides losing power—also remains a permanent possibility and might in some cases be more likely than mutual gains of power. A variable-sum theory of power must keep all of these possibilities in play and not display any general bias toward one type of outcome as opposed to the others. Whether positive-sum, negative-sum, or zero-sum factors predominate depends instead on the specific power relationships under examination.

Not only legitimate but critique existing power structures. From the general premise that power is not altogether harmful, that it may sometimes be necessary and even positively good, it does not follow that one should refrain from challenging a particular regime or system. A variable-sum theory of power can be used to argue in favor of preserving an existing system or practice. But the same premise—that power is not always harmful or oppressive—can also be used to justify the power from below exercised by those seeking to reform or replace that system or practice.

Explain how aggregate gains or losses translate to increases or decreases of power. It is possible to imagine enormous increases in the overall power of a system that places actual power in the hands of very few and disempowers the rest. That would not be a positive-sum power outcome in the sense defined here.

It is tempting to lurch to the opposite extreme and conclude that a genuinely positive-sum outcome must be one that literally increases the power of everyone—all winners and no losers, a kind of Pareto optimality in the realm of power. This sets far too high a bar. To insist that no redistribution of power is justified unless everyone including those currently most privileged and powerful gains (or at least does not lose) power would have the practical effect of legitimating every existing regime and condemning every attempt at reform.

Explain power characteristic of rule-constrained democratic competition. In particular, such a theory should explain whether democratic rules merely redistribute political power or both redistribute and expand political power. It must explain how the system rewards winners with public power while preserving the future power of losers (and how permanent winners and losers disrupt this effect). And it must explain in what ways rival powers actively cooperate to preserve the democratic system—or, alternatively, fail to do so and put democracy at risk. The theory should also shed light on how the peculiar public forms of power that characterize democracy remain rooted in and linked to the harsher, less public forms of power from which it emerged.

A variable-sum theory that effectively meets these criteria, or even one or two of them, would mark an advance over existing literature challenging the zero-sum view of power.

In another work that challenged zero-sum relationships, *The Strategy of Conflict,* Schelling concluded that a lot of the preoccupation with power as a zero-sum game came from game theory applications that focused almost entirely on zero-sum or pure conflict situations.[223] However, he argued that in reality a

---

[223]   T. Schelling, *The Strategy of Conflict* (Harvard University Press, 1980).

pure conflict situation is only likely to arise in a war in which both sides seek the extermination of the opponent. Generally, this is not the case in war. In most cases of conflict, winning does not have a strictly competitive meaning. It does not mean winning relative to one's adversary. It means gaining relative to one's own value system, and one may accomplish this by bargaining, by mutual accommodation, or by avoidance of mutually damaging behavior.

To study the strategy of conflict is to consider conflict situations as essentially bargaining situations. This allows us to avoid preoccupations with pure conflicts or pure collaborations. Both of these are extremes, and it would be a mistake to think of them as limiting cases. In practice, there is a powerful common interest in avoiding situations that would seriously damage the values of either side. For example, a successful employee strike might destroy the employer financially, but more often a successful strike is one that never actually happens. In this work, Schelling traces the definition of *strategy* to game theory, in which there are games of skill, chance, and strategy. In a strategy game, the best course of action for each player depends on what the others do. The focus is on the interdependence of the adversaries' decisions and on their expectations of each other's behavior.

Case Studies

In previous chapters, we have described the situation of the global poor at length. In the next section of this chapter, we will review two case studies to gain a better understanding of how power relations affect this group in the world today. The first case study took place in Mumbai and looked at railroad squatters and how they were peacefully and successfully relocated in a true win-win scenario. The second was an unsuccessful attempt to negotiate pastoral land rights between tribal communities in Ethiopia. Lastly, we will review a case study from the developed world. We will see an example of two tiers of government, central and local, coming together to solve various initiatives; however, the power conflicts inherent in this action create early hurdles to overcome. These three cases provide examples of what can work and what has failed in three very different environments. Most importantly, all three can provide important lessons for implementing legal empowerment.

Revisiting Participation: Win-Win Strategy in Negotiations with Railway Authorities and Squatters, Mumbai, India[224]

In this case study, Sheela Patel[225], of Slum Dwellers International, examines a situation in which squatters, government authorities, NGOs, and commuters came together in Mumbai to create a win-win scenario for everyone involved.

As Mumbai grew, slum dwellings cropped up throughout the city of 10 million, some most precariously beside railroads. These dwellings became a terrible nuisance to the city's estimated 7.4 million commuters, and by the late eighties, stakeholders began to take action to provide a solution.

---

[224] S, Patel.1999. Transport and Communications Bulleti in Asia and the Pacific. No. 69.

[225] Director of SPARC on behalf of SPARC Mahila Milan and National Slum

Here is the situation Patel describes: "There are three suburban rail lines in Mumbai: Central, Western and Harbour. Each of these has a very large number of people living in slums within 30 feet of the railway track ... One consequence of their location is the number of accidents that take place, particularly affecting young children. Another consequence is that in many places people from the settlements and the nearby vicinity walk across the tracks frequently. The presence of these settlements has a considerable impact on the speed of trains."

The settlements were affecting expansion of the railways, commuter time, and the general flow of travel in and out of Mumbai. The slum dwellers in these areas retained poor property security over their land and at many times lacked basic resources.

Patel goes on to describe the actors involved in the struggle to fix the railway lines of Mumbai:

For years, the Railways have argued that they had no part of the responsibility to shift slum dwellers. This was considered to be the job of the relevant authorities, such as the Municipal Corporation or the State Government Slum Clearance Board. Every few years some discussions were initiated by either the Railways or the state government but, in the eyes of the communities and the NGOs involved, nothing emerged as an outcome. In 1988, however, Maharashtra's Housing Department suggested that the Railways, the State Government and the Society for the Promotion of Area Resource Centres (SPARC) undertake a joint survey to assess the number of households encroaching on Railways land.

Based on the survey, SPARC produced in 1989 a report entitled "Beyond the beaten track." Along with its publication

SPARC also organized the residents of these communities into a Railway Slum Dweller's Federation (RSDF). The rationale for the Federation was simple. Unless all the communities developed the capacity to operate as a united group and felt capable of establishing a leadership that could engage in dialogue with the Railways and the state government, they could not expect any changes. SPARC and its two partners, the National Slum Dweller's Federation and Mahila Milan were the main "trainers" in the process.

Along with the 1989 report, they also facilitated a dialogue between the Federation and the State Government of Maharashtra in which communities suggested that if given a secure piece of land with infrastructure, they would be willing to move without other compensation. In 1989, the Railway Slum Dwellers Federation was able to demonstrate its capacity when it worked in collaboration with the state government to assist in relocating a slum of 900 households in order to lay a railway line which linked the city to Vashi or New Bombay.

The alliance of SPARC, Mahila Milan and the National Slum Dweller's Federation also helped 181 households who could not afford the government provided tenement to build their own houses at a lower cost. While this remained a valuable milestone in building credibility and confidence, the alliance did not help any more communities in obtaining amenities or securing housing. However despite that, the Federation worked vigorously, helping communities to form "proposed cooperatives" to save money, plan their own housing and build skills and capability to face a future challenge when they may need to be engaged in negotiations for secure land with the state or Railways.

The section above describes an important example of allies coming to the aid of the poor to form a united front. The increased concentration of power for the slum dwellers allowed them to negotiate successfully with powerful practitioners and to receive some compensation and support. However, as the author notes, this support was somewhat limited.

In 1995, the lessons taken from the SPARC alliance had to be applied to a giant renovation project known as the Mumbai Transport Project II (MUTP II). The project aimed to remake the Mumbai transit system almost entirely and to bring it into the modern age. As expected, one of the main issues that confronted this public-works project was the slums blocking potential road lines and rail lines.

In the case of MUTP II, the World Bank actually became involved and required the government of Maharashtra to formulate a resettlement and rehabilitation policy in mid-1995. Once again, SPARC, the National Slum Dwellers' Federation, other NGOs, and various government agencies became involved. The task force formed by these entities submitted recommendations, and MUTP II approved them. However, after a few years of stalemate with the World Bank, as well as commuter protests and violence, forward momentum stalled.

It took a few successful self-organizational efforts on the slum dwellers' part to reinstill faith in the transport agency: "To demonstrate how organized communities were, in late 1997, near Borivalli station, where slums were almost 10 feet from the track, the whole settlement moved back 30 feet, built a wall for a boundary and realigned their houses."

This effort among the poor led to considerations to move on with the project without international assistance:

At this time SPARC and its alliance partners made another offer to the state government. It was suggested that if the state government gave land and the Railways paid to bring in all the infrastructure, SPARC and the Federation would manage the project and the communities would build houses at their own cost, thus making this a tripartite agreement in which all stakeholders made contributions and played their role.

The Railways identified the fifth and sixth corridor where they sought to lay one additional track as their priority and which they could undertake without World Bank resources. On their part, the state government located a piece of land measuring 2.28 hectares at Kanjur Marg in a suburb called Ghatkopar which was considered very acceptable to the communities. This was sufficient to relocate 900 of the 1,980 families living along the railway tracks. Land for the balance of 1,000 odd families is in the process of being identified and when it is done, all the families currently on the land needed by the project will be shifted.

In view of the earlier involvement of SPARC and its general credibility, the government of Maharashtra issued an order in March 1998, appointing SPARC as facilitator for the resettlement and rehabilitation operations. Land was to be formally transferred to cooperative housing societies of slum dwellers in whose name they were registered. However, regulations stipulated that the land could only be conveyed to the slum dwellers after they lived on the site. Since it would take three years to construct formal housing, it was agreed that the momentum of the initiative would be lost if such a delay occurred.

At the same time, the Railways had project funds amounting to 13.8 million rupees to contribute to the land development (infrastructure) but could not give it directly to SPARC. This problem was resolved when the Slum Rehabilitation Authority, which is a regulatory body, agreed to supervise and "hold" the money for infrastructure development to facilitate this process. The conveyance issue was also resolved when the slum dwellers interested in obtaining the land, suggested that they develop a two phase rehabilitation strategy. In phase one it was proposed that as soon as the land was filled and water sanitation and drainage brought to the site, the slum dwellers would voluntarily shift to the site and build a transit tenement at their own cost with 120 sq. feet per family so that all 900 families could be accommodated.

Patel outlines some general highlights of the experience, which we can use to create an environment that supports the legal empowerment of the poor:

First, all the participants, regardless of where they were located within the state, the community or the NGO operated as a team. This was something which was unique and special because everyone felt that they had helped create a "miracle," a win-win solution, which has been able to take care of the needs of all concerned and improve the situation for all—the city, the commuters, the Railways, and the community. The participants also demonstrated that with such partnerships sharing problem-solving, the crisis actually became easier when each other's needs and aspirations were respected and problems addressed collectively. All the participants became major champions of the process within their own organization and in turn when they had to deal with opposition to the project they contributed to the solution.

Second, the two step relocation strategy is now one which is proposed in a range of venues when relocation is being discussed. Its advantages are several and very obvious. In the past communities never believed in the promise of relocation in which transit accommodation was available elsewhere because people often languished in those transit accommodations for 10-15 years. Often houses constructed for one group of people in transit were allocated to others who jumped the queue because of political and other considerations. In this case, families moved from their railway dwellings of 60-85 sq. ft. to transit tenements of 120 sq. ft. with all amenities. In addition, they were located on the site where their houses were to be built, while owning the land both formally and de facto by their presence. This process increased their housing incrementally, but because they were in the same location, they could build new roots. And because they were all together their social connections were retained.

Third, agencies such as the Railways and municipalities who wanted the land on which the slums were located, could occupy the land almost two years earlier than would otherwise have been the case. To those institutions, the reduced period of waiting to start the project improved the financial calculations. This was a major incentive to work with the communities. Additionally, when communities move by their own choice, there is no crisis of law and order or delays emerging from those situations.

Fourth, the power of the alliance in these negotiations stemmed from its strong presence in the field since the Railway Slum Dwellers Federation is a local people's organization with a membership that covers almost all the families living along the railway tracks. Coupled with a reliable database and links built up with government agencies and senior officials over the years, the credibility of the alliance was of help in solving problems on the ground. When lower-level officials of any department were not forthcoming in their cooperation, senior officials were contacted in order to instruct the field staff to get the job done.

Fifth, as is its practice with any project in which the alliance of SPARC, Mahila Milan and the National Slum Dweller's Federation is involved, Kanjur Marg became a training site for its local, national and international networks. Pavement dwellers from Mumbai, slum dwellers living along the railway tracks in other settlements in Mumbai, slum-dwellers living on the land of the Airports Authority in Mumbai, slum-dwellers from other Indian cities as well have been regularly visiting the site. In addition, government officials from different countries, from Cambodia, South Africa, Thailand and Nepal, have also come and seen the model. As a result, the Bangkok Metropolitan Administration has accepted the strategy of resettlement at Kanjur Marg to deal with slum-dwellers living under its bridges. The transfer and dissemination of these ideas also takes place rapidly in exchange visits and through the publications of SPARC. In the midst of these processes, the dialogue between the World Bank and the state began once more. The process of developing the whole project created a "team" of all those associated with it, and the World Bank team was invited to come and see how much this process had actually contributed to the creation of a truly valuable experience in a multiple stakeholder managed rehabilitation process.

As the plan has continued to progress, it has covered more and more ground. Slums continue to receive respectful negotiating ability in their relocation, and both sides have made efforts to create the smoothest possible process for all. As Patel describes,

The value of the model at Kanjur Marg is in how it optimizes the contributions of communities and the way in which it acts to make the communities central to the solution. In so doing, there has been considerable savings of time and money for the Railways as well as a demonstration that a state government can arbitrate between the interests of the city and its poor. The alliance hopes that the precedent of resettlement in this experiment will be accepted for future Railway operations, whether in Mumbai or elsewhere. If slum dwellers get tenure of land and proper housing, that is the pay-off for the urban poor. The acquisition of information by the community, particularly women, and its use to negotiate practical solutions on the ground by building up the capacities of people's organizations will allow the replicability of the model.

As for any other project, the critical elements are the legal and policy environments, the cooperation of the bureaucracy and a strong, vibrant community network that takes the initiative turns a situation to its advantage and offers a developmental alternative that works for the people, the government agencies and the city. In this particular game, all the players emerge as winners since people's organizations; NGOs and the state develop and forge new partnerships. The Kanjur Marg experiment exemplifies voluntary urban resettlement which secures the entitlements of the poor even as it benefits the larger society around.

Multiple Tournaments and Sustained Defection: Why Do Negotiations Fail to Secure Resource Access Between Pastoral and Agro-Pastoral Groups in Ethiopia?

In the Mieso district of Ethiopia, two main ethnic groups, the Oromo and the Somali, have long had a history of conflict and more recently have encountered land disputes. The Oromo tribe (the Ittu, Nole, and Ala clans), living an agro-pastoral livelihood, has come into conflict with the Somali tribe (the Issa and Hawiya clans), who have a livestock-based free-range lifestyle. Fakadu Beyene analyzes the reasons negotiations between these two tribes have proven unsuccessful and how game theory can make sense of the situation. Local land disputes like the one Beyene examines here are incredibly common throughout the underdeveloped world and are of utmost concern to the legal empowerment of the poor.

Beyene describes the central issue behind the land disputes as follows:

The basic problem does not seem to be the evolvement of co-users of the grazing commons into 'disputants' by virtue of pursuing different production systems. However, it is a lack of legal institutional framework through which claims for access

can be negotiated, settled and sustained. The existing tenure policy of Ethiopia supports private use of land for cultivation, grazing and other activities as stipulated in the national land use and administration proclamation; surprisingly, nowhere does this proclamation entertain communal rural land use rights though it mentions the al and pastoral" (FDRE, 2005). There is also a tendency for the national pastoral policy to support sedentarization and agro-pastoralism (UNCTE, 2004). At local level, allocation of land for cultivation favored by such policy environment contributes to the shrinkage of the grazing area in which the pastoral Issa becomes the loser.[226]
- CONTACT THE SOURCE

In addition to pointing out the absence of a reasonable legal framework for dealing with the conflict, Beyene also notes some other factors that are common among local tribal communities:

The second factor influencing negotiation is the ability of affiliated clans to cooperate. Historically, when conflict was started, Issa divided the three Oromo clans (Ittu, Nole and Ala) in resisting Ittu's access to communal grazing land. The first step taken was to form alliance with Ala and Nole clans to use the communal grazing land in harmony. These two clans were long involved in crop growing unlike the Ittu. The second step was to resist Ala while sharing the resource with Nole alone.

---

[226] Fekadu Beyene, "Multiple Tournaments and Sustained Defection: Why Do Negotiations Fail to Secure Resource Access between Pastoral and Agropastoral Groups in Ethiopia?" *Journal of Socio-Economics* 42 (February 2013): 79–87.

Unexpectedly, this step resulted in alliance among the three clans (belonging to one ethnic group) to resist Issa. In this case, emphasis is being given to Ittu–Issa conflict because Ittu share long geographical boundary with Issa, making the scale of exposure to conflict higher. The other two clans cooperate occasionally.

The third reason for negotiations to fail is the absence of institutional framework within which such negotiated agreements are enforced. The incompleteness of negotiations and apparently incompetent state authority at district level has undermined the potential of local customary efforts from producing positive outcomes in reducing the incidence of conflict. Though the national constitutional rules empower regions to recognize customary institutions to resolve disputes over resources and give them legal guarantee, the regional governments are incapable of translating this into action successfully. As a consequence, negotiations generally lead to promises to refrain from further raids and killings but the outcome has increasingly been observed to be short-lived. For example, an outbreak of livestock raid-related violence is observed sometime after mediation and negotiations. Such violation of commitment on the part of the stronger group is one of the reasons for recurrence of the conflict. For the Issa, the opportunity costs of not raiding are high albeit this creates access insecurity for the other. Under this circumstance, the choice for Ittu is either to shift to confrontation or going for another round of negotiation.

The fourth reason for negotiated outcomes not to sustain is the economic incentives associated with raids. Livestock raid involves an illicit means of taking away one's animal. It

produces a threat to the agro-pastoralists in using communal grazing land. There is a direct link between fear of raids and avoidance (or limited use) of common pasture. The effect of livestock raid is not limited to the creation of livelihood insecurity but also has an ex ante effect leading to range degradation by restraining movements. The gradual increase in the scale and severity of conflict is partly associated with the ever-worsening livestock raiding.[227]
- CONTACT THE SOURCE

As the author points out, these general problems of the limited capacity of the legal system, incentives for players to become aggressive, and poor communication between local groups can lead to dysfunction.

Beyene goes on to apply game theory to the Ethiopian conflict. However, his discussion is somewhat beyond the scope of this work. He does conclude, though, with these final thoughts about the failure of the two tribes to negotiate land usage peacefully:

In theory, distributional conflict can lead to emergence of new institutions that overcome the conflict. This is often seen as a result of bargaining over the distributional outcomes (such as appropriation level and condition). In this case however, group attributes have paramount importance in influencing the success of bargaining over distribution of benefits stream. For this reason, there are no incidences where negotiation and bargaining have led to the creation of stable institutions.

[227] *Ibid.*

Instead, agreements remained unenforceable and the distributional conflict results in inefficient use of the grazing commons. Moreover, the argument of Knight where the weak player is risk averse and refrains from challenging the strong player does not always seem to work. Instead, the weak party's exploitation of ethnic based social capital in mobilizing action resources receives the highest priority. As agro-pastoralists have experienced, this collusion practice of combining forces could instantly yield a positive outcome in terms of ensuring access security and has been a preferred strategy.

In other words, in the case of multiple actors vying for resources, power relations and so-called military or political strength are not the only concern of stakeholder analysis. The characteristics of the actors themselves (such as ethnicity, historical relations, geography, and sociopolitical context) must be worked into the equation and considered as important variables, as these can have strong effects on outcomes. Beyene further confirms this:

The lessons drawn from this study contribute to the growing debate in the resource-related conflict literature by providing new insights on how the dynamics in continuing conflict and interrelatedness of several factors increase complexity in negotiations in search for sustainable institutional solution.

The descriptions of the case have shown that group attributes distinguished along production system and affiliation (ethnicity) has partly contributed to the lack of means for rule enforcement (customary agreements to deter violence). This can be generally ascribed to the lack of effective governance structure in which negotiated agreements can be implemented, regularly monitored and sanctioned.[228]

Win-Win? Early Experience from Local Area Agreements

Although this book has focused primarily on the developing world, this case study demonstrates how the same power relations come into play in any country in the world, rich or poor. Recently in England, there was an initiative to localize funding for certain programs usually undertaken by the central government, such as youth programs, elderly programs, and economic programs. Gillanders and Ahmad studied the early arrangements and interactions of these Local Area Agreements (LAAs). We have included their case study in this chapter because it demonstrates how stakeholders with different power roles (in this case, national and regional stakeholders) can come together to distribute power as best fits the people at large. The process was by no means easy and quick; instead, it was long, repetitive, and slightly disorderly and remains a work in progress. However, the authors praise the initiative for its groundbreaking effort to reorganize some of the English government, and they optimistically await what the future will bring for this program.

The authors specifically are interested not in the effects of the LAAs but rather the negotiation process: "The focus is on governance relationships between the many participants in the LAA process. The article does not explicitly address service improvements and efficiency savings, as local respondents told

---

[228] *Ibid.*

us it was too soon for there to be much evidence of these."[229] The researchers gathered their evidence from interviews with numerous participants and observations of many meetings and negotiations. The authors define the goal of the LAAs as follows:

> LAAs are intended to deliver better outcomes through improved coordination between central government, local authorities and their partners. They are agreements negotiated between individual top-tier local authorities and their partners, and GOs [government offices] acting on behalf of central government. The agreements specify a range of outcomes shared by all partners, along with associated funding; there is also the opportunity to negotiate specific enabling measures (formerly known as 'freedoms and flexibilities'). LAAs provide a mechanism for devolving day to day control of programs from the center to localities, simplifying the number of additional funding streams from central government, removing barriers to the achievement of outcomes arising from central government regulations, allowing greater flexibility for local solutions to match local circumstances and helping to promote efficient use of resources.[230]

The LAAs were very broad in scope and called for definition through the process itself. The authors found that while this may have slowed things down, it also led to better policy making. They describe the evolution of the initiative: "By round three [of

---

[229] G. Gillanders and S. Ahmad, "Win-Win? Early Experience from Local Area Agreements," *Local Government Studies* 33, no. 5: 743–760.

[230] *Ibid.*

negotiations], aims had broadened; the main aim was 'to deliver genuinely sustainable communities through better outcomes for local people.' Secondary objectives were improving central–local government relations, enhancing efficiency, strengthening partnership working, and offering a framework within which local authorities can enhance their community leadership role. As the policy developed, the link with Sustainable Community Strategies became more explicit and the intended role of Local Strategic Partnerships more prominent."[231]

In order to attain these goals, the authors point to certain qualities that the LAAs must meet: "Partnerships are thought to add value in a number of important respects, including through resource gain, enhanced strategic capacity achieved through deliberation, enhanced capacity to deliver services through better co-ordination and 'bending' of mainstream resources. However, building partnerships is difficult and time consuming, and the process of collaboration can generate more costs than benefits. The survival of alliances depends on their ability to create net added value, and the way LAAs impact on the cost–benefit calculations that influence local stakeholders' willingness to collaborate will be important for the success or failure of the policy."[232]

Gillanders'and Ahmad's point here also applies to the legal-empowerment framework. The goal is to create partnerships based on net added value or, as we have called it here many times, a win-win scenario through cost-benefit or stakeholder analysis.

---

[231] G. Gillanders and S. Ahmad, "Win-Win? Early Experience from Local Area Agreements," *Local Government Studies* 33, no. 5: 743–760.

[232] *Ibid.*

The authors go on to describe some of the problems the stakeholders faced from the outset:

> While there was considerable enthusiasm for the general principles behind LAAs, it was clear that stakeholders' aims for the agreements varied widely, and in the early stages in particular there was lack of clarity about their purpose and intended scope.
>
> More ambitious localities sought to use their LAA to shift the power relationship between localities and the center and achieve a significant reduction in the burden of performance management, as well as drive forward radical service redesign. Others saw LAAs primarily as a useful additional mechanism for strengthening partnership working and maintaining the drive for improvement in particular service areas. High initial expectations about freedoms and flexibilities became progressively tempered with pragmatism as hoped-for benefits were slow to materialize.
>
> This diversity of aims and expectations was mirrored in central government. For some departments, especially those with few existing connections with localities, LAAs were regarded as an important new way of engaging with local authorities and partners, situating departmental policies geographically and providing some leverage and accountability in relation to cross-cutting outcomes—such as childhood obesity—whose delivery required partnership working. For some other departments that already had strong relationships with local delivery organizations or that gave cross-cutting outcomes a lower priority, the process was seen

as tangential to their core areas of work or even a threat to delivery of their policy ...

Localities tended to see LAAs mainly as a dialogue, central departments viewed them increasingly as contracts, and GOs were caught in the middle trying to satisfy both sides. There was an obvious tension between the view of LAAs in parts of Whitehall, as described by one senior civil servant: '[LAAs]) are really about getting central government PSA priorities delivered' and the aspirations of localities, as expressed by a local authority LAA lead: 'The long term outcome is genuinely more control locally over priorities and allocations rather than being driven by government, leading to a more coherent strategy locally instead of constantly bending to the latest whim in Whitehall.'[233]

- CONTACT SOURCE

Another lesson to from this study is the importance of articulating clear goals with clear responsibilities. As described above, responsibilities and directives can easily become confused as various stakeholders look out for their best interests. Another example of such confusion over responsibility is the role of the GOs in the LAA process: "One of the critical challenges for GOs was a lack of shared understanding about the extent of their devolved authority. Government Offices expressed frustration: 'We are either in charge of this, or we are not', while officials in Whitehall sometimes felt they were not kept sufficiently informed: 'The problem was that no-one knew how much information should

---

[233] G. Gillanders and S. Ahmad, "Win-Win? Early Experience from Local Area Agreements," *Local Government Studies* 33, no. 5: 743–760.

have been going back and forth ... some GOs were trying to decide things for themselves, keeping it away from Whitehall '[...] this made us nervous.'"[234]

In the context of legal empowerment, the GOs play a part similar to that of intermediaries, such as practitioners or other possible allies of the poor, whose roles should be defined clearly. One of the main challenges to all comprehensive policy changes is the uncertainty actors must accept and deal with. The study quotes one official as saying, "We have no evidence of what LAAs can achieve, but nonetheless are being expected to change what we do in anticipation of future benefits." The authors, on a more positive note, state that amid the uncertainty, innovations and new ways of doing things arose out of the initiative: "LAAs offered an opportunity for departments to free themselves up from day to day performance management of localities and to engage in dialogue about what works, resulting in learning and innovation that improves policy. However, LAAs demanded a radically new way of working, cutting across existing systems and processes and necessitating a culture change that many in central government found hard. Support for the policy from across Whitehall strengthened over time."[235]

The opportunity for spontaneous innovation and change is perhaps one of the greatest attractions of legal empowerment. As described above, once the dialogue of change begins, the possible solutions that dedicated policy makers and other stakeholders can come up with are endless. Of course, realistically, this opening

---

[234] Ibid.

[235] G. Gillanders and S. Ahmad, "Win-Win? Early Experience from Local Area Agreements," *Local Government Studies* 33, no. 5: 743–760.

of Pandora's box could go either way, but the hope is that if the policy goals are straightforward and clear, the policy outcomes are more likely to create the win-win scenarios most desired.

The researches go on to discuss further some of the effects on local-central government relations:

Many found the process of negotiating the stretch element in particular 'tortuous', and were disappointed about the lack of progress with enabling measures. The hoped for reduction in the overall reporting load was also slow to materialize—a finding confirmed by later research, which the new LAAs aim to address. There were also tensions inherent in the LAA policy between devolving responsibility to GOs, and the desire of policy holders in Whitehall to be kept informed and involved. It was unclear whether the more prominent role given to GOs helped to increase understanding between central government and localities and join up central government policies locally, or whether, despite good intentions, GOs added grit rather than oil to the wheels. As one local authority participant commented to their GO, "your people are very nice, but they are stuck in the middle". This was a structural issue rather than one of GO capability [...]

LAAs brought new partners to the table, and unblocked issues that had been blocked for years. One local authority LAA lead commented "We are having discussions that a year ago would have been unthinkable. People moved from denial to 'how can we make this work?'" The benefits were perhaps greatest where partnership working had previously been weak—for one county council "the main benefit of the LAA is that it has brought the district councils kicking and screaming to the table". In addition, LAAs began to produce a more mature dialogue about performance between partners and place a much stronger focus on evidence-based management of performance[236].

Throughout the study, the authors make obvious the slow speed of the process, but they also make apparent many of the unanticipated positive effects that proved beneficial to the local and central governments. Legal empowerment may share these characteristics when implemented in various localities across the world. The researchers conclude their study as follows:

Although our research revealed lack of clarity about the aims and scope of LAAs in the early years, this flexibility to allow for different aspirations, interpretations and circumstances was in many ways a positive feature of the policy. Starting from a position of uncertainty about what would work, it enabled the scheme to be shaped by those engaged in it, and allowed many players to "come to the table" for different reasons. In this context the initiative fits well with the view of LGMA policies as "ambiguous by design".

The LAA policy is an ambitious "whole systems" change process and the early stages of the initiative could be viewed as a valuable transition period, with first generation LAAs paving the way for the more radical proposals in the new LAAs. This period of "trial and error" allowed incremental

---

[236] S.Gallanders and S. Ahmad. "Win-Win? Early Experiences from Local Area Agreements. Local Government Studies.33.No. 5. 743-760.

progress on some issues that were difficult and contentious for government departments, as confidence in the process and the capacity of those involved grew with experience. It also presented opportunities for local partners to seize the agenda and carve out larger spaces in which to act.

That said, it is clear that many of those involved under-estimated the challenge of recasting central–local relationships and found it hard to reconcile the different governance relationships that departments have with different elements of the local system …

Both the difficulties of local partnership working and the rewards from improving it were also initially underestimated. The negotiating timetable for the early LAAs made it hard for the process to be truly participative; the process highlighted weaknesses in local governance, and fundamental questions remain over accountability for cross-cutting outcomes. However, LAAs are beginning to transform local partnership working, as much through their symbolic value as by a tangible shift in the returns to joint working; how robust this change in attitudes and behavior will continue to be in the face of within-sector pressures remains to be seen, and will partly depend on the extent to which local partners start to see real benefits from LAAs in terms of both process and outcomes.

It is clear that many stakeholders (local, regional and central) articulated unrealistic expectations about the immediacy of the impact of LAAs, and in 2006 the balance of costs and benefits was unclear. However, there were significant signs of progress on the ground, and it is important

to recognize how far the policy has travelled in a short time and the fundamental shift in attitudes underlying this.[237]
- CONTACT SOURCE

In their conclusion, the authors point to the positives and negatives of the LAAs. This case study demonstrates quite well the virtue of patience when dealing with political change and negotiations between various stakeholders. Even in a developed, democratic state, power relations and stakeholders affect the speed and quality of political change. The lesson of the LAAs is that attempts to implement complete change will face roadblocks and may require a long period of work before they gain any ground. However, once such efforts do begin to make progress, the opportunities for realistic and positive change become realizable.

Conclusion

In order for the poor to realize their legal rights, especially their ESCR, they will have to face the harsh reality of the entrenched interests of those with power, whether it is political, economic, social, or cultural. Not many of these actors are willing to give up such power and control over the deprived and marginalized. As in most human interactions, they will have to see what is in it for them. Persuasive arguments will be necessary, and in this chapter, we have provided the basis for these arguments. The importance of these deliberations cannot be overestimated, and getting them right will be crucial to legal empowerment and the realization of

---

[237] G. Gillanders and S. Ahmad, "Win-Win? Early Experience from Local Area Agreements," *Local Government Studies* 33, no. 5: 743–760.

ESCR. As Dowding puts it, "Only with political argument can people hope to form societies where they can come to agreement for the principles and rules where they can be justly ruled. Without political argument there can only be power struggles. We need to also consider whether political argument itself is merely a power struggle under another guise. Deliberation provides the conditions for legitimacy of outcomes within a society because it provides the conditions for plurality equality and consensus. Deliberation both ensures that institutions are structured as people wish and enables continued deliberation over all social decisions."[238]

In chapter 4, we described voice as one of the preconditions for legal empowerment. In chapter 8, we will again take up this issue as "articulation" as we present a strategy for integrating legal empowerment into development practice through the sustainable-livelihoods approach. To conclude this chapter, Dowding summarizes some principles to guide deliberation in the context of power relations as follows:

> Each deliberator should recognize and respect the other deliberator's capacity to give reasons and put forward their values. The endpoint of deliberation gives sufficient reason for deliberators to follow decisions since proposals are accepted or are rejected on the basis of the sets of reasons that are put forward. In the deliberative process everyone is recognized as equal since all can participate and give their reasons for the measures they support, there is no hierarchy

---

[238] K. Dowding, "Power and Persuasion: Is Debate Zero Sum?" paper presented to the American Political Science Association Conference, Seattle, 2011.

and each can take part fully. The aim of deliberation is to find consensus based upon reasons. If consensus on the precise measures cannot be reached, then at least consensus on the process by which to decide which rival proposal should be followed. Deliberation in deliberative democracy is about both institution and process as well as about the substantive ways of reaching agreement through institutions and process. One of [the] claimed strengths of deliberative democracy made by some advocates is that it will enable truths to emerge. Well-attested scientific findings will be given due weight as deliberators will have time to understand their importance, the weighing and judging of reasons will enable contradictions and incoherencies in positions to emerge, and the special pleading and forwarding of base self-interest will be more obvious and thus have lower sway. Because deliberation requires the giving of reasons (political argument) conspiracies and special pleading become harder, and where it emerges can be judged on its true worth. Critics of deliberative processes suggest that deliberators will not be as equal as proponents proclaim. Critics argue that we cannot make a clear distinction between reasoned deliberation of deliberative assemblies and the self-interested or coercive bargaining, the pork-barrel and log-rolling processes associated with legislative processes.

Secondly, even if reasons and evidence do prevail, does this not give advantages to those best equipped to explicate their views through reasoned debate. Does deliberation not advantage the educated, the scientists the leisured classes at the expense of others? In Barry's terms some are better at political argument than others because they are better able to provide reasoned justifications for their evaluations. Others might simply be tongue-tied for cultural or personal reasons. In other words, on this account deliberation is just a discursive power game where the advantaged will prevail over others. Is all persuasion; is all movement towards consensus just another power game on a par with manipulation and coercion?

Deliberative assemblies could be [an] arena for rhetorical manipulation, for the giving of false information, for hiding information, for running logical and rhetorical rings around the less educated or naive by those trained in rhetoric and logic. The deliberative assembly could become the playground of the lawyers, the scientists and the philosophers. This sociological possibility does not mean that deliberation as ideally envisaged is impossible however.

But what are the conditions that ensure that not all persuasion is an act of social power? I first want to consider persuasion—the act of changing someone's belief over some issue. We can agree that changing a person's mind changes their incentive structure, and since A set out to change B's mind A has done so deliberately. Why then is that not always a use of social power? If A set out to "change B's mind" then it is an exercise of social power; however, if A set out to "discover the truth", or if that [is] too grand, A set out to see whether A and B can agree then A has not exercised social power. The outcome aim is different in the two cases. If these rules for fair deliberation are stringently established then any agreement that results between A and B would be a kind of emergent truth.[239]

-

---

[239] K. Dowding, "Power and Persuasion: Is Debate Zero Sum?" paper presented to the American Political Science Association Conference, Seattle, 2011.

Women constitute one of the major social groups that have faced hugely disproportionate discrimination in terms of ESCR and power. In the next chapter, we will address the legal empowerment and ESCR of poor women and girls.

7

THE LEGAL EMPOWERMENT OF POOR WOMEN AND GIRLS

The legal-empowerment agenda and the discussion of the realization of legal rights are addressed to the 4 billion people on the planet who cannot use the law to improve their livelihoods because of deficits in their agency or in the opportunity structures they encounter. In this chapter, we give special attention to half of this disadvantaged group, women and girls, because they have been historically disenfranchised relative to their male counterparts and continue to face greater obstacles and, most importantly, because of the skewed power differentials they still face. They lack power in decision making both in the home and in the parliament. They lack control over the assets on which their livelihoods depend and very often over the use of their own bodies. This chapter is not, however, so much about the fight for gender equality as it is about exploring how the law might be instrumental in helping women to achieve their full potential as they choose to define it. This, of course, requires an examination of how the law continues to fail them as well as a broader discussion of their human-rights deprivations. Here we will focus, as in the rest of the book, on ESCR.

The chapter begins with a quote about the emancipation of women. It then reviews the historical struggle for women's rights; the significant successes achieved in the socioeconomic conditions of women and girls, many of which are based of the realization of ESCR; and the challenges that still lie ahead.

The chapter then discusses the international women's rights framework and outlines specific strategies for accelerating the realization of ESCR.

This quote from Emma Goldman sets the tone:

Emancipation should make it possible for woman to be human in the truest sense. Everything within her that craves assertion and activity should reach its fullest expression; all artificial barriers should be broken, and the road towards greater freedom cleared of every trace of centuries of submission and slavery.

[…] those that do reach that enticing equality generally do so at the expense of their physical and psychical well-being. As to the great mass of working girls and women, how much independence is gained if the narrowness and lack of freedom of the home is exchanged for the narrowness and lack of freedom of the factory, sweat-shop, department store, or office? In addition is the burden which is laid on many women of looking after a "home, sweet home"—cold, dreary, disorderly, uninviting—after a day's hard work. Glorious independence!

The movement for women's emancipation has so far made but the first step in that direction. It is to be hoped that it will gather strength to make another. The right to vote, or equal civil rights, may be good demands, but true emancipation begins neither at the polls nor in courts. It begins in women's souls. History tells us that every oppressed class gained true liberation from its masters through its own efforts. It is necessary that women learn that lesson–that they realize that their freedom will reach as far as their power to achieve their freedom reaches.

Pettiness separates; breadth unites. Let us be broad and big. Let us not overlook vital things because of the bulk of trifles confronting us. A true conception of the relation of the sexes will not admit of conqueror and conquered; it knows of but one great thing: to give of one's self boundlessly, in order to find one's self richer, deeper, better. That alone can fill the emptiness, and transform the tragedy of woman's emancipation into joy, limitless joy.[240]

While addressing the requirements of women's self-empowerment, Goldman importantly points to the underlying emancipation needed by both men and women, especially those who are marginalized, but many in the mainstream as well. If legal empowerment of the poor is going to happen—if we, together as a society, are going solve the poverty problem and rise to the full potential of the human being in a flourishing society—then we do well to take these observations seriously.

Much Has Changed, but Much Remains to Be Done for Women's and Girls' ESCR

The 2012 *WDR* provides an up-to-date discussion of what improvements have occurred in gender equality and what remains to be done.[241] While it covers issues broader than the

---

[240] Emma Goldman, "The Tragedy of Women's Emancipation," in *Anarchism and other Essays*, theanarchistlibrary.org/library/emma-goldman.

[241] World Bank, 2012. World Development Report. (WDR)

legal empowerment of poor women and girls, its general findings provide a solid background for the arguments that follow in this chapter. The next few sections, which deal with how things have improved and provide a historical overview of how these changes evolved in both the developed and developing worlds as well as noting what still remains to be done, draw heavily from this report.

Despite the hardships many women endure in their daily lives, things have changed for the better—and at a speed that few expected even two decades ago. In four major areas—women's rights, education, health, and labor-force outcomes—the gains in the second half of the twentieth century were large and fast in many parts of the world. Improvements that took a hundred years in wealthier countries took just forty years in some low- and middle-income countries. Change has also accelerated, with gender equality gains in every decade building on gains from the decade before.

Achieving equality in legal rights in today's high-income countries took considerable time. In contrast, gains under the law have occurred much faster in developing countries, aided by a rising global consensus on formal rights and guarantees of equality for women. In tandem with these gains in formal rights, low- and middle-income countries have seen unprecedented gains in outcomes for women both in absolute terms and relative to men. More women are literate and educated than ever before, and the education gap with men has shrunk dramatically. The gender gap in primary-education enrollments has practically disappeared, and the gains in secondary and higher education have been enormous. Women are living longer and healthier lives in much of the world, in part because lower fertility has reduced their risk in childbirth. And they are participating more than ever in market work. Economic growth has driven much of this progress through higher household incomes, better service delivery, and new labor opportunities for women. But it has not been the only factor: the association between economic growth and better outcomes for women has been neither automatic nor uniform across countries.

Changes in one domain of gender equality have fostered changes in others, influencing the next generation and reinforcing the whole process. For example, the expansion of economic opportunities for women in service industries in Bangladesh and India has boosted school enrollments for girls, which feeds into higher labor-force participation and better educational outcomes for the next generation. This is not to say that all problems have been solved or that progress has been easy.

Women's Rights: A Historical Perspective

Women's circumstances in the eighteenth century were very different from today. In 1789, the French revolution asserted that men are "born and remain free and equal in rights" universally, but the *Declaration of the Rights of Man and of the Citizen* did not include women, and a year later, the National Assembly chose not to extend civil and political rights to women. The legal system in the British colonies, based on English common law, is another case. As Sir William Blackstone stated in his *Commentaries on the Laws of England* in 1765, "By marriage, the husband and wife are one person in law: that is, the very being or legal existence of the woman is suspended during the marriage, or at least is incorporated and consolidated into that of the husband; under whose wing, protection, and cover, she performs every-thing; and is therefore called in our law-french a femme-couvert. For this reason, a man cannot grant anything to his wife, or enter into covenant with her: for the grant would be to suppose her separate existence."[242]

The march toward equal property and suffrage rights has been slow and long. Only in 1857 did the British Parliament pass the Matrimonial Causes Act allowing married women to inherit property and take court action on their own behalf. And not until 1882 did the Married Women's Property Act recognize a husband and a wife as two separate legal entities, conferring to wives the right to buy, own, and sell property separately. Suffrage was not universal until 1928 when, as a result of the Representation of the People Act, women over age 21 received the vote on equal terms with men. The story is similar in Scandinavia: Norway, for example, provided full economic rights to women in 1888 and suffrage rights in 1913.

In the United States, New York was the first state to pass, in 1848, a Married Women's Property Act. Wives' rights to earnings and property gradually spread to other states over the following half century. Political voice was longer in coming. A proposed constitutional amendment guaranteeing women's right to vote was introduced in the US Senate in 1878, but it did not receive a full vote until 1887, only to be voted down. Three more decades elapsed before the ratification of the Nineteenth Amendment to the Constitution guaranteed universal suffrage in 1920.

The struggle against discrimination in other domains, such as labor and family law, picked up momentum in the second half of

---

[242]   World Bank. 2012, WDR.

the twentieth century. In the United States, until the passage of Title VII of the Civil Rights Act of 1964, it was legal to pass over women for promotions in the workplace. Married women needed the consent of their husbands to obtain loans, and marital rape was not recognized as a criminal act.[243] Until the 1980s, female flight attendants were required to be single when they were hired and could be fired if they married. In Germany in the early 1950s, women could be dismissed from the civil service when they married. And through 1977, they officially needed their husbands' permission to work. Until reunification with East Germany in 1990, children of single mothers were assigned legal guardians.[244]

Japan's Equal Employment Opportunity Act of 1985 obliged employers merely to endeavor to treat men and women equally during job recruitment, assignment, and promotion. The mandate for equal treatment came about in 1997. The first domestic violence law was passed in 2001.

Progress Has Been Faster in Low- and Middle-Income Countries[245]

Progress has been most notable for political rights tied to a change in the concept of citizenship. National franchise movements gave shape to a more inclusive paradigm of the nation-state in the first

---

[243] Claudia Zaher, "When a Woman's Marital Status Determined Her Legal Status: A Research Guide on the Common Law Doctrine of Coverture," *Law Library Journal* 94, no. 3 (2002) 459–487.

[244] Katrin Bennhold, "20 Years after the Fall of Wall, Women of Former East Germany Thrive," *International Herald Tribune*, October 6, 2010.

[245] World Bank, WDR, 2012.

half of the twentieth century. Before then, citizenship had long been construed as male. Extending suffrage in already established nation-states involved local social movements and social networks redefining citizenship only after a lengthy renegotiation of domestic political power. In contrast, new nations emerged into a new world order. National and international organizations embraced a gender-neutral model of citizenship with women fully accepted as persons capable of autonomous decisions.[246] Only three countries that became independent in the1900s (Austria, Ireland, and Libya) extended suffrage to men before women.

But Switzerland did not break with tradition and extend the franchise to women until 1971. Among the latest countries to give women the right to vote, Bhutan changed the practice of casting one vote per household and adopted women's full suffrage in 2008. Today, only Saudi Arabia restricts the franchise to men, and removing this restriction for municipal elections is under consideration. Similar progress has been made in women's rights beyond full suffrage. In the Philippines, sweeping legislative changes in the 1980s and 1990s recognized gender equality across a wide array of domains. The 1987 constitution reinforced earlier constitutions by giving added emphasis to the notion of gender equality. The Comprehensive Agrarian Reform Law of 1988 assured equal rights to ownership of land. And a 1989 act amended the labor code to protect women from discrimination in hiring and pay.

---

[246] F. Ramirez, S. Yasemin, and S. Shanahan, The Changing Logic of Political Citizenship: Trans-national Acquisition of Women's Suffrage Rights, 1890–1990," *American Sociological Review* 62, no. 5: 745–755.

Similarly, in 2004, Morocco overhauled its family code to promote greater equality between women and men in multiple spheres. The ratification of CEDAW and other international treaties established a comprehensive framework to promote equality for women. These treaties spurred further progress toward securing formal rights in other domains of women's lives, in large part by facilitating new legislation or promoting the repeal of discriminatory legal provisions. In 2005, the Kenyan Court of Appeal held that there was no reasonable basis for drawing a distinction between sons and daughters in determining inheritance. In 2001, the Tanzanian High Court held that a widow is entitled to administer the estate on behalf of her children. In both cases, principles of equality and nondiscrimination prevailed.

Success in Many Areas

The march for women's rights has gone hand in hand with better outcomes for many women both in absolute terms and relative to men. During the past quarter century, sustained growth in many countries has reduced some gender-based disparities. And the pace of change in these outcomes has been much faster in today's low- and middle-income countries than it was in high-income countries. Indicators as varied as fertility, female education and literacy, and female labor-force participation all show that this is the case.

In most countries where broad-based income growth has combined with better institutions for service delivery and more economic opportunities for women, the improvements in these indicators have been dramatic—and in some cases, they have taken place at rates never before witnessed. Moreover, they have occurred in some categories even in the face of social turmoil or significant institutional challenges.

One of the most dramatic cases cited in the 2012 *WDR* is that of Iran. Human development outcomes among Iranian women have consistently improved along some key dimensions in the aftermath of the Islamic revolution:

- From 1979 to 2009, the Islamic Republic of Iran saw the world's fastest decline in fertility—from an average of 6.9 children to 1.8 (below replacement).
- The female-to-male ratio in primary school is the world's highest, with 1.2 girls enrolled for every boy. The number of women in secondary school as a percentage of the eligible age group has more than doubled from 30 percent to 81 percent; and in 2009, more than half of all Iranian university students, 68 percent of the students in science, and 28 percent in engineering were women.
- Women make up 30 percent of the Iranian labor force today, with the percentage of economically active women having increased from 20 percent in 1986 to 31 percent in 2008.[247]

More girls in school. More women are literate than ever before. In the United States, it took forty years, from 1870 to 1910, for the share of six-to-twelve-year-old girls in school to increase from 57 percent to 88 percent. Morocco did the same in eleven years, from 1997 to 2008.

Tertiary enrollment growth is stronger for women than for men across the world. The number of male tertiary students

---

[247]   World Bank, WDR, 2012.

globally more than quadrupled, from 17.7 million to 77.8 million, between 1970 and 2008; but the number of female tertiary students rose more than sevenfold, from 10.8 million to 80.9 million, overtaking men.[248]

Healthier lives. The second half of the twentieth century also saw large improvements in men's and women's health. Life expectancy at birth most clearly reflects improvements in health in populations across the world. The average number of years women could expect to live rose from fifty-four in 1960 to seventy-one in 2008. This period also saw the world's fastest ever decline in fertility—from an average of about 5 births per woman in 1960 to 2.5 in 2008, lowering the number of deaths associated with maternal mortality.[249]

More women participate in the labor market. Female labor-force participation has grown since 1960, dramatically in some regions. Expanding economic opportunities have drawn large numbers of new female workers into the market. Between 1980 and 2008, the global rate of female labor-force participation increased from 50.2 to 51.8 percent while the male rate fell slightly from 82.0 to 77.7 percent. Consequently, the gender gap narrowed from 32 percentage points in 1980 to 26 percentage points in 2008.[250] Around the world in very poor countries, female labor-force participation is high, reflecting a large, labor-intensive agricultural sector and significant numbers of poor households.[251]

---

[248]   *Ibid.*

[249]   *Ibid.*

[250]   ILO, Key Indicators of the Labor Market, 2010.

[251]   C. Mammen and C. Paxson, "Women's Work and Economic Development," *Journal of Economic Perspectives* 14, no. 4 (2000): 141–146.

In this situation, women are willing to enter the labor force even for low wages, because unearned incomes are also low. As per capita incomes rise, unearned incomes rise (through higher male wages and earnings), and these higher incomes are typically associated with women withdrawing from the labor market. Social barriers against women entering the paid labor force also regain prominence, and their participation rates fall.

New labor-market opportunities can spur investments in education and health for girls. How much parents invest in their children's education partly depends on the returns on that investment. Early studies showed that new agricultural technologies that favored women's production increased girls' enrollment.[252] A new generation of studies extends these insights in a globalizing economy. For instance, the rise of outsourcing in India offers new opportunities for women in the wage sector and increases parental investments in girls' education.[253]

Evidence of greater returns was enough to stimulate greater human capital accumulation. It has often been posited that cultural and social norms (or informal institutions) hold back human capital investments. Consequently, many policy efforts try to change the status quo by trying to alter norms. The results of the 2012 *WDR* present an alternative route—expand economic opportunities, and human capital investments in girls will increase. Markets

---

[252]   A. Foster and M. Rosensweig, "Missing Women: The Marriage Market and Economic Growth," Working Paper Series 49, Stanford Center for International Development.

[253]   E. Oster and M. Millet, "Do Call Centers Promote School Enrollment? Evidence from India," Working Paper Series 15922, National Bureau of Economic Research.

can affect private household decisions even with slow-moving social norms. Recent findings suggest that women's rights and agency play a role in encouraging those public investments. In a world where women care about different things from men (and women do appear to care for children more than men do), it may be that when women have more voice, they can drive institutional investments in a way that favors children. So when women have more rights in the political arena, does the nature of public investment change? Yes.

Much Remains to Be Done

Things have changed for the better, but not for all women and not in all domains of gender equality. Progress has been slow and limited for women in very poor countries; for those who are poor even amid greater wealth; and for those who face other forms of exclusion because of their caste, disability, location, ethnicity, or sexual orientation. Both within particular countries and internationally, the progress in some domains is tempered by the sobering realities that many women face in others.[254]

Across and within countries, gender gaps widen at lower incomes, and in the poorest economies, gender gaps are larger. The benefits of economic growth have not accrued equally to all men and all women for some parts of society. Household poverty can mute the impact of national development, and other means of social exclusion, such as geography and ethnicity, often compound the differences.

---

[254] World Bank, *WDR*, 2012.

Improvements in some domains of gender equality—such as those related to occupational differences or participation in policy making—are bound by constraints that do not shift with economic growth and development. Gender disparities endure even in high-income economies despite the large gains in women's civil and economic rights in the past century. These outcomes are the result of slow-moving institutional dynamics and deep structural factors that growth alone cannot address.

While much of the world has reduced gender gaps in health and education, conditions for women in some low-income countries have not improved much. In many South Asian and Sub-Saharan countries, girls' enrollments in primary and secondary education have progressed little. In Eritrea, the female primary net enrollment rate rose from a very low base of 16 percent in 1990 to just 36 percent in 2008. In Afghanistan, Chad, and the Central African Republic, there are fewer than seventy girls for every one hundred boys in primary school. The Republic of Yemen has one of the world's largest gender disparities in net enrollment rates, and progress has been difficult to sustain.[255]

In addition to household wealth, ethnicity and geography are important for understanding and addressing gender inequality. Even in countries that have grown rapidly, poor and ethnic minority women tend to benefit far less than their richer and ethnic majority counterparts do. Wide gender disparities endure. Many ethnic minorities are poorer and less urbanized than the

---

[255]   T. Yuki, M. Keiko, O. Keiichi, and M. Sakai, "Promoting Gender Parity: Lessons from Yemen," JICA background paper for WDR 2012.

general population. An estimated two-thirds of girls out of school globally belong to ethnic minorities in their countries.[256]

Other factors of exclusion, such as caste, disability, or sexual orientation, also tend to compound disadvantages in ways that affect development outcomes. And gender gaps have not narrowed in control over resources, political voice, or the incidence of domestic violence. In some cases, individual preferences, market failures, institutional constraints, and social norms continue to reinforce gender gaps despite economic progress. Income growth may also have unexpected adverse effects on gender equality through new gendered preferences. In other cases, development outcomes have not always reflected extensive formal gains in securing equal rights. Despite notable improvement in expanding legal guarantees to women and men alike, slow implementation has impeded a move to gender parity. Social norms continue to bind to varying degrees in all nations, and a chasm remains between theory and practice.

Less Voice and Less Power

Some dimensions of gender equality where progress has been slowest fall in the domain of women's agency. Consider three aspects. First, women's ability to make decisions about earned income or family spending reflects their control over their own lives and their immediate environments. Second, trends in domestic violence capture intrahousehold gender dynamics and

---

[256] M. Lewis and M. Lockheed, Inexcusable Absence: Why 60 Million Girls Aren't in School and What to Do about It, Center for Global Development, Washington DC.

asymmetric power relations between men and women. Third, patterns in political voice can measure inclusiveness in decision making, exercise of leadership, and access to power.

Less Control over Resources

Many women have no say over household finances, even their own earnings. The Demographic and Health Surveys show that women in some developing countries, particularly in Sub-Saharan Africa and Asia, are not involved in household decisions about spending their personal earned income. As many as 34 percent of married women in Malawi and 28 percent of women in the Democratic Republic of the Congo are not involved in decisions about spending their earnings. And 18 percent of married women in India and 14 percent in Nepal are largely silent on how their earned money is spent.[257] Husbands have more control over their wives' earning at lower incomes. In Turkey, only 2 percent of married women in the richest fifth of the population have no control over earned cash income, a proportion that swells to 28 percent in the poorest fifth. In Malawi, 13 percent of married women in the richest fifth have no control compared with 46 percent in the poorest fifth.

Less control over resources and spending is partly a reflection of large differences in the assets men and women own. Assets are typically inherited, acquired at marriage, or accumulated over the lifetime through earnings and savings. Women typically earn less than men, particularly when aggregated over a lifetime. This

[257]   UNDESA. *The World's Women*, 2010.

disparity directly affects their ability to save, irrespective of male-female differences in savings behavior.

Inheritance and property rights often apply differently to men and women; gender disparities in access to physical capital and assets remain significant. Land makes up the largest share of household assets, particularly for the poorest and rural households. Women own as little as 11 percent of the land in Brazil and 27 percent in Paraguay. And their holdings are smaller than those of men. In Kenya, as little as 5 percent of registered landholders are women.[258] In Ghana, the mean size of men's landholdings is three times that of women's.[259] In many countries, land ownership remains restricted to men both by tradition and by law. In most African countries and about half of Asian countries, customary and statutory laws disadvantage women in land ownership. According to customary law in some parts of Africa, women cannot acquire land titles without a husband's authorization.[260] Marriage is the most common avenue for women to gain access to land. But husbands usually own it, while wives only have a claim to its use. While property rights for women have

[258] C. Nyamu-Musembi, "Are Local Norms Fences or Pathways? The Example of Women's Property Rights in Kenya," in *Cultural Transformations and Human Rights in Africa,* ed. Abdullahi A. An-Na'im (London: Zed Books, 2002).

[259] Deere and Doss. "Gender and the Distribution of Wealth in Developing Countries," UNU-WIDER research paper series 115 (2006).

[260] E. Katz and J. Chamorro, "Gender, Land Rights and Household Economy in Rural Nicaragua and Honduras," paper presented at the Annual Latin America and the Caribbean Economics Association, Puebla, Mexico, October 9, 2003.

slowly begun to improve in some countries, legislation has often proved insufficient to change observed practices.

More Vulnerable to Violence at Home

Physical, sexual, and psychological violence against women is endemic across the world. A flagrant violation of basic human rights and fundamental freedoms, violence can take many forms. International statistics are not always comparable, yet incontrovertible evidence shows that violence against women is a global concern.

Less Likely to Hold Political Office

Few nations have legal restrictions on women to running for public office, yet the number of women holding parliamentary seats is very low, and progress in the last fifteen years has been slow. In 1995, women accounted for about 10 percent of members of the lower or single houses of national parliaments, and in 2009, 17 percent.

Different Responses to Shocks and Stresses

Whether the source is financial, political, or natural, shocks and hazards can affect men and women differently, a function of their distinct social roles and statuses. First, market failures, institutional constraints, and social norms can amplify or mute gender differences in the impact of shocks. Second, those failures, constraints, and norms can amplify or mute gender differences in the vulnerability to shocks. The mechanisms that produce these outcomes are multiple.

Women, for example, appear more vulnerable in the face of natural disasters, with the impacts strongly linked to poverty. A recent study of 141 countries found that more women than men die from natural hazards.[261] Where the socioeconomic status of women is high, men and women die in roughly equal numbers during and after natural hazards, whereas more women than men die where the socioeconomic status of women is low. Women and children are more likely to die than men during disasters. The largest numbers of fatalities during the Asian tsunami were women and children under age fifteen. By contrast, 54 percent of those who died in Nicaragua as a direct result of Hurricane Mitch in 1998 were male.

International Commitments

The 2010 MDG Summit concluded with a global action plan to achieve the eight MDGs by 2015. It also adopted a resolution calling for action to ensure gender parity in education and health, economic opportunities, and decision making at all levels through gender mainstreaming in the formulation and implementation of development policies. The resolution and the action plan reflect the belief of the international development community that gender equality and women's empowerment are development objectives in their own right as well as critical channels for the achievement of the other MDGs. Gender equality and women's empowerment help to promote universal primary education, reduce under-five

---

[261]   World Bank, *WDR*, 2012.

mortality, reduce maternal mortality, and reduce the prevalence of HIV/AIDS. The 2010 resolution also stresses that achieving the MDGs will require coordinated interventions that target women and other vulnerable groups across sectors:

- taking action to improve the number and active participation of women in all political and economic decision-making processes, including investing in women's leadership in local decision-making structures and creating an even playing field for men and women in political and government institutions;
- expanding access to financial services for the poor, especially women;
- investing in infrastructure and labor-saving technologies, especially in rural areas, that benefit women and girls by reducing their domestic burdens; and
- promoting and protecting women's equal access to housing, property, and land including rights to inheritance.

These are all specific areas of legal empowerment, and we will discuss them as well as related action options later in this chapter. But first, let's take stock of international legal instruments relevant to the legal empowerment of poor women and girls.

International Legal Instruments

Among the most important international instruments geared to the protection of the rights of women and girls are the Vienna Declaration, the Beijing Platform and Beijing +10 review, and

CEDAW. Among these, CEDAW is by far the most important, and we will summarize some of its salient features.

The Vienna Declaration at the 1993 UN World Conference on Human Rights confirmed that "the human rights of women and of the girl-child are an inalienable, integral, and indivisible part of universal human rights. The full and equal participation of women in political, civil, economic, social and cultural life ... and the eradication of all forms of discrimination on grounds of sex are priority objectives of the international community." The Beijing Platform for Action of 1995 was signed by 189 governments, who thereby committed themselves "to include a gender perspective in all policies and programmes." They agreed to take action on twelve critical areas of concern including women and poverty, women and health, the education and training of women, women and the economy, women and armed conflict, and violence against women.

CEDAW: Convention on the Elimination of All Forms of Discrimination against Women

The preamble to CEDAW states that "discrimination against women violates the principles of equality of rights and respect for human dignity, is an obstacle to the participation of women, on equal terms with men, in the political, social, economic and cultural life of their countries." Article 3 dictates that "States shall take in all fields in particular the political, social, economic and cultural fields all appropriate measures including legislation to ensure the full development and advancement of women for the purpose of guaranteeing them the exercise and enjoyment of human rights and fundamental freedoms on a basis of equality with men." The principle of intersectionality is important to bear in mind: gender discrimination intersects with discriminations based on caste, class, disability, sexual orientation, and so forth.

CEDAW has to be understood from the perspective of the dynamics of human-rights treaty law and its domestic application. The dynamics of human-rights treaty law operate on the following principles:

- Treaty law imposes obligations that are legally binding on the state.
- States commit to reordering domestic law and policy as it touches on the subject of the treaty concerned according to universal and international standards.
- States submit themselves to international scrutiny.
- The principles of CEDAW are based on substantive equality—not only formal legal equality but also equality of results. This includes equality of opportunity, equality of access, and equality of results. CEDAW acknowledges that
- discrimination is socially constructed;
- laws, policies, and practices can unintentionally have the effect of discriminating against women;
- women have been discriminated against historically and do not necessarily come into a situation on an equal basis with men;
- women may have less access to resources, less mobility, fewer years of experience, and so on; hence they cannot access opportunity in the way men can. In most cases, men will be more eligible because of the historic advantage they have.

The CEDAW Framework

CEDAW demands a strategic view of women's advancement, a gender-sensitive, rights-based approach. This requires that all interventions for women by the state be based on

- the principles of the universality, interrelatedness, and interdependence of rights;
- the norms of substantive equality and nondiscrimination;
- efforts to ensure equality in the public and private spheres, whether in the areas of private enterprise or the family;
- efforts to eliminate not only individual acts of discrimination but also systemic discrimination as manifested and justified in institutional practices;
- efforts to ensure de jure and de facto rights of women; and
- the principle that it is the obligation of the state to ensure that women's rights are respected, protected, and fulfilled.

While CEDAW forms part of international law and is therefore legally binding on state parties, it has not been incorporated into domestic law in many countries and is therefore not binding on their courts. There are no direct remedies for the infringement of CEDAW in these courts; it cannot be cited alone as the basis for a case against an employer or the government. But it should form part of the principles of interpretation of the courts and should inform the thinking and analysis of the judiciary and the legislature. A challenge for the implementation of CEDAW is to ensure the incorporation of the convention into domestic law.

But apart from the need for greater recognition of CEDAW as a legal instrument, it has great weight as a tool to demand political accountability for states' obligations under human-rights agreements. One way is through participation in the hearings when governments report to the CEDAW Committee on its progress in the implementation of the convention. Another is using CEDAW as part of a strategy to develop a culture of human-rights-based approaches. Using CEDAW in policy work is a way of linking local issues to a global human-rights framework by quoting the obligations that the state has undertaken.

State obligation is legally binding. Article 26 of the Vienna Convention on the Law of Treaties states, "Every treaty in force is binding upon the parties to it and must be performed by them in good faith." Article 27 states, "A party may not invoke the provisions of its internal law as justification for its failure to perform a treaty." States have a legal responsibility to comply. Failure to do so undermines the basis of international treaty law. "All States have a common interest in ensuring that all parties respect treaties to which they have chosen to become parties." The state has entered into this obligation through the legal process of ratification and is therefore bound to ensure that the laws and practices of the country are in harmony with the principles of the treaty. Incorporating the treaty into domestic law is therefore desirable. This provides a basis for individuals to invoke the treaty in national courts and avoids problems pertaining to the translation of the treaty obligations into national law. Thus, though the choice of the means of giving effect to the treaty is left to the state, there must be results, and the CEDAW Committee will review the means that a state has used. It is also possible for women to petition national courts to force their governments to comply with their obligations under the treaty. The obligation of the state is toward all women within its jurisdiction and not only those who are its citizens. The CEDAW Committee has developed jurisprudence through its concluding comments and through its dialogue with states parties.

The Application of CEDAW to the Legal Empowerment of Rural Women

CEDAW is one of the most widely ratified conventions in human-rights history, but as it lacks an enforcement mechanism, many consider its contributions to the actual achievement of women's rights limited. However, it has made an important (and inadequately recognized) contribution in rural areas where law is functionally absent and where it has helped to inspire feminist activism.[262]

CEDAW recognizes rural women as a particularly disadvantaged group in need of additional rights. Article 14 addresses rural women exclusively and specifically, stipulating that they—like their urban counterparts—should enjoy a panoply of rights: education, health care, and an array of civil and political rights. Moreover, article 14 enumerates for rural women rights related to participation in agriculture and development more generally. It also includes the right for rural women to organize self-help groups and cooperatives for purposes of obtaining "equal access to economic opportunities through employment or self-employment," a right not mentioned elsewhere in relation to all women. Finally, article 14 enumerates for rural women a wider range of socioeconomic rights than CEDAW elsewhere recognizes for all women. These

---

[262] M. Vanegas and L. Pruitt, "CEDAW and Rural Development: Empowering Women with Law from Top Down, Activism from Bottom Up," *Baltimore Law Review* 41 (2012): 263–334.

include rights to various types of infrastructure including water, sanitation, electricity, transport, and housing. More specifically, article 14 requires states to encourage and facilitate women's self-help groups in rural areas. These groups have drawn on this article to get states to support their work.[263]

The Role of NGOs

The domestic application of human-rights norms, in particular, requires effective enforcement mechanisms and the creation of a culture that encourages compliance with human-rights principles. A working premise that creates a synergy between the enforcement of rights and the culture of compliance with human-rights norms is that a rights framework does not automatically confer rights; it only legitimizes claims of rights, and women have to be able to claim their rights. NGO advocacy is critical for all of this to happen, as it can improve the flow of information from the international level of legal standards to the local level (including monitoring and facilitating the implementation of the convention locally).

Women's and Girls' Access to Justice and the Rule of Law

Structural inequalities and pressure from traditional stereotypes hinder women's access to justice. The failure of the system to provide justice for women prevents them from filing grievances and suing or prosecuting those who have violated their rights. This remains a significant human-rights challenge. Many women are uninformed about the processes and various possibilities

---

[263] Ibid.

they have to access justice. In many countries, women suffer from a lack of education, which prevents them from reading and understanding complicated legal language. Moreover, they have very limited awareness of their rights, which undeniably excludes women from the judicial system and prevents them from defending themselves and obtaining remedies and reparations. This issue is particularly serious for migrant women: in addition to the lack of information, they also have to face cultural and language barriers if they do not speak the national language.[264]

Police officers often lack guidelines and information on violations of women's human rights. They don't know how to respond to violence against women, because they do not always know what constitutes a violation. There is, therefore, a critical need to combat this lack of education and information among police. Furthermore, women very often endure harmful gender stereotypes, especially when they try to bring complaints to the police. In cases of gender violence, such as marital rape, they are usually discouraged from prosecuting, on the grounds that these are private issues that have to be dealt with within the family, not in a public trial. Police officers and even judges reproach women for clothes and behaviors that they consider provocative, challenging women's credibility as victims and witnesses.[265]

On the one hand, women's behaviors, such as abortion and sex work, are criminalized; while on the other hand marital rape, forced marriages, and honor killings are not always considered violations in many countries and can therefore remain unpunished. It is

---

[264] Women's International League for Peace and Freedom, CEDAW: General Discussion on Women and Access to Justice, 2013, www.wilpfinternational.org.

[265] Ibid.

often easier for women, especially indigenous and rural women, to have access to traditional and informal systems of justice. Yet most of these systems are discriminatory and have a negative impact on women's rights. Discriminatory judicial practices are still very present in some countries (for instance, in some Islamic republics) where informal systems of justice are still prevalent. It is important to take such systems into account to ensure that customary principles do not contradict the CEDAW Convention and that they do not override the principle of equality.

Some have suggested the inclusion of customary justice actors in the formal justice system to encourage both systems to cooperate with each other not only in order to facilitate women's access to justice but also to end discrimination against them.[266] Owing to multiple costs, the poorest populations often cannot afford access to justice. This is especially true of women living in poverty: many of them are dependent on their husbands and therefore cannot prosecute them in case of violations. Justice is incredibly expensive for women living in poverty not only in criminal matters but also in civil cases, since most of the time they do not enjoy free legal aid for such procedures. Moreover, they also risk losing their jobs, since their employers are unlikely to give them permission to leave work for attending sessions at the tribunal, not to mention that some women cannot rely on anyone else for childcare.

There is an obvious and critical need to secure women's access to justice; their rights are violated not only during an assault but also during the litigation that follows. Therefore, it is now time to move from acknowledgement to action.[267] But how? Set out

---

[266] *Ibid.*

[267] *Ibid.*

below are some lessons the International Development and Law Organization (IDLO) drew from case studies intended to understand how poor women and girls can best get access to justice and the rule of law.[268]

Legal-empowerment strategies can improve women's access to justice in both formal and informal systems. One of the key problems for the achievement of gender equality lies in the inability of many women to use existing legal standards to realize their rights. Legal-empowerment strategies, through legal literacy programs, legal aid, or alternative dispute-resolution mechanisms, can help create a culture of justice among women and ensure that principles of equality and nondiscrimination are not only enshrined in law but also translated into practice. Evidence suggests that legal-empowerment approaches to enhance women's access to justice may work well in a variety of legal settings including informal ones. For example, the fluidity and dynamism of informal justice systems can open up opportunities for modernization and progressive reforms around women's rights. Where women have a forum to discuss and (re)interpret cultural or legal rules, the system may be open to positive transformation, particularly when both women and men advocate for a reinterpretation of such rules. Legal-empowerment approaches may also work in informal justice settings, because the customary authority of male leaders generally rests upon their ability to reflect the values and interests of the community. Thus, while customary male leaders often benefit from the status quo and resist positive change for women, they may also have incentives to respond to community expectations. In the same way, bottom-up

---

[268] IDLO, *Accessing Justice: Models, Strategies and Best Practices on Women's Empowerment*, 2013.

legal-empowerment approaches targeting women can pressure community leaders to reform discriminatory practices. When women are informed of their rights and encouraged to discuss or challenge informal laws and practices, they can put pressure on customary justice systems better to protect basic rights. In turn, this can reduce power imbalances and elite capture and improve the transparency of local government decision making.

Legal-empowerment strategies are most effective where implemented in conjunction with top-down measures and through local partners. While the state legal system alone cannot cure gender injustice, it is a key avenue for the achievement of gender equality. Law has the ability to deter discriminatory practices against women with the threat of punishment and the capacity to influence and guide the behavioral norms and social interactions between men and women. A well-functioning and nondiscriminatory legal system can also serve as an accountability mechanism to ensure the compliance of informal practices with basic human-rights standards and to prevent power abuses while at the same time enhancing the predictability of informal decisions. Grassroots efforts to empower women are therefore more effective when coupled with top-down reforms aimed at ensuring that justice systems, whether formal or informal, are in line with international laws and standards pertaining to gender equality. The presence of supportive constitutions and national laws plays a critical role in ensuring the effectiveness of legal-empowerment interventions. Moreover, legal-empowerment projects are most likely to have an impact on gender inequality and women's access to justice if they creatively draw on local knowledge and practices. This contributes to the legitimacy of the reforms and ensures their eventual sustainability.

Barriers to women's access to justice are multidimensional and go beyond legal aspects. Political, social, cultural, economic, and psychological barriers that obstruct women's access to justice and legal empowerment are present at every stage of the justice chain. The case studies clearly indicate that the disempowerment of women is not simply due to a lack of knowledge of laws and legal procedures but rather to a host of economic, social, and cultural practices that perpetuate inequality in the community and broader society. Programs that encourage women to object to discriminatory practices are unlikely to provide meaningful relief unless they also address the broader economic, social, and security context. Research indicates that legal-empowerment projects targeting women work best when combined with activities addressing a rule-of-law culture, women's economic autonomy, and discriminatory attitudes within the community. While legal empowerment is not the panacea to the wider problems of inequality, discrimination, and the poverty of women, it can make a positive contribution, which, if properly integrated with other initiatives, will place women on a better trajectory toward effectively addressing discriminatory practices.

Legal-empowerment programs designed to address women's access to justice need to be context-specific. Women's experiences in the justice system are diverse. There are no ready-made formulas for empowering women to assert their rights and act as agents of sustainable social change. Rather, reformers should ask a number of questions: What is the best entry point for women to be empowered to use the legal system to advance their rights? What is the forum in which a community deals with women's core concerns? Is that system open to reform, or would legal empowerment have limited results in that context due to deeply entrenched gender stereotypes, vested interests in the status quo, and power inequities? Each intervention should carefully examine where the opportunities are in a given context. For example, opportunities may lie in the formal or the informal justice system, and it may be most effective to target procedural or substantive aspects in any given situation. Ultimately, projects designed to be pragmatic, realistic, and reflective of the local context demonstrate a higher rate of success.

The IDLO summarizes the policy implications of these lessons as follows:[269]

- Consider legal empowerment approaches as part of the solution to advance women's access to justice. Invest more resources to identify and design effective, context-specific strategies to promote gender equality.
- Explore the interface of informal and formal justice settings. Efforts to address discriminatory laws and obstacles to the use of the formal legal sector need to complement empowerment strategies.
- Engage with informal justice systems, despite the challenges of program design. Informal justice systems should not be positioned against formal justice systems in a zero-sum game.
- Engage with civil society and support local ownership to ensure the legitimacy and sustainability of measures targeting women's access to justice.
- Adopt a multidisciplinary approach to women's access to justice. Investigate the potential of partnerships with nonlegal

---

[269] *Ibid.*

service providers, in particular those working in the areas of women's economic empowerment and income generation, protection from violence, and food security. Best practices include legal aid providers teaming up with nonlegal service providers—for example, by collaborating with domestic violence counseling in women's shelters or bundling legal-aid delivery with existing services women frequently access, such as midwifery services or micro credit schemes.

Property Rights of Women and Girls

International law unequivocally recognizes women's equal rights to access, own, and control land, adequate housing, and property.[270] However, the persistence of discriminatory laws, policies, patriarchal customs, traditions, and attitudes in various countries still prevents women from enjoying their rights. Even where statutory national laws recognize women's rights to land, housing, and property, traditional values prevail among judges, police officers, local councilors, and land officials. They often interpret statutory laws in "customary ways" that deprive women of the rights they should enjoy under statutory law.

The UN special rapporteur on adequate housing confirms the dire situation of millions of women across the world: "In almost all countries, whether 'developed' or 'developing', legal security of tenure for women is almost entirely dependent on the men they are associated with. Women-headed households and women in general are far less secure than men. Very few women own land.

---

[270] UN Habitat, *Rights and Reality: Are Women's Equal Rights to Land, Housing and Property Implemented in East Africa?* 2002, http://www.unhabitat.org/tenure.

A separated or divorced woman with no land and a family to care for often ends up in an urban slum, where her security of tenure is at best questionable."[271]

Women who are potentially able to meet their subsistence needs on their own may threaten to leave the household if they do not receive a large share of the surplus.[272] However, due to patriarchal property rights and husbands' control over the allocation of wives' labor time, husbands can make decisions that reduce the value of their wives' alternatives to marriage. The rights to manage land and control income from production have implications that reach far beyond than mere access. For many women, access to land and property are essential to the production of food as well as sustainable livelihoods but are dependent on natal and marital affiliations. In many countries, women can lose rights to land when there is a change in marital status including marriage, divorce, or even the death of a spouse.[273]

Because of the worldwide prevalence of patrilineal inheritance customs, both productive resources and property like household goods have ended up in the hands of men and not women. When only men have rights of inheritance or family succession, women

---

[271] UN Special Rapporteur on Adequate Housing, *Study on Women and Adequate Housing*, April 2002, E/CN.4/2003/55, 9, http://www.unhchr.ch/housing.

[272] Elissa Braunstein and Nancy Folbre, "To Honor and Obey: Efficiency, Inequality, and Patriarchal Property Rights," *Feminist Economics* 7, no. 1 (2001): 25–44.

[273] Renne Giovarelli and Beatrice Wamalwa, "Land Tenure, Property Rights, and Gender: Challenges and Approaches for Strengthening Women's Land Tenure and Property Rights," Property Rights and Resource Governance Briefing Paper no. 7: 2011.

have little opportunity to improve their status or living conditions within the family and community. Consequently, they are dependent on male relatives for survival and have little say over how property is used to generate income or to support families. Additionally, within patrilineal communities, there is a strong resistance by men to endowing women, especially daughters, with rights to land access.[274]

While a growing number of contemporary laws give inheritance rights to daughters and recognize them as individuals within communities, the process of marriage and traditionally patrilineal customs have remained largely unchanged. Thus, there remains a mismatch between marriage practices and inheritance laws, with the strength and biases of marriage customs often overriding inheritance laws. Dowry practices are further evidence of this mismatch. In many cultures, families view a daughter's dowry as her direct portion of the inheritance even though the new husband and his family typically absorb it. Thus, while in some communities women do have the formal rights to inherit land, the social representation of inheritance in the form of dowries and the strength of the practice of marriage trump formal laws.

In communal land-tenure systems, women had significant indirect access and rights to communal resources through their roles as household managers. Registering lands in the name of heads of household (almost invariably men) further excluded women. Without legal protection, women are at risk of suddenly becoming landless, which often happens when a husband sells the family land.[275]

Low levels of education, often the product of restrictions on women's interactions with institutions primarily composed

---

[274]   En.wkipedia.org/wiki/womens_property_rights.

[275]   *Ibid.*

of men, create a mystique and illusion about legal actions. Additionally, ideologies about the conduct that a woman should display (normally, the expectation is docility) can bring shame to the idea of challenging persisting gender inequalities in law, policy, and land rights.[276]

The fact that property rights have a degree of fluidity and dynamism not generally seen in other areas of the law further complicates the situation. Laws affecting women's property rights can run the gamut of the legal spectrum. From family codes to land-titling regulations, constitutions to personal-status codes, and civil codes to gender-equality laws, a multiplicity of overlapping laws—some of them contradictory—affect women's property rights. Thus, any number of legal provisions can protect or undermine women's ability to acquire, possess, manage, and transfer property.[277] The intersection of statutory and customary law also can create confusion about what property rights women possess. The disharmony in the formal legal system, coupled with the mix of legal frameworks, can lead to inequitable outcomes for women.

Research has found strong links between property rights, access to finance, and business productivity. In particular, data shows links between women's access to land and gains in family welfare and children's health. Property rights are even more essential in low-income economies, where women are more likely to work in family businesses and their income is more likely to be determined by how much property they own. Though it is

---

[276] John. L. McCreery, "Women's Property Rights and Dowry in China and South Asia," *Ethnology* 15, no. 2: 163–174.

[277] World Bank, *Women, Business and the Law*, 2010.

difficult to measure the global gender asset gap, several studies document significant regional and local gender asset gaps in property ownership.[278]

Labor Rights of Women

The ILO standards that seek to protect the labor rights of women include the following:

- The Equal Remuneration Convention (no. 100) guarantees equal remuneration for men and women workers for work of equal value.
- The Discrimination of Employment and Occupation Convention (no. 111) states that governments should "uphold equality of opportunity and treatment in respect of employment and occupation, with a view to eliminating any discrimination in respect thereof."
- The Maternity Protection Convention (no. 183) protects women from safety risks during pregnancy and guarantees paid maternity leave.
- The Domestic Workers Protection Convention (no. 189) aims to end abuses of migrant domestic workers.

However, while increased access to employment has provided new economic and social opportunities for poor women, the jobs they occupy remain unregulated and unstable. Women workers are systematically denied their rights to regular pay and regular working hours; equal pay for equal work; permanent

---

[278] *Ibid.*

contracts; safe and nonhazardous work environments; and freedom of association. Sexual harassment in the workplace and workplace-related sexual violence are a particularly egregious and widespread form of discrimination against women. Forced sexual relations and pregnancy tests, which become a precondition for employment, significantly reduce a woman's ability to demand a living wage and break out of poverty. Working mothers face everyday barriers as they try to support their families. Organizing against abuse is also particularly difficult for women because of the highly gendered nature of subcontracting and other forms of flexible work.[279]

In a recent call for papers on the on the subject of "Women's Empowerment, Gender Equality and Labor Rights: Transforming the Terrain," the Solidarity Center summarized the search for solutions as follows:

> In a global context of economic crisis, uncertainty and political change, women workers are uniting in different ways and under different banners to fight for and widen their labor rights and to claim a role in their nations' social, economic and political structures. They are bringing demands for inclusiveness, new ways of building power and often their own experience of discrimination and exclusion into a hard-nosed and, at times, deeply conflicted battle to actualize a broad agenda of economic and labor rights. As such, women workers are helping to define a new economic citizenship— one that integrates political and union activism, labor rights,

---

[279] International Labor Rights Forum, Rights for Working Women, www. laborrights.com/labor-rights-for-women.

social and economic justice, and gender equality. Rooted in the rank and file, these efforts offer practical insights into how women can exercise their rights and shape the meaning of participatory democracy and just economies.[280]

Conclusion

This chapter has surveyed the significant progress toward the legal empowerment of poor women and girls but also has identified tremendous challenges that they still face. The successes show up in areas ranging from increased school attendance of girls to women's inheritance rights in some countries. But the obstacles are many: traditional cultural norms and practices that are used as excuses to violate the fundamental human rights of poor women and girls, lack of access to institutions of formal law and prejudices in customary law, discriminatory laws, lack of awareness of rights, marriage practices that subordinate women, and men who still think of their wives as their property. Approaches that can help the empowerment of this half of the human population include international instruments, systemic programs, policy shifts, and feminist activism.

[280] The Solidarity Center, 2013, www.ifwea.org.

8

BRINGING IT ALL TOGETHER:
REALIZING LEGAL RIGHTS THROUGH
AN INTEGRATED HUMAN-RIGHTS
AND DEVELOPMENT FRAMEWORK

Introduction

The goal of this book is to catalyse and accelerate action on the legal empowerment of the poor. It is clear that the most significant communities of practice in a position to advance the agenda are those in human rights and development. However, these communities have not formed a strong bond in the past and have not been phenomenally successful in their respective fields. The largely unrealized potential of the human-rights-based approach to development is ample testimony to these failures. The human-rights community has been strong on advocacy, while the development community has developed technocratic strengths in program design, implementation, monitoring, and evaluation. Bringing these strengths together in an integrated approach could be quite powerful.

This chapter uses two relatively radical concepts in human rights and development—governance and sustainable livelihoods—to provide a framework that hopefully will help these communities work better together and help advance the legal-empowerment agenda. The legal-rights agenda can then find a place in the mainstream, gaining access to significant resources and receiving significant political attention. To be successful, this framework must bring together a broad array of concepts including poverty action, informality, ESCR as legal rights, the legal-empowerment agenda, and self-empowerment through changing power relations. Let us see how well we can make this happen.

Sustainable Livelihoods

The evolution of sustainable livelihoods (SL) as a key concept of development confirmed the beginning of a new era in international development cooperation. This concept stresses that development simply does not work for people unless they are the ones who conceive and realize it. The days are gone when development was just a top-down affair organized by government institutions for the people. So are the days when poverty eradication took the form of redistribution of public resources to meet the anticipated needs of the poorer segments of society. SL embraced such concepts as ownership and empowerment, both associated with a bottom-up approach where access to resources and incentives to action replace the redistributive approach of the past. Multilateral and bilateral agencies have yet to operationalize fully this remarkable shift in development thinking, this silent revolution. Their actions do not always match their rhetoric. By focusing on how governance relates to the realization of sustainable livelihoods, this chapter uses the SL framework to show how the legal empowerment of the poor might be put into practice in development circles not only in international cooperation but within developing countries and among the poor themselves.

The Brundtland Commission first proposed the idea of SL as an approach to enhancing resource productivity, securing ownership of and access to resources and income-earning activities, and ensuring adequate stocks and flows of food and cash to meet basic needs.[281] The commission saw sustainable-livelihood security as a precondition for stable human populations and a prerequisite for good husbandry and sustainable management of natural resources. Agenda 21 expanded the concept and was the first intergovernmental forum to demand sustainable livelihoods for all as a universal objective. By integrating SL into poverty eradication strategies, Agenda 21 also contributed to incorporating the concept into mainstream economic development thinking.[282] Subsequent fora, such as the Social Summit in Copenhagen[283] and the Beijing Conference on Women[284] have made use of SL in their program statements, as have an increasing number of agencies, both multilateral and bilateral, as they have increasingly turned their attention to poverty eradication.

At the core of the SL approach are two broad principles. First is its integrative potential. The concept allows policies to address issues of jobs and employment, sustainable resource management, access to or ownership of assets, and poverty eradication simultaneously. Second is its emphasis not just on jobs but also on the full complexity

---

[281] Report of the World Commission on Environment and Development (1987) chaired by Gro Harlem Brundtland.

[282] Agenda 21 was one of the main outcomes of the Conference on Environment and Development in Rio in 1992.

[283] United Nations, World Summit on Social Development, 1995.

[284] United Nations, Fourth World Conference on Women, 1995.

of livelihood systems in the context of families, households, and communities. The overall policy objective of the SL approach must be to identify the livelihood systems, survival strategies, and self-help organizations of people living in poverty and to work with such organizations to develop programs for combating poverty that build on their efforts, ensuring the full participation of the people concerned.[285] Individual scholars, notably Chambers and Conway,[286] Davies,[287] and Singh and Titi,[288] have continued to buttress the concept and developed participatory methodologies that facilitate the implementation of SL.

The SL approach has evolved in recent years as a cornerstone in the program thinking of many agencies. Growing out of the concern with human development—and the desire to link that to Agenda 21—SL have gradually become a major policy objective with the following principal dimensions:

- use of self-empowerment;
- focus on community assets and strength (including local knowledge and coping and adaptive strategies);
- improved access to resources;

---

[285] United Nations, World Summit on Social Development Outcome Statement, 1995.

[286] R. Chambers and G. Conway, "Sustainable Rural Livelihoods: Practical Concepts for the 21st Century," IDS Discussion Papers, 1995, 296.

[287] S. Davies, "Versatile Livelihoods: Strategic Adaptation to Food Insecurity in the Malian Sahel," IDS, February 1993.

[288] N. Singh and V. Titi, "Adaptive Strategies of the Poor in Arid and Semi-Arid Lands: In Search of Sustainable Livelihoods," IISD Working Paper, 1994.

- recognition of the cross-sector nature of the approach and the need, therefore, to find levels of analysis and action commensurate with its complexity and dynamics;
- livelihoods as a function of activities, assets, and entitlements people use to make a living;
- emphasis on the capacity to cope with shocks and stresses as well as the ability to deal with economic efficiency, social equity, and ecological integrity; and
- recognition of the links between small, local actions and broader conditions and policies.

When we place the emphasis on what poor people can do by and for themselves, it becomes obvious that we must adjust the system to serve them. There is no reason to pursue a general or vague state policy objective that means little or nothing to the poor because they never see it implemented. The SL approach has the potential to bring public policy closer to the real interests and demands of poor people. In order to do so, however, institutions at the macro level must revise their strategies. Here governance comes in, because it draws attention to the rules that determine the conduct of public affairs.

Governance

Broadly speaking, governance refers to the way a country gets things done. The UNDP, for example, defines governance as the exercise of economic, political, and administrative authority to manage a country's affairs at all levels.[289] From this perspective,

---

[289] UNDP, Governance for Sustainable Human Development, 1997.

governance comprises the mechanisms, processes, and institutions through which citizens and groups articulate their interests, exercise their legal rights, meet their obligations, and mediate their differences. The UNDP definition considers governance to have three legs: economic, political, and administrative. Economic governance includes decision-making processes that affect a country's economic activities and its relationships with other economies. Political governance is the process of decision making to formulate policy, while administrative governance is the system of policy implementation. Consequently, governance is an all-encompassing concept; it permeates all sectors—public, private, and voluntary—and all phases of making public policy. It has the same vague ring surrounding it as development management had in the 1970s.

Adopting such an all-encompassing definition has its advantages when it comes to providing justification for a broad program. Governance, so defined, helps legitimize a wide-ranging portfolio of programs. As suggested above, the SL approach is a radical departure from previous perspectives on development and poverty eradication. Starting with the constraints and opportunities facing individuals, households, and communities creates a rationale for a coherent understanding of governance that suits this objective.

We must rethink two aspects of governance in relation to an SL approach. The first is that governance—as it is broadly understood, especially in the academic literature—is associated with the actions of regimes rather than state or civil society. This means that the concept refers to the constitution or reconstitution of normative rules that guide public or political action. Governance is just one aspect of politics; it focuses on the basic—or constitutional—rules that determine behavior and action. The second is that governance is different from policy making, public administration, or project management. As suggested in table 1, governance takes place at a meta-analytical level, meaning that the rules established at the regime or governance level circumscribe the other activities listed above.

Governance and its relation to other concepts and activities

Level	Activity	Concept
Meta	Politics	Governance
Macro	Policy	Policy making
Mesa	Program	Public administration
Micro	Projects	Management

It is important to emphasize that these different levels are empirically interconnected, but there are good reasons for keeping them analytically distinct. Rules are, empirically speaking, set at different levels. For example, a community may decide to change its rules in order to improve the prospects of enjoying sustainable livelihoods. Such a revision of rules at the level of the local community regime affects policy making and Implementation as well as project management. Governance is also present at higher levels, ultimately establishing and managing the constitutional principles of a given country.

The more precise meaning given to governance here makes it possible to distinguish between two sides of politics. One is the distributive side, which addresses the perennial question of who gets what, when, and how. This side of politics is usually referred to as political economy, because it focuses on how public resources are allocated in society. The other side is the constitutive side, which addresses the question of who sets what rules, when, and how. This is what we call here governance, because it focuses on the rules of the political game. This distinction is particularly important in relation to SL. The conventional needs approach relies on the distributive side and does not ask for changes in the rules of the game to achieve its objectives. The SL approach, on the other hand, which focuses on empowerment and enhanced access to resources, calls for a change in the rules and, by implication, a shift in power relations. An SL approach to poverty reduction therefore requires attention to the constitutive side of politics—that is, to governance.

Governance for Sustainable Livelihoods: An Action Framework[290]

From this perspective, it is important to treat governance not just as a loosely connected set of activities (or a portfolio of programs) but as a tool that can promote SL. As a management tool, governance is the analogous to strategic management in business administration. Governance deals with coping and adapting to an uncertain and changing environment. In business, these conditions arise most often from changes in the market and in technology. In politics, such changes also emerge from the wishes of empowered groups of people to change the conditions under which they are ruled. Governance, then, encourages

---

[290] Adapted from: G. Hyden. 1998. Governance for Sustainable Livelihoods. Paper prepared for UNDP.

actors to think beyond business as usual or the need for merely incremental adjustments that do not call for a change in the regime. Governance, like strategic management, becomes a way of looking at a problem in the context of the big picture, of adapting systems of rule to changes in the environment (political, economic, technological, and sociocultural), and of encouraging leaders to find consensual—and positive—solutions to problems their constituents or followers encounter. Governance, engaged in this manner, becomes a way of engaging politics including the need for changes in power relations rather than hiding political issues behind a set of generalized phrases.

At a first glance, this revised use of the concept may appear controversial. It implies getting involved in support of changes in the internal political arrangements of sovereign states. Such fears, however, are exaggerated. First, virtually all multilateral and bilateral agencies are already involved in such transgressions. The democracy and governance programs of such agencies do exactly that whether they explicitly recognize it or not. The difference between such programs and engaging with governance in the context of an SL approach is that governance here becomes more than an end in itself. Good governance exists when rules related to specific SL objectives are successfully implemented. This is a hands-on way of approaching governance. It also demonstrates a direct relationship between democracy and development that current uses of the concept of governance do not really allow, because they are too vague and, when disaggregated, refer to a set of program activities that typically do not reinforcing each other.

It is precisely the ability to identify how different types of program activities may be mutually supportive that has been missing in past uses of the concept of governance. We must apply the concept in a more practical manner if it is to serve the objectives of erasing poverty and promoting sustainable livelihoods. This chapter identifies one (but by no means the only) way of doing so.

This is only a first step in the emergence of an alternative approach that starts with the individual, household, or community. Because actors enter the marketplace differently endowed, it is not an even playing field. Those who are already rich have an initial advantage, and only special measures enable the poorer segments of the population to succeed. With low public levels of confidence in government and public-sector institutions in general and a trimmed-down state machinery, compensatory interventions by governments are not likely to play the role in development thinking that they did in the past. That is why the SL approach emphasizes greater reliance on local resources and strategies to cope with social and economic issues, the empowerment of local actors, and the need to improve their access to additional resources that can help them make progress on their own. Reducing their sense of vulnerability and powerlessness implies realigning power relations and creating an environment that is not only enabling (a concept that is a product of economic liberalization) but also reassuring (a concept that more closely relates to an SL approach).

Governance, understood as management of the rules of the game at different levels in a society, is an important aspect of realizing SL but not enough on its own. It needs to function in the context of other potential measures, such as technological enhancements of the local resource base and the right policies to encourage greater self-reliance and the prudent use of scarce public resources. However, a concern with the strategic aspects of change—the big picture—is especially important in order to provide a vision of and justification for changes in the relations between public authorities and citizens as well as among groups of citizens. It is also important to acknowledge that governance in the context of an SL approach means working both at macro and micro levels. There must be leaders with a vision and the political courage to challenge the status quo—at whatever level it manifests itself—in order to realize the conditions that will allow a successful implementation of SL objectives. At the same time, it is clear that local citizens themselves have an active and meaningful role to play in improving their own livelihoods in a sustainable fashion and thereby contributing to sustainable human development at the national level.

Making the Framework Operational

Since the ultimate end of constitutive politics—or governance—is the realignment of relations between public authorities and citizens with a view to enhancing the legitimacy of the regime, it is important to point out that the SL approach can deal with programs in several different ways. We suggest a four-pronged approach that takes into consideration that changes in power relations are the result of leadership interventions from above as much as citizen demands from below. The first aspect of changing power relations is *articulation*, or the readiness and ability of individuals to demand the freedom to make decisions of their own on issues that concern the use of shared or public goods. The second aspect is *mobilization*—that is, the readiness and ability of groups of citizens to work together to maximize gains for themselves without doing so (in a zero-sum fashion) at the expense of others. Like articulation, this aspect refers to the generation of citizen demands from below. The third aspect is *distribution* of power, which becomes important as more and more groups begin to compete for influence. In order to accommodate this growth of demand for freedom and the right to organize for enhancing SL, it is important that the leadership be ready to distribute power in such a way that the political system becomes more pluralist and groups have access to complementary resources through the market, the state, or other relevant institutions. The fourth aspect is *confirmation* of power. This typically takes place through the decisions taken by judicial institutions but is more generally dependent on the readiness of both citizens and public institutions to respect the principle of rule of law. This aspect is important in an SL context, because it points to the importance of a rights-based approach to development.

The operationalization of governance in relation to SL grows from the realization of these four aspects of power in the context of specific programs. Table 2 below summarizes how this happens:

Table 2. Operational aspects of governance in the context of SL

Power Aspect	Governance Focus	Program Concern	Institutional Issue
Articulation	Self-organization	Ownership	Empowerment
Mobilization	Social capital	Capability	Civil engagement
Distribution	Social space	Access	Pluralism
Confirmation	Strength	Rights	Rule of law

We shall now discuss how each of these four aspects actually translates into a set of mutually supportive programs that develop and enhance sustainable livelihoods. As indicated above, this is not necessarily the only way of doing it, but it is an effort to provide a coherent governance program that is associated with and supportive of the SL program objectives.

Articulation. Being able to articulate one's own views on a public issue is the first step on a long path toward realizing SL. When individuals begin to articulate their own views, a meaningful discussion and dialogue with others emerges and the prospects for spontaneous organization of efforts become real. If an SL approach—like human development—means expanding the choices for all people in society, it also implies increasing the opportunity for both men and women to participate in and endorse decisions affecting their own lives. To be sure, it is unrealistic to assume that every person will be able to participate in all decisions affecting them, but it is important that, as a means of increasing such opportunities, they are able to organize themselves freely at the local level and claim ownership of the decision-making process. Governance, therefore, means changing the rules to the extent that such self-organization is becoming increasingly possible.

A governance measure may not, in itself, be enough, but it is an essential part of any effort to realize SL. Such measures may include new rules for who can participate in community affairs and decide on such matters. For example, in many patriarchal societies, the idea of extending opportunities to women on an even basis—and taking complementary measures to realize that objective—is one relevant case in point. Studies have shown that women in such societies are especially hesitant to voice their opinions in public unless they have had a chance to learn how to speak and thereby have gained confidence to interact with men. Another example might be a group of peasants or workers initiating a move to have the rules changed in order to allow them greater influence over what transpires in a factory or on the farm where they work. They may then begin to feel that they are stakeholders in the exercise. This is not only a matter of enhancing social equality but also one of prudent management. A member organization may often be a more efficient way of getting things done than a regular corporate structure.

The important thing here is to use governance as a lever. The idea that governance deals with the big picture may demonstrate ways of raising parochial issues to a new level and thereby open up opportunities for change in the relations between members of a given community or group. An emphasis on the strategic role that governance plays in public affairs is also important for demonstrating the commonalities rather than the differences between communities or groups. Governance itself, therefore, can have an empowering effect when it serves as a catalyst for organization of efforts at the local level.

Especially when one deals with poor people, it is important to stress that any governance measure must be complementary to other supportive measures. For example, many people live in such poor circumstances that aspiring to greater freedom and control over their own destinies is a lower priority than other concerns, notably just getting by. In Africa, for example, it is quite common for the men to have lost interest in working together because they no longer trust others. They have retreated into an existence where each lives and works pretty much for himself. Readiness to organize with others has all but vanished. The result is often that the burden of securing livelihoods falls upon the shoulders of women, who organize in groups with the sole purpose of earning a meager income that allows them to buy food and clothes for themselves and their children. In these circumstances, it can be argued, the likelihood of self-organization in communities is very low, and only the development of indigenous technologies that are not costly and that the local population itself can use and develop will achieve improvements in SL.

People may find it somewhat easier to organize when the enemy is social rather than purely a matter of inadequate resources. For example, wherever there is a legacy of one group's exploitation by another, antagonisms typically have crystallized into feelings of solidarity that can form the basis of new group action. In this situation, the local actors themselves may take action together to change the circumstances of their lives regardless of their economic resources. In so doing, they are also likely to change the rules of public conduct. Such self-organized action may lead to rights—whether civil and political or social and economic—that have been previously denied.

Institutions have acquired experience working with participatory methodologies that may be particularly suitable for promoting this type of governance measure. Some such methodologies, however, are likely to be more successful than others, as not all of them necessarily emphasize the ownership dimension of such approaches. It is important, therefore, that program staff be familiar with various participatory analysis approaches and can arrange for a proper assessment of how appropriate they are for a specific application of governance to achieve SL.

Mobilization. Articulation is only the first step in an approach that emphasizes the need for greater local initiative and ownership.

It focuses on making the individual ready to take initiatives of his or her own. Self-organization is evidence of the search for power if not power itself. These local initiatives, however, stand little chance of becoming truly empowering experiences for the people involved unless they lead to the mobilization of social capital. Social capital here means trust and readiness to engage in reciprocal action. Trust is an outcome of reliability in social interactions. When individuals realize that they have something in common and stand to gain from concerted action, trust may not be too difficult to develop. Such conditions, however, are not omnipresent. Very often, people start interacting with each other in a climate of distrust. This makes the task of creating trust much more difficult.

Since an SL approach implies the use of local knowledge and information, the principal challenge is more often social than technical. People usually have the requisite technical know-how, but the social skills that translate into sustaining local initiative and power often are missing. That is why the concept of capability is more appropriate than that of capacity, which connotes technical or physical ability. By referring to capability, the approach emphasizes the importance of institutional or social dimensions in realizing the objectives of SL. Particularly significant is the readiness and ability of people to engage each other in a civic manner—that is, in a way that is consistent with the rule of law and tolerant of the views of others. While a good deal has been written about the need to scale up successful local initiatives, the point here is that equally important—and maybe a prerequisite for scaling up—is scaling out. The idea is for people to extend their contacts beyond the scope of their primary social organization—household, village, or community—and work or interact with people whom they may not have known before. Such branching out is necessary if local actors are going to have access to more resources and challenge monopolies or entrenched social forces that otherwise may subvert or destroy local initiatives.

The mobilization of local power and the formation of social capital are sensitive processes that require both tact and integrity from those responsible for implementing SL programs. The governance aspect of this process is not the technical issue of establishing, for example, savings and credit institutions or other community-based initiatives but the task of encouraging a revision of the rules that guide who is responsible for what and who can interact with whom. One consequence of this observation is that leaders must be credible to their followers. Trust and confidence in organizations grow only when leaders show respect for their followers and the latter understand both the constraints and opportunities that their leaders face. Again, therefore, governance measures alone won't necessarily make the difference. They have to work in the context of other inputs or measures that help realize local aspirations. These include ensuring prompt delivery of goods or services that are important for enabling local groups to sustain their own project initiatives, better use of local resources, and avoidance of high-cost solutions that local stakeholders cannot sustain.

These measures notwithstanding, it is important not to overlook or downplay particular governance dimensions. As suggested above, governance deals with realigning relations between the authorities and citizens and among groups of citizens in society. A mere stroke of a pen will not achieve such interventions. They need to be carefully nurtured and followed up. Donor program staff cannot be in the middle of such an exercise, but they can help such a process along by assisting local groups of people to gain strength by allowing them to get involved with others and to become more efficient. This does not mean creating large-scale—and bureaucratic—types of organization around a successful local initiative in order to replicate it elsewhere. Rather, it implies nurturing loose local partnerships or alliances based on dialogue and reciprocal interaction, where learning comes at a pace that is commensurate with local capacities and processes. The rules that need to be reformulated, therefore, are not administrative but political. They should make various actors mindful of the need to respect local ownership while at the same time feeding new ideas and other resources into the minds of various stakeholders. This typically requires more patience than many actors, especially in government, are ready to allocate to the exercise. Yet one of the principal lessons of previous attempts to foster development is that accelerating the process in an artificial manner without local understanding and support leaves it unsustainable.

Social capital forms when actors have enough time to get to know each other and learn from each other's experiences. Trust, confidence, and reciprocal action emerge in a manner that supports civic engagement, especially when the autonomy of local action is respected and not neglected, and builds on local initiatives without others perceiving it primarily as a threat to their own livelihoods. Current efforts to strengthen civil society need to become especially sensitive to this aspect. Success in this field does not consist merely of tangible, measurable material improvements but also of more diffuse—yet important—process outcomes, such as greater trust among stakeholders and better understanding and appreciation of each other's constraints and opportunities for action.

Distribution. As suggested above, both the articulation and the mobilization of power are prerequisites for the pursuit of SL. The provision of opportunities for local actors to set their own agendas to suit their circumstances is at the core of an SL approach. This is not to advocate some form of local autarchy. That is neither desirable nor feasible. What the previous two sections have advocated, however, is the need for local actors—individuals, households, groups, and communities—belonging to the poorer segments of the population to become empowered vis-à-vis other actors in society by relying more on their own resources and skills. Still, it is inadvisable to pursue an SL approach exclusively from the bottom up. Even if local groups are empowered and begin to take charge of their own destiny, they will sooner or later encounter the limits of their new power set by other groups in society. To avoid choking local initiatives, therefore, it is necessary to enlarge the social and political space that they enjoy. The political leadership plays an important role by offering the poor greater access to resources provided by the public, private, or voluntary sectors. This implies realigning the relations of power in society in such a way that access to public goods becomes easier and more even. More specifically, governance for SL involves two measures of special significance: (a) delegation of power and responsibilities and (b) the institutionalization of political pluralism.

The delegation of power and responsibilities must aim at ensuring that locally elected bodies play a greater role in administering development. Many pronouncements of decentralization in the past have amounted to no more than administrative decentralization—de-concentration of administrative authority—rather than delegation of real political power and responsibility. What we need is a much more genuine decentralization that involves the delegation of power to autonomous local authorities with the right to collect their own revenue. Such authorities may be at the district level, but it is important to emphasize that at that level, these institutions are still far from the poor. A genuine decentralization, therefore, should also include dispersal of authority to levels below the district, where the opportunities for poor people and their representatives typically are greater.

Too much power in the past has been concentrated in central government ministries and other state institutions. Most of these have been accountable upward to authorities rather than to the public. Very few of these have worked in the public interest. The vast majority have been inefficient and corrupt. In many countries, delegation of power and responsibilities has therefore included privatization of such state institutions. Privatization is no panacea, because there is always a risk that individual tycoons with little interest in the public welfare will take over privatized enterprises, but as long as there is competition, the prospect is there that such hegemony can be challenged. Whatever one thinks of the market, it has at least one characteristic that is helpful in the context of the SL approach: the rules of the market tend to be less restrictive than those in the political arena. In the market, it is typically also easier to arrive at split-the-difference compromises over the content of such rules. The market is therefore an important counterweight to the state and a potential ally of an SL approach as long as it provides opportunities for local actors to have more influence over their own affairs. A genuine political decentralization is the best way of ensuring that local authorities increasingly handle matters like building schools, health clinics, and roads and have the right to control their own revenue or at least a substantial part of it. Organizations—both private and public—that provide complementary resources for local development, such as credit and technical services, are also part of the institutional landscape that will support SL.

What are typically needed here are not big and expensive investments but relatively small amounts of money that local actors can use prudently. The UNDP, for example, has already worked with small-grants programs for some time to promote community-based initiatives. These include LIFE, the Partners in Development Programme, the Sustainable Agriculture Network, Africa 2000, and Asia-Pacific 2000. National selection committees have been involved in decisions concerning these programs and their implementation, which ensures inclusive and participatory decision making and implementation.

It seems important for donors to build on this experience as they consider adopting an SL approach. In the interest of enhancing partnership in member countries and as a means of promoting a demand-driven approach spurred by groups of local—and typically poor—people, there is good reason to evaluate experiences with small grants and revolving loan funds for rural development and take the necessary steps to institutionalize measures that encourage greater local responsibility for development. The idea of public but politically autonomous funds that focus on a particular sector or thematic concern, such as women and children, is a natural extension of what donors have already done and fits the ideals associated with the SL approach. Such funds would be registered as legal entities in the member country and administered by boards of trustees drawn from government, civil society, and the resource providers. It is important, however, that a single donor does not provide and control these funds, as that tends to reduce the sense of local stakeholder involvement. Such funds should serve as catalysts for multi-donor funding in a given sector or for a given thematic concern. That way, local stakeholders will have a chance to experience ownership with the resource providers as a minority influential enough to blow the whistle (if necessary) and serve as a moderating factor in any unresolved issues between the various local stakeholders represented on the boards. These funds would require governance intervention to ensure that impartiality rather than partisanship determines resource allocation. This issue has taken on increased importance as most countries around the world have moved in the direction of multiparty democracy. In this new political dispensation, it is common for governments to deny groups of people access to public resources as a punishment for having voted for the opposition. The autonomous-development-fund model would transcend partisan loyalties and make available to any group, regardless of political stance, the resources necessary for development.

Managing a multiparty regime has proven to be complicated and difficult in many countries where a democratic legacy is absent and where ethnic or religious divisions in society provide a fertile ground for politicization. Yet a politically more pluralist dispensation is, in the long run, an important ingredient in the SL approach. People must feel free to express themselves in public and to organize without fear. These freedoms do not necessarily come without demand from the citizens themselves, but it is important that the leadership be ready to guarantee such freedoms. This means that the government and other prominent actors in society must be ready to respect human rights and freedoms enshrined in the constitution. Donors have already engaged in a multitude of activities, typically through governance program, that relate to this SL concern. For example, in Guatemala, after years of civil war, donors have assisted in the restoration of individual dignity by fostering programs aimed at a more active citizenship. In South Africa, donors have supported the Women's Development Foundation, which focuses on the political participation by women in local government. In Eastern Europe—and other places, for that matter—donors have worked with national organizations to establish human-rights mechanisms and other fundamentals of a functioning legal system. These are all part of governance measures that aim at reconstituting rules that promote a more popular and participatory approach to development.

Confirmation. Confirmation of realigned relations of power is perhaps the most challenging of all governance measures. At stake under this heading is the institutionalization of power relations meant to give greater social space and strength to groups that previously may have been both ignorant and placid. Changing the rules of the game will do little if the institutions in society cannot guarantee the new rules. Such a process does not happen overnight. It takes time, and it involves finding ways for actors to engage each other without sensing that they are losing face. This is particularly important if one is concerned with poverty eradication and SL. Because of their comparative weakness, these groups are particularly prone to fall victim to the abuse of power by other actors in society. The latter often take action as if the poor do not matter. This is true, as history tells, in both the economic and the political spheres. An unregulated market tends to cause its own failure, because actors do not start with the same endowment of resources. The result is the marginalization of many who cannot manage to compete in such a context. Similarly, a state-controlled system where the market has no role in allocating resources also leads to a skewed distribution of benefits, because those in power have no one to challenge them. What we need, therefore, is a regime in which rules that respect each person on an equal basis and take into account the conditions of the poor and disadvantaged in society minimize the costs of a market or state failure.

Fortunately, the global political climate is beginning to change so that new opportunities exist for the first time to make headway in this direction. That is why the governance dimension of the SL approach is so vital to the realization of its objectives. Being able to put in place a system of rules that (a) allows actors in society to realize that politics is a positive-sum game and (b) guarantees that the rights of the poor cannot be trampled upon with impunity is the highest priority in order to make SL work.

The SL approach has the great advantage of being comprehensive and thus viewing the condition of the poor not only in socioeconomic but also in civil and political terms. This means that in tackling poverty, this approach invites actors to bring into consideration concerns about both socioeconomic and civil and political rights. There must be a growing political understanding that not allowing the poor to develop on their own terms is a cost—not to mention an embarrassment—to society. This means that the economic and social systems need to cater to the interests of such people.

Governance measures to redress previous imbalances in the social and economic sectors must view development in these sectors not in a patronizing manner as meeting perceived needs but in terms of activist rights. An activist-rights approach emphasizes that states are not solely responsible for the destiny of their people but that the people themselves, through their own organizations, share in this effort. Such a redefinition of how to do development, however, requires a broader understanding and recognition of the rights that go with it. Various social and economic rights that improve living conditions for the disadvantaged in society, especially women and children, must attain a higher level of political significance. They must be interpreted in the context of the big picture, which means explaining that these rights are helpful not only to those particular groups but also to society as a whole.

Although it is not clear to what extent courts can assure such rights, it is not at all beyond reason to hope for step-by-step progress toward making such rights justiciable. It would be a mistake to attempt to do so with all the various social and economic rights approved in international conventions in the last few decades, but some of them are clearly more likely to be possible to work with. Such positive rights may include the right to education or the right to housing. The importance here is to work with cases that may set precedents for future instances. Having a progressive judiciary that sees its role as creating new rules for how society conducts its affairs becomes important. Judicial power does not have to contradict popular power. If imbued with the notion of how rights fit into the bigger picture of securing more sustainable livelihoods for a larger percentage of people, judicial power can play a very constructive role. In short, judges can be on the side of the poor, as the public-interest approach of the Supreme Court in India over the years demonstrates.

If work on social and economic rights entails both creating and securing rights for the poor, any effort in the domain of civil and political rights should focus on reassuring people that these rights apply equally to all. The international community has adopted a multitude of conventions that reaffirm these rights, even though the ratification of these instruments and their incorporation into national legislation still falls far short of expectations. One issue facing those working on SL, therefore, is to ensure that these conventions become part of national laws and that court systems implement them effectively. This is not going to be an easy task, because with a more complex human-rights regime in the making at the global level, there is also scope for different interpretations of which particular set of rights apply in a given situation. For example, in recent years, there has been an interest in securing the rights of indigenous peoples or minorities; the International Human Rights Conference in Vienna in 1993 confirmed this interest. This has been an important step forward in the broader context of development, but it is clear that such a rights regime can also be called upon to challenge the notion that rights are universal. This is what has happened, for instance, in Fiji, where the indigenous population, a de facto minority but in control of the army and most other instruments of the state, has invoked the new rights of indigenous peoples to challenge the political powers of the immigrant Indo-Fijian majority.

Such contestations notwithstanding, the important point about the emergence of a global rights regime is that it challenges state sovereignty. After the Second World War, the international community recognized the rights of all people to enjoy political independence within the context of their own state; since then, the notion of sovereignty has shifted away from state and territory toward people or communities that are especially vulnerable. This gradual change in outlook has led both governments and nongovernmental organizations to refer to universally adopted declarations on human rights as justifications for getting involved in the plights of people who are being oppressed or exploited by state machineries or unscrupulous individuals with economic power. The idea of interference in the affairs of another state is no longer a principle that everyone endorses. While it is true that the notion that what happens to people in one country is a concern of all, regardless of whether they are citizens, may be abused—or at least applied in a way that allows the strong to bully the weak—it opens up important opportunities for governance measures to implement an SL approach. Program officers in donor organizations cannot ignore such opportunities but should—and must—support initiatives in the interests of SL even if it means challenging those in power. It is in this context that support of strengthening judiciaries becomes important. The more judges are able to act free of fear or favor, the greater the chances that the social capital and social space organizations of the poor and disadvantaged have obtained for themselves can be adequately confirmed. There must be a firm and fundamental sense of agreement regarding which rules apply to relations between state and citizens and the interactions among the latter. Without the institutionalization of such an understanding, the poor and disadvantaged will continue to face problems in realizing greater control over their livelihoods.

Governance measures under this heading, however, are not necessarily confined to strengthening state institutions like the judiciary that have an official role of adjudicating on how rules apply to specific cases. It is equally important that these confirmatory measures include attention to institutions that can challenge efforts by those in state power—or those with money—to influence court judgments in a particular direction.

This means supporting not only human-rights organizations that work to educate the public on their civil and political rights but also organizations that can ensure that the market itself becomes more social—that is, considerate of the interests of the poor and disadvantaged. Such organizations have a particularly important role to play in teaching society that the market is a potentially constructive institution in which conflicts over resources can be resolved in a positive-sum manner. Proposing and institutionalizing new rules for the market's operation can secure considerable progress toward ensuring that SL become a reality for the poor.

More difficult but equally important is the task of getting political actors to view themselves from a positive-sum perspective. This involves making them more inclined to see political compromises as victories rather than defeats (viewing compromises as defeats is still common in many countries where autocratic tendencies remain). This may involve organizing seminars or workshops that expose such actors to techniques for negotiating and resolving conflicts. The problem so far has been that leaders have few opportunities to learn these techniques until they are involved in a crisis. Learning on the job in such circumstances does not lend itself to internalizing these methods. Donor organizations should consider measures to help leaders learn these techniques in more congenial circumstances as part of an SL approach.

The task of helping societies realize that politics can be a positive-sum game is both sensitive and difficult. It may require, therefore, a special study (the literature review for such a study comprises chapter 6) that would indicate precisely how an organization may move ahead in this area in order to realize its own SL objectives and thereby help member countries to become more effective in doing that on their own.

Conclusion

This chapter has attempted to suggest an SL approach to human rights and sustainable development as an essential element to achieve the legal empowerment of the poor. It has teased out the conceptual and practical shifts that must take place for actors in these communities to become supporters of the legal-rights agenda. The empowerment agenda includes the four steps of articulation, mobilization, distribution, and confirmation. The SL approach in practice boils down to the following four steps:

- multidimensional assessment of the livelihood base of the poor including jobs, small businesses, coping and adaptive strategies, assets, and the transformation policies and institutions including macro-micro linkages, placing special emphasis on their strengths and assets (not needs) to set the stage for self-empowerment;
- articulation of the vision of a more sustainable livelihood;
- establishment of what the poor can do on their own to get to their vision from their current situation; and
- discussions to establish what help is required from outsiders, such as the government, donors, NGOs, and so on.

These steps mesh well and can be integrated during implementation.

This chapter has therefore hopefully answered the question of what the human-rights and development communities should do differently in the post-2015 era.

CPSIA information can be obtained
at www.ICGtesting.com
Printed in the USA
FFHW022214041218
49769679-54237FF